Mimetic Criticism
and the Gospel of Mark

Mimetic Criticism and the Gospel of Mark

An Introduction and Commentary

Joel L. Watts

WIPF & STOCK · Eugene, Oregon

MIMETIC CRITICISM AND THE GOSPEL OF MARK
An Introduction and Commentary

Copyright 2013 Joel L. Watts. All rights reserved. Except for brief quotations in critical publications or reviews, no part of this book may be reproduced in any manner without prior written permission from the publisher. Write: Permissions, Wipf and Stock Publishers, 199 W. 8th Ave., Suite 3, Eugene, OR 97401.

Wipf & Stock
An Imprint of Wipf and Stock Publishers
199 W. 8th Ave., Suite 3
Eugene, OR 97401
www.wipfandstock.com

ISBN 13: 978-1-62032-289-5
Manufactured in the U.S.A.

To all of those who write the changes of the world

What is an epigram? A dwarfish whole, its body brevity, and wit its soul
—SAMUEL TAYLOR COLERIDGE

Contents

Foreword by Dr. Jim West ix
Acknowledgments xi
Abbreviations xii

1   Introduction   1

Part I   Foundation
2   Our Kopis: Mimetic Criticism   9

Part II   The Constant
3   His Kydoimos   47
4   His Pedagogue   83

Part III   Application
5   Reading Mark Mimetically: Jesus against Vespasian   105
6   Reading Mark Mimetically: Jesus against Simon Bar Giora   153
7   Reading Mark Mimetically: A Lucan Reading   195
8   Reading Mark's Scholia   211
9   Conclusion   238

Bibliography   239
Author and Subject Index   251

Foreword

Joel Watts' book will not 'fall on the playground of the theologians' like Karl Barth's 'Romans' did. It will not shake the theological or exegetical worlds to their foundations and it will not mark a turning-point in the way biblical scholars do their work.

And those are good things. Barth's 'Romans' was more Barth than Romans (as many early critics of the volume showed quite clearly). That is not the case here for Watts doesn't offer readers Watts or 'Wattsianisms', he offers readers a sure, steady, stable, sensible, and useful methodology for doing Gospel criticism in particular and biblical exegesis in general.

The theological and exegetical worlds do not need to be shaken to their foundations: they need to be utterly and thoroughly demolished and rebuilt from the bottom up. The way scholars have engaged the biblical text for the past 200 or so years has gotten us virtually nowhere. Fad methodologies have come and gone and we still can't assert with any sense of assurance that 'this biblical passage means this' (indeed, many would suggest these days that texts don't mean anything, it is only what the reader thinks that matters). Nor can we confidently insist that this or that biblical author wanted to communicate this or that idea. A new approach is needed. We need not build on the shaky and uncertain foundation of historical criticism: we need a new paradigm. It may well be that in halting first steps Watts' effort might lead us to at least the proper path.

Yet being something of a realist I understand that most biblical scholars will continue to utilize tools developed many, many decades ago. And that is a shame. Medical specialists utilize new tools and so do other professionals. Biblical scholars alone seem fixated on making use of methods long since abandoned in other fields of research. Biblical scholars are, it seems, excessively conservative.

If we at least were to entertain the possibility that Watts is 'on to something' (and I am not yet fully convinced that he is) then we might

Foreword

finally break free from our shackles and discover new facets of biblical texts which we have not yet seen.

The book at hand is a starting point. A first step. It is not, and shouldn't be imagined to be the 'last word' or 'the definitive treatment'. But as a first step, it is in fact quite bold. As the first salvo in a demolition operation, it is worthy of consideration. Let the demolition commence.

Jim West
Petros Tennessee

Acknowledgments

A SPECIAL THANKS TO my wife who insisted that I write a book. She is Polla Argentaria. To my children—Abigael, Landon, Sophia—do your homework. I want to thank Dr. Robert M. Foster, a true teacher. His kind words and care in constructing my own proper boundaries are appreciated. To Dr. Adam Winn, I offer my sincerest thanks as one who first inaugurated my interest in the Gospel of Mark. I want to thank those who suffered with the earlier manuscripts, Dr. Mark Goodacre, Dr. Jim West, Kelly West Figueroa-Ray, Robert J. Wilson, Rodney Thomas, and Mike DeVries. And a special thanks to Ric Hardison. Throughout the book, I make odd references to teachers and their students, so I want to now thank mine. First, let me thank all the teachers whose names I have long since forgotten. Lessons more than scholastic taught by Deana Peake and Edgar Beauchamp from Central High School (Baton Rouge, La) and Dr. Samuel C. Hyde Jr. (Southeastern Louisiana University), are still with me throughout the many intervening years. To Dr. Vivian Johnson, a friend, mentor, and thesis advisor I owe a great deal of academic shaping. To the members of Christ Church United Methodist and to the Pathfinders class (Charleston, WV), I owe a debt of gratitude for allowing me a place to think—and for not burning me at the stake when I thought out loud. To J.K. Gayle who first helped me to see beyond myself in the text. To the readers of my blog, I offer my sincerest thanks for your support over the years. To a select view, your friendship has rescued me from a dark night of the soul. Finally, because all should find a way to live on,

> The Gospel of Mark was the first draft of a doctoral candidate's dissertation. He submitted it to his advisor who suggested the need for more background information about Jesus' birth, maybe some more teaching material, and a stronger ending. The student rewrote his dissertation and submitted the Gospel of Matthew.

Acknowledgments

His advisor thought the revision was much stronger but felt that the teaching material should be better integrated into the narrative, thought a story about Jesus' youth might be helpful, and suggested that the genealogy could be expanded back to Adam, etc. The PhD candidate did another major revision and produced the Gospel of Luke.

Once again the advisor was critical and asked for major revisions. Frustrated, the student took drugs and wrote the Gospel of John.—Jordan R. Scharf (d. 1982 after a battle with leukemia)

This work uses the abbreviations as found in *The SBL Handbook of Style*

1

Introduction

. . . however, this is the beginning of that conclusion.

Several recent works have attempted to introduce the rhetorical tool of mimesis to Gospel criticism. This volume depends heavily on these works, but when it comes to criticism centered on the practice of mimesis, scholars have barely scratched the surface. Therefore, I will attempt to begin the introduction afresh. In (re)introducing mimesis to Gospel Criticism we will establish a better understanding of what it means to use mimesis as an examining tool. Ancient grammars were based on imitation, the practice of imitating previous texts to shape the Greco-Roman student. This tool also helped select sources for the imitator. If we are to examine the Gospels in their time and place, then we will need to take a sincere look at the normative educational practices of the time. If we are to look for sources, then we need to know the natural and artificial sources supplied to them.

This book will show Mark appropriates not only written sources, but manipulates several external situations to answer a crisis through the rewriting of history. Do not mistake my words; I do not mean to imply Mark makes use of a proto-document. Q does not exist and neither does Mark need to go beyond the Septuagint for a structuring source; however, by using mimetic criticism, we will discover not only the well watering Mark's imagination, but something more daring. We can know Mark's authorial intent; no longer are we left with merely a historical sketch of Jesus or a scripted theological treatise, but a colossal literary work deserving more attention. The failure to realize Mark may not have intended to write a factual report—but instead capitalized upon the plethora of literary tools at his disposal to shape *his*tory by rebelling against social constructs forcing his community into crisis—limits historical criticism.[1] What is Mark's purpose here? Does Mark want to re-craft a story as an unoriginal compiler—or is he up to something more? What if Mark is not relating a biography of Jesus? I suggest Mark writes to *effect* future history and to rescue the present from the past. Mark does not mythologize Jesus (the past) in his Gospel (future), but mythologizes the present in such a way as to bring an end to an ideological crisis. This book sets the stage for Mark to display his innovative originality in an epic Jewish-Roman tradition. It is, although purposely brief, only an introduction.

Philosophy

A sound methodology is important to any criticism. To that end, I want to establish the basic philosophy of the book, beginning with the greatest fear about the future of my criticism. The threat of "parallelomania" remains ever present in any commitment to uncover the mystery of ancient literary sources. The concept was coined by Dr. Samuel Sandmel during his presidential address to the Society of Biblical Literature. He writes, "The key word in my essay is extravagance. I am not denying literary parallels and literary influence exist as source and derivation. I am not seeking to discourage the study of these parallels, but, especially in the case of the Qumran documents, to encourage them. However, I am speaking words of caution about exaggerations about the parallels and about source and derivation. I shall not exhaust what might be said in all the areas which members of this Society might be interested in, but confine myself to the areas of rabbinic literature and the gospels, Philo and Paul, and the Dead Sea Scrolls and the NT."[2] He encourages scholars to move past abstract thoughts and into the realm of likeliness. Sandmel still speaks to us today, warning the historical critic and theologian alike to walk carefully in dissecting the evolution of a literary work so as to not embarrass themselves and to cast doubt upon their work.

Often, scholars find it tempting to stretch out similar details best explained through normal conventions, such as language, forcing them together to create a false sense of parallelism, such as in the work of Kersey Graves, the infamous nineteenth century skeptic. In

---

1. *His*tory means to reflect "Mark's story," or Mark's contextualizing of history.
2. Sandmel, *Parallelomania*, 1–13.

his estimation, the Evangelists simply repeat cultural myths following other pagan sources when creating their stories of Jesus. His work goes too far in assigning parallels without understanding contextualization and thus even modern mythicists, surprisingly, dismiss him.[3]

I too find it titillating to wonder as I wander across Mark's landscape what else I might illicitly pull from the Gospel. For example, in discussing Mark as a counter to Roman imperial ideology, the possibility is tempting to see the twelve apostles not as a reminder of the twelve tribes of Israel, but as reference to the twelve Caesars of Rome.[4] Perhaps we could do as many cultural critics do and suggest a speculative connection between Christianity and Roman cults or Greek mystery religions. Christianity becomes nothing more than a hodgepodge of pagan religions synthesized without any accounting for its independent origins in Early Judaism. This, like Graves, fails to consider the extremely important concept of intertextuality, contextualizing, and the social memory. To avoid the legitimizing of pseudo-scholarship like Graves and other mythicists this book will resist unclear connections. Only clear and purposeful connections are made.

Mimetic criticism does not subsist only of mimicking or mirroring; therefore, connections simply appearing to look alike are not identified through this form of examination. After all, contextualization prevails as a very human attribute still common today. For example, just pay attention to those who examine the daily news through the lens of the Book of Revelation. One is not the source of the other, only a poor view.

Before we continue, I want to focus on the use of Classical Studies in approaching the New Testament. If we are to treat the New Testament honestly, then we must not remove it from its historical Greco-Roman-Judean setting. The New Testament is a theological book used by Christians if taken as a whole, and before this, there was some

---

3. Several recent works have attempted to portray the search for the Historical Jesus as seriously flawed, not because of modern criteria, but because Jesus never existed. This goes from the more outlandish view that Jesus is a spiritual being only in heaven to the idea that one can use mathematical formulas to determine the probability of the existence of the Historical Jesus. See, Carrier, *Proving History: Bayes' Theorem and the Quest for the Historical Jesus*; Thompson, *The Messiah Myth: The Near Eastern Roots of Jesus and David*; Thompson and Verenna, *Is This Not the Carpenter?* A forthcoming work by Maurice Casey aims to put nails in the coffin of mythicism. Entitled *Jesus: Evidence and Argument or Mythicist Myths?*, it is scheduled for publication sometime in 2013.

4. Suetonius's work provides for twelve Caesars from Julius to Domitian, fitting well a very late date for Mark's composition.

assembly required. It exists as a whole *because* of Christian theology. These parts were hardly *Christian* theology at the outset. The *Epistle to the Romans* existed first as an ideological letter to convince those in Rome who already believed in Jesus to adopt Paul's gospel and thus become his students. He would maintain he had the proper theology of Jesus, Israel, and Scripture against others who were preaching about Jesus. To get to the heart of Paul's letter, we must move past the patina of the Christian theology of Calvin and Luther and instead understand the author's rhetorical investment, not with Christianity, but with a mid-first century Roman persuasive style the author used to counter mid-first century Jewish sectarianism.[5]

The Gospels and Jesus need a likewise examination. Scholars must treat Jesus as a historical figure apart *from*—but sympathetic *to*—early Christian tradition. The Gospels are literary compositions similar to forms existing in late first century milieus of Roman and Judean schools of rhetoric and religion. Whereas studying Second Temple Judaism helps us to understand the nature of rewritten Scripture and the role Scripture played in the Jewish community, Classicism helps us position the audience in the Greco-Roman world. Thus, Classicism gives us a better edge in discovering how the audience in classical antiquity would hear, appreciate, respond to, or perhaps even laugh at the production of the Gospels. Scholars are not meant to judge the truthfulness of the text's proclamation, only to measure how the author aroused the passions of the audience in the text to disseminate the message.

This book expects to engage Classicists, New Testament scholars, and theologians alike. The philosophy remains unadulterated in this regard because the premise is modest. First, Mark writes among others of the Silver Age of Rome. Second, Mark's Gospel dates half a generation after Paul writings, and most likely, had Paul in view as he birthed his creation. Unlike Paul, Mark faced a severe crisis centered on the person of Jesus—a person somewhat interpreted through the Pauline (and Petrine, although we know little of the actual Petrine influence) community. Therefore, I will contend for a synthesis (Christianity) of Roman propaganda (thesis) and Jewish resistance (antithesis) in reading

---

5. Christian theology is meant to represent theology formed from the New Testament through Christian tradition. This involves such matters as the Trinity and Justification. New Testament theology is the theology in transition. It is moving from sectarianism Jewish theology to a theology of Scripture and events seen through the experience of Jesus.

Mark's Gospel. Real theology is built upon a proper understanding of the context and historical meaning of Scripture. What I hope to do with this book is to primarily help further the significance of mimetic criticism as a basis for reading the *Gospel of Mark* through Mark's context. It will also help to decipher the Historical Jesus in Mark's Gospel. What the theologians do with the results, if they decide to accept them at all, will be up to them.

One final word concerning the philosophy of this book. Christian Tradition has assigned the authorship of this Gospel to the canonical John Mark. This book is not about identifying the author of the work, something otherwise impossible, only the rhetorical strategies of the author.[6] The author, for no other reason than Tradition, will simply be named Mark and thus the Gospel will retain this name. We need not judge Tradition as too ideological to serve a purpose, but must make use of it cautiously. No doubt, this author was a male, given the period, so inclusive language is not used unless otherwise allowed. Further, this book will not attempt to judge the author of the work for faults or failures of the work, neither any of the characters contained therein.

Overview

The book is divided into ten chapters. We will give hope to the wayward Gospel critic and (re)introduce mimetic criticism in chapter 3. We will begin by summarizing several recent critiques of the Gospel using imitation, as well as enunciate the limitations of these studies. We will then examine mimesis so that moving forward the reader will have a firm historical understanding of the role imitation has played in Plato, Aristotle, Virgil and others in literary and cultural phenomenon. Once established, we will explore the tools of mimesis such as intertextuality and allusion. Our hope is to cement the difference between borrowing preexisting patterns (intertextuality) and building a work mnemonically and metonymically out of these devices (mimetic), as well as establish that allusions are purposeful tools of the author. The purposed creation is important to mimetic criticism. This chapter concludes with a clear definition of mimetic criticism.

The third chapter explores various details about Mark, such as his social situation, the crucial impetus for his writing, and his sources

---

6. While the name of the author is never revealed in the text, the author does make an appearance.

(ante- and memetext). This brief chapter is not meant to argue exhaustively for the finer critical points of recent Markan scholarship, only to establish the proper boundaries. These chapters are important because the wrong time and place of composition will hinder proper mimetic criticism as it gives the critic a false starting point. If we assume the early forties as Mark's *terminus post quem* we are likely to see Mark as history, and while palatable to many, this removes the proper authorial intent of the work. If Mark is dated too late, say into the second century, then we miss the crucial impetus driving Mark to compose his *courante* and thus are left with a heavily mythologized and reasonably suspected work of nothing more than fiction. If we are able to better place the Gospel into a proper time and place of composition, we will find the mimetic elements of Mark's Gospel are pertinent to his situation and thus find a necessary and natural limitation to our wild and abundant imagination (or imaging-ation). Establishing Mark's proper boundaries also serves another purpose: it allows us to identify whom Mark is using as a stylistic model. Chapter 5 will seek to introduce a Roman poet as Mark's exemplar. Further, we will examine his innovation upon Virgil's mimetic use of Homer.

Chapters 5, 6, and 7 demonstrate the application of mimetic criticism to the Gospel of Mark. In chapters 5 and 6, this will take the form of a commentary, but only on those passages managing a manifestly mimetic meaning. The concern for parallelomania abides with us as an internal control keeping the reader from getting too far off course. The seventh chapter will read Mark through the eyes of his rhetorical master. The teacher should always be able to recognize something of himself in the work of his students, after all. These chapters will also draw together the controversies surrounding dates and sources, showing the applicability of mimetic criticism to solving several of these problems. Chapter 8 will prove the value and validity of mimetic criticism by Mark's first reader, Matthew, while tackling the issues of Q. In this chapter, we will show how mimetic criticism can help cast light not just on the sources of Matthew and Luke, but also on the Historical Jesus. And of course, the conclusion is chapter 10.

Introduction

Key Terms

Before we go on to the next chapter, there are a few terms to discuss. Throughout the book, the word *source* is used. An original source is not always a written document, but the motivation of the author. When referring to an original written work we will use *antetext*. This source of the author's imitation provides the intertextual framework, acting as a structuring document, and possible allusions. Here, redaction criticism helps us to limit the *antetext* to a literary source but we need not waste too much time in searching for a line-by-line connection, only a broad correlation of structure. In mimetic criticism, we understand the *antetext* as a written text supporting the community through social constructs such as religious fidelity. However, we may find an author countering a non-textual source. If we identify an example of a non-textual antithesis we refer to this source as a *memetext*. The *memetext* comes from the crucial impetus, the social crisis answered in some way by the author's composition. In this, the source no longer exists just as a literary source, but is transformed into a *mimetic source*.[7] *Hypotext* will refer to *antetext* (thesis) and *memetext* (antithesis) while *hypertext* will refer the finished product (the synthesis). I will explain this in chapter 3.

Mimesis, mimicking, and *imitation* usually refer to the same concept of the rhetorical practice of an author borrowing or otherwise using a source to create a new work. Do not confuse *mimesis* with the idea of *re-authoring*. Generally the translators of the Septuagint are referred to as *re-authors*. I will explore this more when we examine Isaiah 65 as a mimetic source. If a text in the LXX is different either in scope or intent from the Hebrew text, the translator is referred to as a re-author.[8] The *Septuagint* (LXX) is the designation for the Greek Old Testament.

---

7. A modern example of the memetext is found in the debacle that is *Star Wars III: Return of the Sith*. George Lucas inserted various strong allusions to the then-current political situation in the United States wherein it was all but impossible not to see Emperor Palpatine as the symbol of George W. Bush. Lucas was not using written sources to mimic his crisis, but "real life" situations, something that both his and his American audience shared. Mark's memetext, then, needs not be a written source, but a social situation shared between him and his audience.

8. For example of recent work completed in the field of rewritten Scripture, which the Septuagint must be included with, see Zahn, *Rethinking rewritten scripture*; Crawford, *Rewriting Scripture in Second Temple times*; Lange, *From Qumran to Aleppo*; Koskenniemi and Lindqvist, *Rewritten Biblical Figures*.

Finally, there are the terms *mnemonic* and *metonymy*.⁹ Mnemonic devices help students memorize literary and oral works. In the New Testament, mnemonics and *merisms* are replete and often serve to mentally expand the details of the passage beyond what is read.¹⁰ For example, in the Passion narrative, Jesus quotes a small portion of Psalm 22, but it is more likely the author intends for the audience to recall the entire psalm. This overshadows the Passion narrative and is not to be missed. This includes the scourging, piercing of the hands and feet, and the soldiers gambling over garments as well as a hopeful rebirth of the speaker and the birth of a new generation. Metonymy, however, is a rhetorical device taking one object as a stand in for another. For instance, Caesar represents Rome. All of these concepts build upon historical criticism to decipher the author's use of layered forms in his rhetoric. By using these devices, the shortest Gospel becomes like a police-box. The outside appearance gives off an unassuming perceptive, but on the inside, where we expected a stuffed and cramped box we find only a never-ending space of who knows what.

I have not written this work to abolish historical criticism, but to fulfill it. Some of the conclusions are nothing new, but only serves to give rhyme to the reason of why Mark would make use of what we perceive as fictive sources. My iambic cadence, however, is new I will show Mark does not merely record history, but writes history as master poet, who, had the stars aligned differently, would find a place in our pantheon of literary heroes next to Homer, Virgil, and most of all, Lucan. I will now tell you why.

---

9. Jakobson holds that metonymy is intimately connected to realism, similar to romanticism and metaphor. He further suggests that while metaphor is ideal for poetry, metonymy offers a "line of least resistance" for prose. (Jakobson, *The Metaphoric and Metonymic Poles*, 47.)

10. For merism, see Longman, "Merism," 464–6. For recent a recent study of merisms and their role in the New Testament, see Jackson, *New Creation in Paul's Letters*. Merisms are otherwise known as enthymemes; however, I want to reserve the sound of the word "meme" for memetext whenever possible.

2

Our Kopis

Mimetic Criticism

Introduction

PREVIOUS METHODOLOGIES ARE NOT sufficient in offering a full examination the Gospels. They all lack something. Using rhetorical criticism as a way to seek out the ultimate message of the Gospels, I suggest form criticism is the primary vehicle allowing us to peer underneath the text to discover the origin of the word-images. This being said, my hesitation in aligning too closely with either of these, or the rhetorical form criticism of Berger, et. al, is the limitation of the historical trustworthiness of the text.1 Rhetoric does not just concern itself with shaping existing forms to fit a message—something found in form criticism, but selects forms according to the message. We need to discover, especially for Mark, his imaging-nation. To do this, we need a new criticism.

    The failures of historical criticism are augmented by narrative criticism, allowing the audience to sit front and center. Unfortunately the audience is usually constructed from within the text. If mimetic criticism can make use of narrative criticism, both will then use the historical-critical method as well as rhetorical criticism in examining episodes as parts of a whole as well as the reality figured by the composition. Then we can focus on the audience. Rhetoric is meant to shape a perception and to force a promulgation of something. Perhaps it is used for the ideal law (deliberative), a judicial decision (forensic), or even the memory of a person in such instances as a funeral oration (epideictic). Seeking the context of composition we will find their intended promulgation is directly related to their crucial impetus. However, historical criticism is limited when we continue to suggest that historical continuity exists between the Jesus of history and the Jesus of the Gospels, namely, even if the text is a mythologized account, heavily edited through theological reflection, there is some kernel of historical reality. Narrative Criticism introduces us to the story as a whole, but we must not assume that the surface is the complete story.

Writing was not just a medium of communication, but a highly developed process for the ancient author. To find out what happened before the Evangelists wrote, we will need to understand certain tools, particularly *imitatio*, or 'mimesis.' This is the literary tool employed by Homer, Virgil, and others in the production of literary works, a tool that is experiencing something of a rebirth in scientific studies.[1] The use of mimesis as a literary tool in the reading of Mark is not new, although I argue this approach has not reached its full potential. My first step is to migrate Dennis MacDonald's conception of "'mimesis'" criticism" to mimetic criticism.[2] Thus, the needed (re)introduction. To secure this (re)introduction, we will need to examine mimetic theorists in the ancient world as well as modern literary theorists. We will shape this ongoing narrative and tie it to the emergence of mimetic criticism. Whereas literary theorists and others may doubt that one cannot fully know the authorial intent, we will envision the mimetic critic as one who establishes the intent, sources, and method of the author.

---

1. Plato roundly criticized Homer for being nothing more than an ignorant mirror, but in more recent times, Laura M. Slatkin has provided a serious study on the combination of creation and allusion in Homer's Iliad. See Slatkin, *The Power of Thetis: Allusion and Interpretation in the Iliad*. Recently scientific research suggests that mimesis is an essential part of human physical and social evolution. The suggestion that mimesis is an essential part of human physical and social evolution, see Dawkins, *The Selfish Gene* and Garrells, ed., *Mimesis and Science*.

2. I have purposely moved mimesis from the noun to the adjective because mimesis is a misunderstood process; the noun simply does not accurately reflect with the critic or the author's continued work. Mimetic is what the author, and critic, does with mimesis. MacDonald's 'mimesis' critic appears to look only for the use of a specific form of mimesis rather than the multiple types of mimesis and the overarching goal of the author.

Part I: Mimesis and Imitation Criticism in the Gospel of Mark

I am not the first to identify imitation or mimesis in Mark's Gospel, nor is Mark the first biblical sculptor to mold his story with mimesis. Imitation is a natural inclination in storytelling and is found in our canonical sources. For example, simply compare the story of Yael in Judges (4–5) with the deuterocanonical *Judith* or the countless times Deuteronomy suffered reexamination in the period of the Second Temple. Rewriting Scripture to fit the current need becomes almost expected. I would suggest that it is needed for a community who is trying to establish itself after continuity with a previous tradition is broken. The real explosion of Christianity into the Gentile world did not take full expression until after the destruction of the Jewish Temple. Once Jewish Christianity transitioned to Gentile Christianity, it reacted to and incorporated responses and traditions of Greco-Roman literature. While I disagree with Dennis MacDonald in no small way regarding his conclusions, his methodology of introducing ancient literary theory to Gospel Criticism is well worth any Gospel critic's examination. Thomas Brodie has provided help in narrowing down methodology and to offer some correction to previous conclusions. Adam Winn's continuing push into the undiscovered country has helped beyond words to clarify my own position. It is to these three giants that I shall now turn.

Dennis MacDonald and Mark's Homer-textual Problem

Dennis MacDonald's *The Homeric Epics and the Gospel of Mark* has thus far played an allusive role in this present volume. While it is not my particular crucial impetus, it is nevertheless an intertext and my dialogue partner. After initially dismissing Homeric influence in the New Testament, MacDonald writes that he found "parallels between Jesus and Odysseus, then between Jesus's disciples and Odysseus's crew, then between the Jewish authorities and Penelope's suitors, and then between entire episodes in the two works."³ His basis of seeing Homer in Mark is his assumption of a theological crisis pitting the Hellenist against the Jews. To counter this, for MacDonald, Mark steals from Homer's protagonist for Jesus's biographical sketch. MacDonald goes on to suggest the victory of Jesus over death (and his foes) is analogous to the victory Odysseus achieves.⁴ It is rather too Hellenistic-centric to attribute every modeling of a hero after Homer's poems. In reality, victory over defeat is a constant strain of the human creative voice, especially in times of desperation, persecution and apostasy. MacDonald, however, persists and calls Mark a hypertext. This is an accurate description, I concede, of Mark but the Gospel's hypotext is not Homer. MacDonald's issue at this point is one of self-fulfilling prophecy. He suggests his solution is the one needed to the then-present problem—that of identifying Mark's original sources—of Mark's Gospel, but he does so without asking the important questions—questions with answers leading him *away* from Homer as a hypotext, such as Why is Homer important to Mark? If Homer and his imitators write epics, why does Mark not? MacDonald merely concludes, "Mark wrote a prose epic modeled largely after the *Odyssey* and the ending of the *Iliad*."⁵ He leaves no room for anything else, although we have plenty of evidence from the time period of authors who wrote easily enough without a direct Homeric influence. A further fallacy suggests Mark is writing to a community overcome with a theological crisis caused by Homeric ideologues. Not even Rome cared much for Homer.

Not long after measuring Homer's influence on Mark by certain criteria, MacDonald endeavors to destroy his own thesis. MacDonald acknowledges the historical use of Homer by Greek and Roman poets, such as Virgil, Quintas Smyrnaeus, Nonnos of Panopolis, and even identifies two Jewish poets who composed their works in "dactylic hexameters."⁶ Prose, for MacDonald, is also based on Homer, although,

---

3. MacDonald, *Homeric Epics*, 2. Mark is not MacDonald's first foray into Homeric Christian authors. He begins his first work on Homer and the New Testament by drawing attention the mid-second century Acts of Andrew. No doubt, this later work could very well have epic undertones. Given that it was preserved by the Manichean community, these may have appealed to them; however, one must question what bearing this has on the Gospel of Mark.

4. Here, I would alert the reader to the above mentioned concern with parallelomania.

5. MacDonald, *Homeric Epics*, 3.

6. MacDonald, *Homeric Epics*, 4. It is not until the third century that we find

with no slight to Philodemus intended, the story does not have to come from Homer even if the style supposedly does. MacDonald moves into the Jewish realm, suggesting the author of *Tobit* (composed in Aramaic) and Josephus both imitated Homeric prose to tell their stories. When it comes to the Gospel, however, MacDonald removes breaks with traditional uses of Homer (see below) and suggests Mark's Jesus is in competition with Homer's *Odysseus*.

An author may choose a style based on a theological crisis. Virgil and other Homeric mimics adopted his style and his images because, in part, they challenged not the characters of the story (external crisis), but the ancient poet (internal crisis). However style is not always reminiscent of crisis. Grammar students selected their texts to imitate based on their teacher. Style, while a part of imitation, is an elementary tool used to develop a writing unique writing style. Mark was in crisis, no doubt, but MacDonald fails to establish how such a great theological crisis is in anyway connected to a Hellenistic poem with mythological heroes foreign to the Jews. If we refuse to continue to take into account the theories and psychology of narrative as well as how orality functioned in the ancient world, we will continue to rob the Gospel of any sort of cognitive basis. To suggest Homer as a hypotext, especially when no one knew Homer was in Mark's Gospel, is to do one of two things. First, it is to suggest that Mark was not a very good writer, in that his writing failed to produce mimicry and failed to notify his readers of his epic journey. Second, it is to suggest Homer was not as huge a theological crisis in early Christian as MacDonald would have us believe, caving in his theory. After all, if Homer plagued the Markan mind, then where is the calming of the seas?

One of the most difficult aspects to overcome in accepting MacDonald's work is his definition of mimesis. There were, according to MacDonald, "no limits obtained to what features of the hypotext an author might imitate: its genre, characterizations, type-scenes, poetic conventions, distinctive motifs."[7] There is nothing wrong just yet, but MacDonald instead of relying on these words turns to Stephen Hinds who misread Richard Thomas in assigning to the idea of allusion nothing more than a mere psychological echo of the author's experiences. If this is the definition of allusion, we are all lost in interpreting even

---

Christians using Homer's stylistic innovations.

7. MacDonald, *Homeric Epics*, 5.

the most transparent of works. Because of this failure MacDonald's synthesis suffers fatally. MacDonald has latched on to Hinds's first work, without a due examination of Hinds's second work, following so closely Hinds's cordoning off territory he repeats the negative terminology and the erroneous literary theory of Hinds. [8] Allusions are tropes, not mimesis. MacDonald contradicts himself when he allows for a host of mimetic possibilities but then insists only philological fundamentalists require them. While he attempts to dismiss charges of literary relativism, he is unable to escape. MacDonald, following Hinds, created for himself a theoretical problem because allusion is not what mimesis is, but rather, only a pointer to the author's use of intertextuality. This is why, when in reading MacDonald's work, we discover his use of a word here or there to create unnatural intertextual relationships, supporting the initial thesis. Even with my severe disagreement with MacDonald's liberality of allusion, his developed criteria are our muse. These criteria are "accessibility, analogy, density, order, distinctiveness, and interpretability."[9]

Accessibility is always the main literary criteria for imitation; one cannot imitate what one does not know. Here, MacDonald is correct, that if a Greek author could own any book, or have it accessible through a sponsor, Homer is the first choice. However, this is where the idea of cultural synthesis is pushed too far. The Jews, for the most part, were not known for their accommodation of foreign culture, with this anti-Gentile focus growing stronger the closer history comes to 70.[10] Not only did the stories of the cultural-purists Maccabees exist, but also the community of Qumran existed outside of what they considered tainted Jewish culture, and of course, the most obvious fact that should prevent us from easily accepting Jewish accommodationism is the Jewish Revolt. Mark was not a Greek, nor a good Roman. If anything, he was a Roman-educated Jew, but more than likely an educated Jew living in a Roman world of epics and rhetoric. Further, Greek rhetoric and pedagogy was not as easily

---

8. See Hinds, *The Metamorphosis of Persephone*.

9. MacDonald, *Homeric Epics*, 8.

10. I do not mean to suggest that the Jews were exempt from cultural synthesis, only that a willing embrace did not happen. Subtle changes happened, but nothing on the scale of the Greco-Roman synthesis, a synthesis that allowed, and expected, the borrowing of Homer.

adopted into Roman life as MacDonald would have us believe.[11] So while Greek readers chose Homer, the cultural milieu around Mark did not allow for many readers of high Hellenistic literature.

Charles McNelis would caution anyone on too stringent of an idea that Homer was used by all. The influx of Egyptian educational practices into Rome after the battle of Actium, McNelis urges, should make use consider a "broad geographic and chronological range" in looking at the educational practices of Rome. He does this, noting the Latin grammarians who served as educators hailed from a variety of places, but rarely from Greece proper. Grammar, the use of words as power, was considered a rhetorical device.[12] Education was used to cement Rome's power and to replicate the elite social structure, something very necessary in the so-called melting pot. While the Romans used the Hellenistic inheritances, they nevertheless Latinized it through acculturation. Bloomer adds to this fact that Homer was not as important as MacDonald would make him when he writes, "Ancient education is sometimes said to have focused on Homer or more generally on literary texts; yet whereas students learned to read and write from their Homer, the culmination of education was not the production of poetry but the performance of prose speeches."[13] Other authors outpaced Homer in educational use as a matter of reality, even if tradition and nostalgia held otherwise.[14]

---

11. Sarah Culpepper Stroup notes that as Greek professionalism met Roman amateurism, something new was created. There is also the fact that Stoicism played a large rule in late Republican/early Imperial Roman rhetoric. Greek rhetoric, with its ornamentation was despised. It was feminine and unlike the later Latinitas style of rhetoric, filled with euphemisms. This is supposedly Plato's problem with mimesis, in that it was too feminine, too full of embellishments. The Stoics refused to solicit emotions from their audience. As a matter of fact, in 161 BCE, near the time of the Maccabean Revolt against their Greek overlords, Rome expelled Greek orators. In 92 BCE, Latin rhetoricians were censured by the Senate. Nearly 180 years later, the Emperor Vespasian would name Quintilian as the chief Roman Rhetorician, the first to hold the post.

12. Elementary students would learn through the progymnasmata how to take various genres and mold them into persuasive pieces (Witherington, *Art of Persuasion*, 12).

13. Bloomer, *Roman Rhetoric*, 300.

14. A quick summation of why we should exclude Homer as an antetext or memetext is needed. First, the borrowing of Homer is almost restricted not to archetypes, but to stylistic designs. We see repeated in the ancient grammar books when the student learns the use of poetry and prose to produce a new work. Second, Homeric poems were not Scripture, allowing that myth was oral and fluid over the breadth of the Roman Empire. Third, Homer was used in education of the elites. By the time of the high

Corbeill makes a strong case for the inclusion of Euripides in the ancient educational canon. His work, *Phoenissae*, serves better than Homer's poems, although we must admit that *The Phoenician Woman* does contain some Homeric elements.[15] *Phoenissae* was accessible because of language and because it served as a circle of education. Students started and finished with it. If *Phoenissae* was the antetext for Mark, it could provide us a better foundation than the use of Homer. After all, it is about a Phoenician Woman (Mark 7.24–30). It contained *gnomai* (maxims) as does Mark in the parables of Jesus. Women are not inferior to men in *Phoenissae*; in the Gospel of Mark, they are seen as the model disciples. The woman in question, Jocasta, is concerned with justice and truth and is against *philotimia* (injustice) much like Jesus is in the Gospel. Indeed, if we were to consider the transposition between *Phoenissae* and Mark, we might delude ourselves into thinking we have discovered the perfect antetext. However, would *Phoenissae* have given Mark a theological crisis? Hardly, as it was for educational purposes, much like Homer.

One of the major prohibitions in using Homer—or *Phoenissae* for that matter—is the role of education in the Roman Empire. As Scipio states, "Roman education is neither fixed by law, nor set forth publicly, nor uniform."[16] It was not merely the lack of uniformity in the educational system, but so too the restrictions placed on it. Education was an elite activity. It was centered on rhetoric, poetry, and what we consider the classics. Average citizens, then, had no need for such things because their goal was not public service. Thus, education was for the elite to keep them in the elite class. While some educational principles were adopted from Greece, the transition was not as smooth as we might think. According to Corbeill, the Roman acquisition of Greek practices came at a cost. Rome was antagonistic to and deemed the Greeks as

---

empire, the original mythological meanings of Homer were long-forgotten and their existence buried in under allegory and reproduced not best in theological crisis but in murals on the walls of the elite. Not for edification, but for decoration. Mythographies were invented to relate the reader to the original meaning of Homer. To suggest, then, that Homer and his characters presented a theological crisis to Mark is deny the course of history concerning Homer, education, and the Roman Empire. Homer was simply not the powerhouse he once was. While Homer is accessible, he was not crucial. See Rives, *Religion in the Roman Empire*, 28 and Cameron, *Greek Mythography*, 190.

15. Corbeill, "Education," 241.
16. Cic. *Rep*, 4.3.

untrustworthy.[17] Rome took from Greece what it needed. Homer was not always what it needed and what was used of Homer was generally found in the upper classes, as the average Roman did not have the time or space to learn Greek or the Greek myths in such a way as for them to be used feasibly in allusions.[18]

Tessa Rajak again adds something to the discussion. In writing regarding the connection between Homer and the Septuagint as educational sources, Rajak notes the similarities in that both served as a foundational tool of education.[19] Whereas Homer was the source for Greek, and even Roman, children of the upper elite, the Septuagint, and even the Hebrew Bible, served as a tool for all Jews who came to the synagogues where they spoke Latin, Aramaic, or Greek. As mentioned before, refugees fleeing Alexandria settled in Rome. Some of these were of no doubt Jews who brought with them their text, the Septuagint. She notes, "Homer's high status simply cannot match the supremacy and ubiquity of scripture in life." She also reminds us that Plato had banned Homer from his Republic, something not said about Scripture in any Jewish sect. Jewish sects revolved around Scripture, not Homer.[20]

Analogy is another of MacDonald's criterion. He is correct, that other authors used Homer; however they made use of other sources as well, and yet, MacDonald has no need to examine them or to have Mark base his Gospel on them. Imitation was a common educational tool (see below); to suppose, then, that this is a real criterion to base Mark's Gospel on Homer is a bit of a stretch, after all, we have already established Euripides for Greco-Romans and the Septuagint for the Jews. Analogy is best used to suggest style, rather than compositional sources. His third and fourth criteria, density and order, respectively, are pre-weighted by MacDonald to provide basis of his argument. He does not need extended evidence (we see this when MacDonald compares Mark 5.1–20

---

17. Corbeill, "Education," 264.

18. Corbeill, "Education," 270. If allusion is to work, then the people would have to understand it. Corbeill suggests that unless the student was in school, then s/he would have not acquired the Greek elements needed to fully understand the stories. If this is the case, then the permeation of Greek mythology into the lower classes is not as deep as we might think. Add to this the usual method of Romanization of Greece and we find Homer replaced nearly a century before Mark as the literary tool molding the Roman writers.

19. Rajak, *Translation and Survival*, 216–20.

20. We see this in the New Testament as well as exemplified by Paul, the writer of the Epistle to the Hebrews and the unknown author of the Apocalypse.

and Isaiah 65.1–7), but "as few as two or three weighty similarities may suffice."[21] Distinctiveness, the fifth criterion, is based on the occasional *hapex legomenon*, in that a one-word allusion is all that is required. His final criterion, intelligibility, requires the audience pick up on what the author is doing in the new creation.[22] His methodology is helpful, but fortunately we have others to move us further along.

Thomas L. Brodie and Mimetic Reorientation

Thomas L. Brodie began his work on the sources of the Synoptic Gospels with the publication of *The Crucial Bridge* in 2000—a work detailing the unity of the Elijah-Elisha narratives in the writings of the Evangelists.

---

21. MacDonald, *Homeric Epics*, 8. His refusal to seek real evidence is dependent upon Hinds's recommendation that allusion is unintentional.

22. Others have elsewhere critiqued MacDonald's thesis. Karl Olvan Sandnes and Adam Winn have both issued critiques of MacDonald's work. Sandnes makes quick work of many of MacDonald's claims, including the "slippery slope of emulation." Sandnes follows Quintilian in noting the mimicking a work should bear some semblance to the original, something no one can see in the supposed connection between Mark and Homer. Further, Sandnes is correct to note that MacDonald suggests that a work should advertise if it is going to employ such methodology. Mark does not, at least for Homer. Winn also takes up this charge, showing that it is nearly impossible to say that Mark is advertising Homer, but readily accessible that Mark is advertising his connection to Elijah-Elisha. Both seem to follow Watts in suggesting that Mark is opening his Gospel up with what is a broad advertisement. Sandnes concludes, as does Winn, that MacDonald fails to take into account emulation as practiced, but does highlight "reader-orientated exegesis." MacDonald's critics are not without a direct answer, however. Sandnes issued his critique in JBL 124/4 (2005) 715–732, while Winn's critique is part of his second work.

MacDonald's reply to his critics solidifies terminology and concepts. He starts by identifying what he means by "'mimesis' criticism." "Simply stated, a mimesis critic assesses a text for literary influences that one might classify as imitations instead of citations, paraphrases, allusions, echoes, or redactions." Unfortunately, this takes the wind out of the sails of mimesis. Further, he admits that his first criterion is not one he follows closely. Responding to his critics that he does not make proper use of the Septuagint, he acknowledges his avoidance of the LXX, unless it is "unassailable." His first choice is "classical Greek literature." This is a subjective choice, allowed by Hinds, but is one disingenuous to Mark's social situation. He responds directly to Mitchell's criticism that he has failed to show purpose by restating that he believes that Mark is seeking to show that Jesus is culturally superior to Greek myths. Was the declining influence of classical mythology, and indeed, Greek-style rhetoric, that much of a danger to Mark that he had to answer it by so cleverly hiding mnemonic clues that his closest readers did not understand? It is doubtful but MacDonald has introduced mimesis into the discussion of the Gospels.

Before that Brodie briefly explored the use of mimesis in John's Gospel with his 1993 work on the sources of the fourth gospel. His 2004 work, *The Birthing of the New Testament*, exploring his answer to the creation of the New Testament, stands as a masterpiece. His thesis is rather remarkable and easily within the realm of Roman literary tradition. He suggests a document exists, Proto-Luke, interpreting Jesus according to the Elijah-Elisha narratives. He sees this in Luke-Acts as fully defined, but Mark is the originator of the process who uses this document to write his Gospel. I agree with Brodie's concept of a Matthean "Deuteronomizing" of Mark, but I am unable to fully acquiesce to the concept of a needed source document such as Proto-Luke.[23] I find that this needed source document is too close to Q, something we shall dispense with below. To be sure, Brodie's work in *Birthing* is not so much about Mark, as it is about the fully defined New Testament; however, as he has provided us with a better methodology, we will continue.

The strength of Brodie's thesis is the use of the proper source material for the Gospel, namely, the Septuagint. He does not shy away from the Jewish background of the New Testament writers, but places it within a Greco-Roman light. It was their grammar of life. While the writers were in an atmosphere that was more Roman than Greco-, they were still firmly in this environment as Jews. Thus, they used the Septuagint in their studies, even if they did learn rhetoric at the feet of the Latins. Further, this use of the Septuagint as an intertextual source allows us to consider the full range of mnemonic devices at the hands of the author, a technique Brodie appropriately names the literary backbone. As the backbone of Mark, the Septuagint provides us with a certain structure that cannot be found in other literature of the social context of Mark. If we stray too far from this backbone, we will suffer collapse and uncontrollable internal hemorrhaging.

Brodie begins by noting that imitation moves beyond style and into content. It is an ancient practice directed at preservation, a key motivation in elementary imitation of texts.[24] Of course, a concept is not the definition of the theory and as we know, therefore mimesis takes on different forms in ancient literary theory. Recognizing the need to prevent a set of boundaries akin to redaction criticism, Brodie gives us a brief survey of literary mimetic models. Three of his models contain impor-

---

23. Brodie, *Birthing*, xxviii.
24. Brodie, *Birthing*, 1–6.

tance to this study on Mark's Gospel. The first is *inventio*. This is the idea of creativity that moves the style or original text forward. We may say that mimetic criticism is *inventio* of mimesis criticism—because I am adding to what others have done something just a little more qualitatively new. Second, emulation is about rivalry, something MacDonald understands but misdirects. As we have seen, the Romans competed with the Greeks in the literary field, something Virgil does against Homer. Finally, Brodie lists contamination, or the mixing of several literary sources. This would allow the combination of several texts to produce a final form, using both structure and key words from various works to build a new one. One of the highlights that cannot be stressed enough, is Brodie's acknowledgement of the twofold exercise of imitation. The student writes; the teacher inspects. This is the idea of transformation, or the synthesis of texts.[25] Imitation with *inventio* is understood as something more than telling the same story differently. The new story, then, becomes a way to transform and to make use of by preserving the original.

In response to the idea of preservation of original material, Brodie again offers us fertile ground to grow mimetic criticism. He cites several practices including substitutions of images, positivization, and form-exchange—all types of *inventio*.[26] Virgil is the prime example this, and through another Latin innovator we will discover, so is Mark. While many like to see history as devoid of what we would call fiction, in reality it is not.[27] Virgil used poetry to relate the "history" Rome. Cicero demanded that orators cast history in rhetoric. Then there is Livy, who conflated history and drama in his work on Roman history. This is the vital *inventio* of the author.

I want to turn more fully to the practice of *inventio*, that tool of the author that should always cause inquiry. *Inventio* and historiography are not always the warmest of bedfellows but have from time to time been found sneaking around the other's back door when one is in need of another. A historical imagination enjoying *inventio* does not concern itself with accurately molding fact into literature, but mythological

---

25. Brodie, *Birthing*, 7–8.

26. Brodie, *Birthing*, 10–13.

27. To borrow from a modern analogy, we could look to George Washington's apocryphal biography. The famous story of the cherry tree is one told to school children to prove the character of Washington while urging students to follow in his footsteps. It is fiction, but as part of historiography, it demonstrates the idealist moral view of Washington many Americans have held.

narrative. Cynthia Damon suggests *inventio* was an almost expected feature of historiography suspecting for the most part, what was fiction was easily known.[28] She quotes Wiseman in suggesting late Republican or early imperial Roman historiography *needed* rhetoricians to write it due to the expected inclusion of *inventio*.[29] Even Tacitus who had great volumes of history present to him was known to flavor history with his own personality. Of course, as Quintilian reminds us, *inventio* is acceptable if it is plausible and germane to the topic at hand (*Inst.* 4.2.34). *Inventio*, as part of *imitatio*, gives us two suggestions while reading Mark. First, we understand why even the most invented stories have some semblance of truth; and second, why Mark makes an appearance from time to time in his Gospel using the biographical footnote. It is unfair to dismiss *inventio* as untrue, but instead as, Daman says, truth-like.[30]

As with MacDonald, Brodie has developed his own set of criteria for judging literary dependence. "External plausibility" is the first criterion. His view is that external factors, such as compositional context, can decide literary dependence. Brodie's second criterion, "significant similarities," is a bit more detailed. Theme, pivotal clues and leads, similar plot, completeness, order, linguistic details, and complex coherence form these similarities. His final criterion is the "intelligibility of differences." This criterion is defined by what the differences represent. Here Brodie uses the key words of reverse, reinterpretation, and refocusing—words that will become second nature to the mimetic critic. Further, the critic must consider general familiarity. One should not exclude similarities because a certain model was not followed. Brodie also advises against dependence upon oral tradition, and follows his discussion here with one on oral tradition, something he considers "radically problematic."[31]

---

28. See her chapter in Dominik and Hall, *A Companion to Roman Rhetoric*.

29. For a fuller discussion, see Wiseman, *Clio's Cosmetics*.

30. Michael Goulder established two criteria for judging the historical truthfulness of events in Acts. Appreciating Luke's symbolic intrusions into the narrative, Goulder insisted that any passage with "no apparent root in symbolism" is considered factual, while if symbolism is detected, it is ahistorical (Goulder, *Type and History in Acts*, 181–2). This is a little unfair to the human memory and need for contextualization or the historiographical approach. For a respond to various examples of scholars and other theorists attempting to dissect the historical and the ahistorical, see Le Donne, *Historiographical Jesus*.

31. Brodie, *Birthing*, 44–9.

Mimetic Criticism and the Gospel of Mark

Adam Winn and Textual Disintegration

Adam Winn's second monograph on Mark is one of extreme importance to the development of the concept of mimetic criticism. He follows the work of Brodie, particularly on using the Elijah-Elisha narratives as an antetext for Mark. He also takes MacDonald respectively to task, leveling much of the same criticism as others. He, as MacDonald and Brodie before him, establishes a set of criteria for discovering literary dependence. He uses Virgil's imitation of Homer to do this. These criteria are: plausibility of imitation, shared narrative structures and order of events, shared narrative details and actions, verbal agreement, and the weight of combined criteria. He sides with Brodie that, to a certain degree, differences between the shared texts do not detract from dependence. The plausibility of imitation is based on dating the texts, as well as the accessibility of the hypotext. The second and third criteria are based on Virgil's episodic nature, which of course the Gospel contains as well (episodes, not Virgil). Unlike redaction criticism, there is some flexibility between the hypo- and hypertexts allowing for the *inventio* of the author. Verbal agreement is not always readily accessible, especially if the author of the hypertext is using a different language than the author of the hypotext. Verbal agreement, then, is rightly next to last for apparent reasons. Finally, as with any good scientist, a hypothesis is dependent upon the combined weight of the tests. Winn's contribution to imitation and Gospel Criticism points to a working model of how to read Mark mimetically—and this is crucially important. His criteria are more applicable than we find in MacDonald and Brodie, propelling us to the needed evolutionary progress for mimetic criticism.[32]

---

32. While these criteria are near perfection I find that it lacks one key aspect, purpose. If Mark is using the material only to tell a different story, possible in the time and place of composition, then any interpretation is unnecessary (that it is unnecessary is not Winn's point); however, if the author is using imitation to create a different reality or to counter ideology, then this purpose will guide the interpreter into determining the lengths of imitation, the historical value of the final work, and original sources. I am not saying Winn is not interested in the purpose, but it was not included in the criteria. In fact, Winn's first work is interested in Mark's purpose. Unless we are willing to forgo any hope of understanding the initial reception of the work, we must add to Winn's criteria the "why." For Virgil, the reasons are implicit. As Roman culture began to mimic Greek culture, Homer saturated the Latins for a time. Using Homer, then, gave Virgil's poem of Roman ascendancy an initial high standing in the minds of his audience. For Mark, Winn begins with 1.2–3 to suggest, and rightly so, that Mark has left enough clues for his audience keep in mind Elijah-Elisha; yet, no mention is made

Our Kopis

Dennis MacDonald gives us mimesis to study Mark, but we are unfortunately lost along the way as he seemingly restricts the use of criteria to fit his goal of a Homeric antetext. We cannot read Mark as one who eavesdrops on a telephone call. Hearing only one part of the conversation, we are liable to supply our contextual lexicon and definitions of our own unique social circumstance. Admitting that he has spent several years studying Homer and Homeric influences in later Christian works, MacDonald has seen his *langue* filled with nothing but Aegean spices. Rather, we must allow that this atonal method is not the best in reading Mark, not if we are to discover Mark's purposed cantata. Mark does not allow us our own improvisation, but requires us to follow a rather rigorous agency, one literary theorists assent too. Interpretation and application may allow for a rather monologic method of reading Mark, where we decide Mark's meaning, but a dialogic method requires us to consider the grand libretto performed before us and we can only consider it with a heavy measure of intertextuality. MacDonald's use of theological rivalry, synthesized with Brodie's *inventio*, emulation, and contamination as well as Winn's criteria of looking at the text for the required clues offer us our present development in mimetic criticism. Brodie and Winn have given us solid criteria from which to move forward—and finally we will.

Part II: History of Mimesis

While previous studies have shown the validity of examining literary imitation in the *Gospel of Mark*, we will narrow the focus to the rhetorical device of mimesis, attempting to move past the idea that it is merely a literary tool for imitation. Mimesis is at once a literary, rhetorical, and psychological tool as recent studies have dictated. Arne Melberg defines mimesis as a repeating action. This repeating action, an almost natural occurrence, moves slowly away from the original until it becomes something completely new.[33] Matthew Potolsky allows that no "one translation, and no one interpretation, is sufficient to encompass its

---

of his previous work in which he has laid down the challenge meant by Mark 1.1.

33. "Mimesis is inherently and always already a repetition – meaning that mimesis is always the meeting-place of two opposing but connected ways of thinking, acting and making: similarity and difference" (Melberg, *Theories*, 1).

complexity and the tradition of commentary it has inspired."[34] He does suggest, however, "mimesis describes the relationship between artistic images and reality: art is a copy of the real." Stephen Halliwell calls it a rarity to discuss the *philosophy* of mimesis, especially those developed by Plato and Aristotle, but it is "indispensable for any understanding of ancient views of representation."[35]

Halliwell understands mimesis as something more than imitation. *Homeric Hymn to Apollo*, tales of maidens who "bewitch" their audiences with songs, "treats mimesis not as a mere clever trick or knack but as a type of artistic accomplishment—the mastery of different styles of (poetic) language. . . . Mimesis is here, therefore, some kind of representation, rather than simple simulation, of vocal and musical sounds."[36] The representation of voices drove Plato to issue anathemas against mimesis by railing against mimesis in the voice of Socrates in his book, *The Republic*. If taken as less a treatise on the perfect political state and more about *representation* of the perfect political state, Plato's mimesis becomes more of a rouse than sadistic laws meant to create mundane individualism. Plato embodies the perfect form of mimesis—so cleverly even Aristotle, who would go on to define mimesis through performance of tragedy *against* Plato, could not see.[37]

Let us pause for a moment and reconsider Plato. Elizabeth Belfoire calls attention to the subtle maneuvering of Plato between Book 3 and Book 10, so that we may begin to see something of a difference.[38] She posits that Plato has invented new words to separate the good imitation from the bad. The bad form is based on versatility crafted by one with no skill or care, and thus continues to re-image everything that s/he sees. Good imitation is one based on knowledge. Here, Plato sees a difference between artifacts and Forms. Plato is not a fan of those who

---

34. Potolsky, *Mimesis*. 1.

35. Halliwell, *Aesthetics*, viii.

36. Halliwell, *Aesthetics*, 18.

37. "Whereas Plato regards mimesis as a dangerous and potentially corrupting imitation of reality, Aristotle treats it as a foundational aspect of human nature, with its own internal rules and proper effects." (Potolsky, *Mimesis*, 7) Plato, according to Potolsky, sees nothing but violence in mimesis while Aristotle sees catharsis. Might we conflate these two wide-ranging views of Plato and Aristotle? Plato's psychological war lends itself to a cathartic expression in Aristotle, who is the first to directly suggest that mimesis is a performance.

38. See her chapter in Laird, *Ancient Literary Criticism*.

replicate the image, but is partial to those who can design art about the truth of the image. It is appearance against reality, external against internal. While this is a deeply philosophical way of approaching mimesis, it is nevertheless the basis for what follows Plato, as we have seen with Aristotle. Plato and Aristotle suggest mimesis can be used to bring about the truth. For Aristotle, this comes as tragedy, but for Plato, except for Homer, he allows that literary works may bring about truth through mimesis.

If we consult Plato, the master of an ideal existence, we might see in him and his notion that the grand designs in the heavens, the ideal, are mimicked on earth.[39] As with most religious rituals and dogmas, there is the teaching of ethics. Mimesis, then, is a way to mold the children of his city into the guardians he needed through mimesis; it instills ethics through the sharing of stories. Gods and goddesses as well as heroes are pictured at various times in error, or glory. This helped to guide the children into stately citizenship. Potolsky writes, "Indeed, mimesis is an effective educator precisely because it is false. Its power to circumvent reason turns ethical training into a matter of automatic and unthinking imitation rather than rational choice."[40] Mimesis does not necessarily produce virtue, but it can produce ethical citizens. There is also mimesis in narrative. Through the voice of Socrates, Plato strikes against the use of another's voice to instruct, or to participate in Greek tragedies. Socrates argues forcefully that all such poets must be expelled from this new city. Images, too, are removed. Only philosophy will remain because only philosophy reveals the reality under the images. Yet, all of this is said while Plato uses Socrates's voice to create narrative images to build ethics.

There is real political power in the control of images. The mimetic master who understands how to control images can thus control his or her audience. Plato is well known as an antagonist against the influence of Homeric poetry in Greece. Potolsky writes, "Plato's criticisms imply that poetry held a monopoly over social and political life."[41] This is brought to life in Socrates's words at the end of Book Ten when he refers

---

39. This also makes an appearance in both Leviticus and Hebrews, if not in Revelation as well, when the heavenly is the perfection of the early. Further, is the notion of idols.

40. Potolsky, *Mimesis*, 20.

41. Potolsky, *Mimesis*, 30.

to "an old quarrel between poetry and philosophy."[42] Plato engages with a dialogue in *Phaedrus* against the art of writing. Plato demanded only staged discussions, although this was at some point written down. Aristotle, who failed to grasp his master's point, writes *Poetics* in response to *Republic* countering Plato in arguing for mimesis *as* reality, poetry is the product of mimesis, and as such it is something treated as worthy of closer examination, not as a replication, but as a new object, a part from what it represents.

Aristotle sees the poet as an artificer, able to take images, narrative, and other styles and combine them to produce something new. In epic, tragedy, and comedy, the poet shapes people into different molds to fit his ultimate purpose. This new thing is not merely an imitation of a previous existing object, but a perfection of it. Voices are used—the poet, the narrator, the characters in the story—but so are the voices spoken through visible images, giving added weight to the author's. Further, it allows the audience to remain a safe distance away from the story itself. This entices the audience to participate by making them a part of the story. Aristotle writes, "Thus the reason why men enjoy seeing a likeness is that in contemplating it they find themselves learning or inferring, and saying perhaps, 'Ah, that is he.'"[43] We invoke Aristotle in the modern arena when we as an audience are brought to empathic responses to a person or situation in a performance by an author, causing a cathartic reaction. Our emotions and sympathies are abused, creating a sense of attachment between us the audience and the characters. Our attachment is not true—neither is it false; nevertheless, it is very real. In a much worse arena, this is also the explanation of why we enjoy more often than not, the dead body on the screen that otherwise would cause us to recoil in terror if faced with a similar circumstance in our "off-camera" life. Mimetic theatre, then, allows for the audience to become so interwoven into the story that they feel the pains and joys of the characters. The basic component of mimetic theatre, mimesis, allows the author to bring to the performance well known and already emotional attached scenes, employing them to reach his or her audience quicker than those who have to create everything from the start.

Mimesis is also about impersonation. In the *Iliad*, a scene involving the priest Chryses sees the priest begging Agamemnon to release

---

42. Potolsky, *Mimesis*, 30.
43. Aristotle, *Poetics*, IV.

his daughter, causing Agamemnon to become angry. Before the prayer to Apollo for aid, Homer acts as narrator. In the prayer, however, he speaks in first person, impersonating the priest.[44] Plato and Socrates lashed out at this form of narrative. For Plato/Socrates, this imitation is troublesome because it removes the voice of the narrator allowing one person to have multiple descriptions. Yet, this breakthrough of voice is something we see even in the Hebrew Scriptures, especially in Jeremiah and Isaiah when the prophets are praying and suddenly the voice changes, or in Mark, when the narrator breaks character to remind the reader to make note (Mark 13.14) or to interpret something (15.34). The natural voice of the narrator speaking only as narrator or through the voice of a character comes through to jolt the audience, letting them realize that they are still characters themselves in the performance.

Mimesis is not a stable, hegemonic theory. Mimesis continued to change after the generations of Plato and Aristotle, adopted by various cultures, philosophers, and religions. That is, after all Melberg's basic definition of mimesis. Groups like the Stoics, when they encountered mimesis, applied their groupthink to it and changed it incrementally. In chapters 4 and 7 we will come across Stoics who changed mimesis, but for now let us examine briefly how Stoicism received and passed on mimesis. The Stoic philosopher Posidonius suggested he was able to successfully synthesis Stoicism and Platonic mimesis. Poetry was a function of language, and of course, language a function of the truth, and truth the description of reality. Thus, poetry became a subset of philosophy for the Stoics. Strabo began to use mimesis in his philosophical understanding of Homer, combining it slightly with allegory. The ancient geographer did not see mimesis solely as allegory, but he was able to use mimesis to suggest that language, specifically the language of the poet philosopher (specifically Homer), aimed to give a more true account of reality. This involved myth, or a way of speaking not of the way things appear, but of the reality behind the image—the ideal. Factual accuracy, a hallmark of Stoicism, was changed to include semiotic language systems. This also includes religious rituals helping to reveal on earth the divine reality, or, perhaps, the actions of heaven as related to the actions on earth. Thus, literalness is no longer attached to

---

44. Reading a story that moves from the third person to the first person would place the reader into the story. After all, is it Homer, Chryses, or the reader praying to Apollo?

factual accuracy. The Stoics began to use mimetic interpretation to discover deeper meanings in poetry, especially Homer, although I would argue not to the extent as previously thought.[45]

Approaching the time of Mark, we find the Latins beginning to use imitation. Quintilian was a contemporary of the Gospel writers and the first chief rhetorician of Rome. The great Roman rhetorician and author of the *Institutes of Rhetoric* cited what he called the appeal to emotions through imitation. The summary of VI.2 is simply that the orator must know the proper uses of emotion in appealing to a judge. The Roman Rhetorician begins the book by starting at the end of the argument, the peroration, advising the reader that this part in particular is "chiefly concerned with the feelings."[46] Like Aristotle before him, the nature of human emotions entertains a part in the decision making process of the audience; perhaps to the extent that it is one of the greatest assets to the author. To this end, Quintilian cautions against treating these emotions "cursorily," urging instead the position that nothing greater than the emotional appeal is found in the "whole art of oratory." He goes on to cite the "number of pleaders" who could establish proofs, but is warmer to those who can "seize the attention of the judges." He writes, "Proofs in our favor, it is true, may make the judge think our cause the better, but impressions on his feelings make him wish it to be better, and that he wishes he also believes." In this, we find that Quintilian is speaking more in regards to the forensic style of rhetoric than other forms of rhetoric; and as such, is concerned with using emotional appeals to declare someone innocent. The emotional appeal must incite the judge, regardless of proofs, to connect to the person on trial, perhaps to even see himself on trial. Of course, there is danger in this as Quintilian notes, "passion overpowers the sense of sight, so a judge, when led away by his feelings, loses the faculty of discerning truth; he is hurried along as it were by a flood and yields to the force of the torrent." To this end, the Roman Orator notes that *pathos* in the conclusion will excite judges, but the use of *ethos*[47] will soothe them. *Phantasiai*, or visions, are defined by

---

45. This is summarized from Halliwell, *Aesthetics*, 266–78.

46. The translation I will be using is John Selby Watson's found in Honeycutt, *Quintilian: Institutes of Oratory*.

47. Quintilian notes later, 2.14, that the "ethos ought especially to prevail between persons closely connected." Perhaps if there is no ethos, or if the ethos is muted by the prosecution being closer in connection to the judges, then pathos is the only appeal left.

Quintilian as "images by which the representations of absent objects are so distinctly represent to the mind that we seem to see them with our eyes and to have them before us." He goes on to give credit to the orator who can represent things so vividly that one can actually "see" them. This is important for the judge, then, in order to establish both *pathos* and *ethos* so that the jurist can feel the evils "of which we complain."[48]

Regarding imitation, he encourages his students to adopt "a stock of words, a variety of figures, and the art of composition." His caution, however, is one that should be heeded by critics and judges alike, "imitation is not sufficient of itself." For him, imitation for imitation's point alone is a mark of "indolent nature." He was careful to suggest imitation requires improvement upon and a desire to excel past the previous text, that a student should consider what lies within his grasp, and ordered history and poetry should not mix with imitation.[49] Perhaps he had learned from his predecessor not to use history and politics as a source of imitation.[50] He was not so strict, however, to dissuade the use of images, "But imitation (for I must repeat this point again and again) should not be confined merely to words. We must consider the appropriateness with which those orators handle the circumstances and persons involved in the various cases in which they were engaged, and observe the judgment and powers of arrangement which they reveal, and the manner in which everything they say, not excepting those portions of their speeches which seem designed merely to delight their audience, is concentrated on securing the victory over their opponents." Imitation is not limited to the use of words but in using what I have called the memetext. He goes on, "We must note their procedure in the exordium, the method and variety of their statement of facts, the power displayed in proof and refutation, the skill revealed in their appeal to every kind of emotion, and the manner in which they make use of popular applause to serve their case, applause which is most honourable when it is spontaneous and not deliberately courted. If we have thoroughly appreciated all these points, we shall be able to imitate our

---

48. Quint., *Inst.*, 2.29–36.

49. Quint., *Inst.*, 10.2.21.

50. This connection, that with Lucan which will be examined below, is not missed by Jorge Fernandez Lopez who writes, "The fact that so much interest was focused on matters of form (rather than content) has been interpreted since antiquity itself as a result of the political constraints imposed by the imperial regime." (Dominik and Hall, *A Companion to Roman Rhetoric*, 317.)

models with accuracy." Imitation was a form of seeking glory as well as increasing the arsenal of the present orator, "But the man who to these good qualities adds his own, that is to say, who makes good deficiencies and cuts down whatever is redundant, will be the perfect orator of our search; and it is now above all times that such perfection should be attained when there are before us so many more models of oratorical excellence than were available for those who have thus far achieved the highest success. This glory also shall be theirs, that men shall say of them that while they surpassed their predecessors, they also taught those who came after."[51]

Mimetic Criticism

Henceforth, *Mimesis is the purposed use of intertextuality and allusion employed by ancient writers to fashion a new reality out of the old through imitation, representation, or creative emulation.* I want to now take some time to explore this fully. However, first, why should we call it mimetic criticism and not simply leave it as rhetorical, form, or narrative criticism? Abrams defines mimetic criticism as a view of the literary word "as an imitation, or reflection, or representation of the world and human life, and the primary criterion applied to a work is the "truth" and "adequacy" of its representation, or should represent."[52] It is based on imitation, "the relationship of one literary work to another literary work which served as its model."[53] Narrative Criticism cannot fully explain what is happening behind the text but only the normalizing activity in the text. Form criticism teaches us to look at passages as individual developments of previous traditions present in the community. This is well and good, but it still does not fully explain intertextuality and other tools of mimetic composition. Rhetorical criticism helps us to understand the shaping of the story to the audience, but it does not take into account the rhetorical use of imitation to combat ideological crises (external), instead focusing on persuasion (internal). I may weight mimesis too ideologically, but considering rhetoric as a whole developed to meet three goals, each of them purposeful and crafting, we cannot refrain from understanding the psychological aid offered by mimesis

---

51. Quint., *Inst.*, 10.2.27–28.
52. Abrams, *Glossary*, 69.
53. Abrams, *Glossary*, 171–2.

in a rhetorical work. It is not merely about the use of proper words, but about the "why" of the writings.

Mimetic criticism is at once a part of rhetorical criticism, form criticism, and narrative criticism. But, there is more to it. We must take into account not just what the audience heard, but so too how they would have reacted to the authorial intent. We must seek out not just the public transcript (thesis) and the hidden transcript (antithesis) but how the hidden transcript is making use of the public (synthesis). James Scott has provided for two normal transcripts, those written or unwritten methods of communications, among societies in the cycle of resistance. His public transcript is the transcript of the ruling elite while his hidden transcript is one the oppressed use to maintain their freedom. However, there is another transcript. Scott described it as "a politics of disguise and anonymity that takes place in public view but is designed to have a double meaning or to shield the identity of the actors." Unlike the hidden transcript, this double-meaning transcript allows for the hidden transcript to appear in public so those who know it will recognize it.[54] If Mark directly challenges his readers to understand his intention, as he does at 13.14, then the reader is of the utmost importance and in *some* respects as equally important as the author because the power is shared between the two. The author brings expertise and technique, but it is the audience that is the validator of the author's message. Reception history is important, then, and reception is shaped by persuasion.

Thus far I have followed mimetic theorists in allowing mimesis as a representation of reality. I have also pre-positioned the reader to see Mark as using mimesis to reverse reality. I do not intend a paradox by this, but I do intend to suggest that Mark is using mimesis, the accurate representation of reality, to reverse course. Mimesis is reality's representation, but what is reality? Without waxing too philosophically, we must accept perception is always reality, understanding through a rather strict Hegelian-Fichte dialectic that reality is always faced with anti-reality, so that our views are challenged by what others consider reality. This is called antimimesis, although I would recommend something more positive such as the mimetic reversal or phenomenological mimetic perception, but as we are all Hegelians at the moment, mimesis and antimimesis will work fine. Antimimesis is the use of imitation to

---

54. Scott, *Domination*, 18–19.

create the paradox of life imitating art.[55] This wild distinction is first qualified by Aristophanes of Byzantium some 200 years before the birth of Jesus. He, speaking to a dead poet, wondered aloud, "O Menader and Life, which of you took the other for your model (*imesato*)?" Halliwell suggests that this is nothing more than the continued proclamation of the poet giving truth to life.[56] Aristotle considered mimesis essential to historiography in *Poetics*. We identify antimimesis in ancient writings when mimesis is used to expand the details of lives. Dionysius allows for mimesis to represent the truth, without a need for literalness. He brings together the poet and the orator into a single creature who conjures "up a supposed reality in which the hearer or reader will be persuaded to believe."[57] Plutarch worries that mimesis is confused with the Platonic notion of truth, but upon closer study, it is Plutarch's high-wire act of that fine line between reality and truth.[58] Antimimesis is akin to Plato's positive use of mimesis, as noted above.[59]

What is antimimesis? Antimimesis is the Hegelian philosopher's antithesis. As Lacoue-Labarthe writes, "Anti-mimesis is what will finally be revealed in the last, Hegelian dream of philosophy: absolute (in) sight, the subject theorizing its own conception and engendering itself in seeing itself do so – the speculative."[60] I would refuse the separation of antimimesis from mimesis since you cannot have the former without the latter. We cannot understand our reality apart from the perception of others therefore we must include antimimesis under the banner of mimesis. For example, in chapters 5 and 6, I will show that Mark uses the Septuagint to contextualize Jesus (mimesis), but he is doing so as an ideological resistance to a psychological encroachment to *effect* a better reality (antimimesis). The disappearing line between the Histori-

---

55. The titular phrase often repeated was first proposed by Oscar Wilde in his 1889 essay, "*The Decay of Dying: An Observation*."

56. Halliwell, *Aesthetics*, 287–8.

57. Halliwell, *Aesthetics*, 293–4.

58. Heirman, *Plutarchas De Audiendis Poetis*, 131–2 and Schenkeveld, *Strabo on Homer*, 67n15.

59. For a more canonical example, we need to look only at the Apostle Paul who, in his written letters, urged his hearers to shape themselves around what he presented. In 1 Corinthians 4.6, Paul urges the congregation to imitate him, but more forcefully, in 1 Thessalonians, he reminds the readers of their imitation of the Apostle and the Lord when they "received the message."

60. Lacoue-Labarthe, *Typography*, 127.

Our Kopis

cal Jesus and the Historiographical Jesus produces the *Gospel of Mark*, solidifying key concepts in the life of the early Christian community. If we were fundamentally Hegelian and feeling more neologic than we should, then we might consider that the product of mimesis and antimimesis as *synmimesis*. That is for others to decide at another time, of course, but for now we should consider antimimesis as Eco's picture of the hidden labyrinth when he writes, "How beautiful the world would be if there were a procedure for moving through labyrinths."[61] After all, "Books are not made to be believed, but to be subjected to inquiry."[62]

What of the mimetic critic? Dennis MacDonald terms his student the "mimesis critic."[63] MacDonald is right is suggest that our critics do more than examine the form, or genre of the passage. The mimetic critic—and I am imitating MacDonald here—"will compare it with earlier texts, one or more of which might have served the author as a model." I want to go further. The mimetic critic is not meant to account for the truthfulness of the story or any number of stories. To suggest that because the Elijah-Elisha narratives underlie Mark's telling of Jesus expressly in Mark 6—8 then the story is false is rather out of our realm of knowledge. The mimetic critic provides evidences of contextualization, or historicity, not of the historical fact of the story.[64] We might compare what MacDonald says about accounting for stories and what the proper role of the mimetic critic is. I did not invent the word critic or mimesis, but I am using them to contextualize my thoughts. These are still my thoughts and my words, but I have to have them supported, and frankly, neologisms only go so far. Another way at looking at the limits of contextualization is the modern use of academic sources. Ancient contextualization through mimesis acts as a way for the author to source the authority of the story. If the mimetic critic does her job well enough she will discover whose

---

61. Eco, *Rose*, 178.
62. Eco, *Rose*, 316.
63. MacDonald, *Four Cases*, 2.

64. Historicity is not historical fact, but is the interpretation of our position in history. Williams defines it well when he writes, "Historicity is our innate condition as caring begins who are constantly seeking ourselves in the past (thus we know satisfaction, regret, and guilt) and the future (thus we know hope and anxiety)." He goes on, "Historicity as I mean it is a human phenomenon in which language, historical and natural influences, and motives are interwoven in the human project of looking to the past and envisioning the future in order to confirm value and identity in the present (Williams, *Gospel Against Parable*, 13)."

33

authority the author of the hypertext borrowed. I have borrowed the authority of MacDonald, Winn, Brodie, and in the chapter 8, Farrer, Goulder, and Goodacre by using their work to contextualize mine through the modern need of academic sourcing.[65] Finally, the mimetic critic is the one who discovers not just mimesis as many literary critics are apt to do, but so too the antimimesis—while walking a fine line between revealing the concealed and interpretation.

Tools of Mimetic Criticism:

The author is indeed dead.[66] The language of the author has swallowed up the author and the referent so we may never really identify the intent of the author, leaving us to our own devices for interpretation. We, in this post-modernist age, no longer need to force an interpretation upon the text. We are free; the text is free!

I must disagree. Reading a text is not forcing an interpretation; we do not force interpretation upon a text in an aggressive manner but are passively coerced through our cultural dynamic so as to read the author in a wave that swells around us and attempts to drown us in the rip-current of "this must mean." This is the usual course; however, when we read a text in a such a way as this, we kill the author. Perhaps not intentionally, but as we take the text and read it in our own voice, with our own experiences shaping the words before us, the author slowly slips from life. We must remove ourselves from this drifting about on the arrogant literary sea and instead seek the shoreline of the author. We are not the first to engage a culture. Indeed, the author strategically engaged his or her culture, preserving the past and looking to the future while preserving his or her culture, audience, and crisis. Just like us, the author is understood to have intent knowable alongside his or her methodology. Just like us, the author is alive, intentional, and methodological.[67]

It is more sensible, rational, and empirical to attempt to identify the authorial method instead of the intent, but only a partly so. After all, methodology is important and very much a part of the intent as

---

65. Of course, the audience—you—will need to decide if I have made proper use of the authority or if I have simply stolen it.

66. Barthes, *Music*, 142–8.

67. Pucci, *Full Knowing*, 8–9.

noted above with the selection of sources for imitation. If we discover the contextualizing backbone of the author, we can hope that the methodology will lead us to the original intent. What might Mark's method be? The scope of this volume is to (re)introduce mimetic criticism, but in this new discipline are several preexistent tools to help us, including intertextuality and allusion—aiming at a better interpretation based on a proper methodology. Methodology is how intent is contextualized. Intent is the interpretation of external facts while methodology is measurable within the framework of the author, testable within the author's social situation, and is the interpretation of the internal factors.[68] Granted, in a work like Mark's Gospel, we know a reasonable sense of the intent because we know Mark's social situation. Identifying the social situation becomes what the constant is for the scientist who seeks to simultaneously prove and disprove her hypothesis—it gives us a set boundary for the intent and the tools. As this is the case, we can feel more certain about what the author was attempting to contextualize and the way he did it.

The interpretation of a text is not only the reader's responsibility, but it is the author's proper duty to insure that his audience will receive his or her work, even with the manifold hidden meanings buried in the text, properly. The audience of a text should not need a lexicon and key to decipher what the author is trying to say. If the author fails in this, then those in his community (his immediate audience) will find that they have no hope of ever reconciling the hidden meaning of the text; this authorial anxiety produces a careful composer who uses intertextuality and allusions to leave necessary clues to communicate the text's meaning. Later readers must walk circumspect around the boundaries set by the author so not to find themselves in the wrong place. Umberto Eco notes legitimate boundaries of interpretation. He writes, "A text is a place where the irreducible polysemy of symbols is reduced because in a text symbols are anchored to their context."[69] The purposed clues in a text are based on its context anchored well in a certain time and place. While the text is open to various applications, there is the distinct probability that if you do not take into account the author's editorial context, you will create

---

68. After all, *inter arma enim silent leges*. This is why assigning a set genre to Mark is too presumptive to be considered valid. Mark's methodology is directly tied to his intent, an intent shaped in a crisis.

69. Eco, *Limits*, 21.

wild and baseless interpretations with no connection to reality. We have a pre-existent echo to this thought in Livy. Kraus writes, "That *Preface*, in which Livy repeatedly challenged his readers to evaluate and use the historical text in front of them, also sets up certain boundaries between the legendary and the historical, the plausible and the true."[70]

Language is a powerful thing. With it, we are able to read literary works with our own lexicon and draw from them as we need too; however, if we care about original intent, then we are still limited to the context of the author and should seek to understand the author *before* we read the story. Thus, language is both freeing and imprisoning. If we are able to measure out the author's methodology, we will soon discover what is and what is not proper as an interpretation. This is our prison. Part of the areas of concern for proper interpretation is intertextuality and allusions. These are our jailer's keys. We must continuously inquire as to whether or not we are seeing something not there or the reverse as we attempt to use these keys, however. We should also understand the proper role of intertextuality and allusion in pointing to the audience *and* the author. These are two different concepts. As Duncan Kennedy noted, there is a cold war between the concepts of intertextuality and allusion, and while many have attempted to bring peace, peace is likely to never be attained, and most certainly not in this volume.[71] I would add that if we continue to ignore the cold body of the author, the war will only escalate. Instead, we should attempt to resurrect the author and hear what s/he has to say. In the section below, we will discuss the tools of mimetic criticism in an attempt to sift through the rather muddy waters hiding the body—original intent—of the author.

Intertextuality

What is often confused for mimesis is intertextuality just as allusion is often confused for intertextuality.[72] There is no denying that intertextu-

70. Kraus, *Historiography and Biography*, 249.

71. Duncan, *Greece and Rome*, 46

72. The term, was first introduced by Julia Kristeva in 1969, originally meant to describe something different from allusion. Intertextuality was the method of normalizing the works of authors. This term was later used to refer to a host of literary devices. For the purposes of this volume, I define intertextuality as the structuring text of another, just slight a part from the original meaning. For evolution of intertextuality, see Pucci, *Fully Knowing*, 14–15).

ality is an important tool, but it is a tool still within the box of mimetic criticism. It helps, sometimes, to identify shared sources, but if one relies upon it too much, it develops the same restrictions of redaction criticism. For this volume, the discipline of intertextuality is defined as identifying connections between texts and more broadly as the effects of the connection. This connection occurs between the audience and the shared text wherein the later author is pulling into his work the emotional attachment, either through passion or even structure, of a previous author into his work. As opposed to direct citation, intertextuality allows the author to use older texts not in unoriginality but in a creative manner to expand his text. We will explore how the mimetic author uses this later, but for now, we should note that recent critical theory is moving intertextuality away from the simply borrowing of textual formations to the examination of what the new creation would mean to the audience.[73] Thus, intertextuality is the dialogue between the author and the audience.

Intertextuality is also related to form criticism, a criticism former SBL President James Mulienburg suggested needed to become more sensitive to the hearing of the texts, "To state our criticism in another way, form criticism by its very nature is bound to generalize because it is concerned with what is common to all the representatives of a genre, and therefore applies an external measure to the individual pericopes. It does not focus sufficient attention upon what is unique and unrepeatable, upon the particularity of the formulation. Moreover, form and content are inextricably related. They form an integral whole. The two are one. Exclusive attention to the *Gattung* may actually obscure the thought and intention of the writer or speaker. The passage must be read and heard precisely as it is spoken. It is the creative synthesis of the particular formulation of the pericope with the content that makes it the distinctive composition that it is."[74]

The great modern literary theorists have developed several working theories of intertextuality. I do not intend to explore these fully but will attempt to give an adequate summary of the theories most useful to

---

73. For example, see Brunson, *Psalm 118 in the Gospel of John*; Hays, *Echoes of Scripture in the Letters of Paul*. One may consider the example of Philippians 2.5–11 and the story in Genesis 3, or the songs of Mary compared to Hannah. Intertextuality has been identified in the Old Testament as well. Psalm 113 has a connection to 1 Samuel 2.1:10.

74. Muilenburg, *Form Criticism and Beyond*, 5.

this present volume. Bakhtin formulated intertextuality as a dialogism, or the idea a literary text is a conversation. Indeed, it is difficult to see any true monologic text.[75] Martin Buss addressed intertextuality to its proper home when he began to steer form critics to considering the relationship constructed between interrelated texts shared with the final forms.[76] If we consider all literary texts as communication between the authors and the audiences (as literary theory holds), then we must truly look for the conversational phenomenon. It involves an entire study of semiotics, but in the end, it comes down to the use of object X so that the audience will feel, see, or understand Z. Barthes notes intertextuality issues a "disconnected, heterogenous variety of substances and perspectives." This plurality brings together a "variety of citations, echoes, and cultural codes" that act as "a network of signifiers of which no part can be arbitrarily separated as possessing unity."[77] Intertextuality is the plurality framing the work of literary communication. Kristeva goes too far in attempting to avoid the rather simple traditions of influence and sources, but she is near to perfection when she recommends understanding intertextuality as moving "the passage from one sign system to another."[78] The old text is destroyed and preserved in the triumphal new text, but this triumph is only appreciated in the study of context, influence, and sources—only by understanding the old text as a literary artifact. For the text to transition to intertext, it must rely upon the previous text and even challenge it with some form of polemical dialogue. Virgil challenged Homer. Lucan challenged Virgil.[79]

Unlike allusion, the intertextual structure is not a word here or there, but takes on the structure, feature, characters (even if the characters exhibit subtle reminisces), writing styles, and basic plots anchored in the time of the author. This is the role of intertextuality, that is, the scaffolding of the literary work. The meanings assigned to these various memetexts are not by the author's own choosing, but is temporally fixed

---

75. Bakhtin, *The Dialogic Imagination*, 259–422.

76. Buss, *Context*, 255–6.

77. Habbib, *Criticism*, 647.

78. Kristeva, *Revolution*, 59.

79. No doubt some sort of tribal ritual is long embedded into our literary genetics, whereby we prove ourselves literary talents by deposing our masters, so that we as students then become the masters.

with the cultural system of the author and initial audience.[80] Granted, the author is not responsible if later audiences have so abused a text as to cloud the original meaning, but this does not remove the impetus of the author who exploited specific language to meet a specific social situation. Bakhtin observes "the very presence of the utterance is historically and socially significant."[81] These utterances, Graham Allen following Bakhtin writes, are not understood "as if it were singular in meaning, unconnected to previous and future utterances."[82] This is where the idea of the dialogic text comes into play, because we must find the conversation partner of the text through the intertextual clues left to us.[83] Intertextual works are anchored, and once we find the proper chain we can begin to pick apart real intertextual structures to listen in on the polyphonic conversation.

There is a greater idea here than the simple use of hypotexts to create a hypertext. Kristeva suggests that all texts are not from the author's original mind but are compiled from previous texts so "several utterances, taken from other texts, intersect and neutralize one another."[84] This is the emergence of the social text and thus acts as a limit on the discipline of source studies. We may suggest an author subconsciously chose this or that text and thus, no hypothesis will suffer annulment; but an utterance is linked to a specific time and place and while the meanings are not stable across time and in other places, the original time and place remains fixed—in the author and audience. As Barthes suggests, the literary text is only the "phenomenal surface of the literary work." He goes on to form this concept into the shape of things to come. For Barthes, and for us, the text is the surface that connects the reader and the author on one plane but through a mirror. The author interprets the social situation,

80. The author makes a conscious choice to use certain images, but s/he did not apply meaning to those images, but acquiesced to their intention.

81. Bakhtin, *Marxism*, 120.

82. Allen, *Intertextuality*, 18.

83. Jakobson sees this dialogic communication in the parallelism of biblical poetry, noting what he calls "on objective criterion of what in the given speech community acts as a correspondence." This dialogic communication, however, is attended by not just the author and the audience, but all of those tasked with "psychopathology, psychology, linguistics, poetics" and of course, semiotics. (Jakobson, *The Metaphoric and Metonymic Poles*, 43–6).

84. Kristeva, *Desire*, 36. I do not equate this with Harold Bloom's allowance "no poem has sources and no poem merely alludes to one another." See Pucci, *Fully Knowing*, 10–11.

transmitting the sign through the text. This gives the author's reply some permanence.[85] S/he can do this through intertextuality, but as with any good reply, it must include the answer in some way, and it does this by including structures, characters, and plot points.

Allusion

If intertextuality provides for the construction of the texts, allusion provides for the highway signs warning the reader that construction is taking place just ahead. Allusions are, according to Bula Maddison, markers "in a text pointing to an antecedent text and thereby invoking "intertextual patterning" between the two texts as the reader ponder the meaning(s) implied in the relationship."[86] Gian Biagio Conte, the teacher of Richard Thomas, writes "Allusion… functions like the trope of classical rhetoric. A rhetorical trope is usually defined as the figure created by dislodging of a term from its old sense and its previous usage and by transferring to a new, improper, or "strange" sense and usage."[87] Edmunds tells us that allusions function as a part of intertextuality, that it is a reference. He goes further to suggest "there is nothing *in addition* to the alluding words that causes the allusion or the reference to be made.[88] Allusions are words, but they are not the whole of classical imitation.[89] Baldick takes

---

85. Barthes, *Untying*, 31–47.

86. Maddison, *Bakhtin*, 162; Perri notes much the same thing as I intend, "Allusion is a way of referring what takes into account and circumvents the problem of what we mean when we refer: allusion markers act like proper names in that they denote unique individuals (source texts)." She notes the danger for the author if the audience misses the reference (intertextual) but this is why the markers are present (allusion). Perri, *On Alluding*, 291–2.

87. Conte, *Imitation*, 23.

88. Edmunds, *Roman Poetry*, xvii.

89. Pucci sees the allusion as something retrievable. His view comes the conclusion of a few decades worth of waltz, ending with definition of allusion as given by The New Princeton Encyclopedia of Poetry and Poetics (1993): [The allusion is a] poet's deliberate incorporation of identifiable elements from other sources, preceding or contemporaneous, textual or extratextual. Allusion may be used merely to display knowledge, as in some Alexandrian poems; to appeal to those sharing experience or knowledge with the poet, or to enrich a poem by incorporating further meaning." (*Full Knowing*, 3–4) Pucci follows this up with a discussion of the changing view of allusion and authorial intent common in New Criticism. The boundaries began to break down that had once allowed the allusion to stand on its own as a tool of the author. The New Critics viewed the

us to the precipice when he defines allusion as a "passing reference" left unexplained and forced to rely on "the reader's familiarity with what is thus mentioned." Calling it an economic technique, Baldick then separates allusions into two species—imitative and structural.[90]

Allusion is a tacit clue shared between the author and the audience with intent. For instance, the shield of Aeneas may at times represent an allusion to the shield of Achilles, in an intertextual scene shared between Virgil and Homer.[91] Virgil employs the allusion to present Aeneas as Achilles to the audience, robbing them of their Homeric attraction.[92] To bring it closer to home, as Winn has shown, Mark purposely inserts Jesus into intertextual structures to invoke the Elijah/Elisha narratives, perhaps as a way to highlight the prophetic role of Jesus. Allusion comes into play in such things as geographic locations or even as a woman and a child in a foreign land.

R.O.A.M. Lyne has given us something to build on as well. Of his five textual signals, three are pertinent. First, allusions are intentional.[93] Second, they are invitational.[94] Third, allusions force a decision. The author is intent on pointing to his brilliance, or if we would like to think the author humble and shy, then we should consider allusions as pointing to the author's meek attempt at gaining the audience's attention. In other words, allusions are the internal component shared between the audience and the author pointing to the two texts and inviting comparisons.[95]

---

allusion as manipulated by the author who controlled everything (10).

90. Baldick, *Literary Terms*, 9.

91. Elsner calls attention to the literary reality that often times in works, the *ekphrastic* description of something, such as the shield, is a mark of allusion or even intertextuality. See Elsner, *Art and Text*, 312.

92. I use the imagery of robbing at this point for two reasons. First, because Virgil attempts to displace Homer. Second, if Virgil is successful, the audience transfers the emotion and loyalty from the hypotext to the hypertext.

93. Pucci, *Full Knowing*, 4–14.

94. Lynn, *Further Voices*, 102–4.

95. Here, I follow the work of Pucci who has stylized the use of allusion (and intertextuality) as exploitive of the reader and controlled by the author (Pucci, *Full Knowing*, 28). The reader is the important, however. The author has power to shape and guide the story, but the power is derived only from a fully knowing audience. The author must first borrow from the audience's context the language s/he needs to write the work, and if this is an audience in crisis, careful attention is paid to the social meanings of words. These borrowed words are used as references to the author's

The great Roman rhetorician did not think enough of allusion to include it as a section of study, but gives us some structure as to allusion in moving forward. Quintilian does not name allusion, but gives the idea, requiring it structured just so to enlighten the judge, or in our case, the audience. While Quintilian allows for light mimicry, it is still targeted. Untargeted allusion appearing out of the author's social situation would render the work pointless. Quintilian suggests that the writer must "defer the discussion of some points, laying them up as it were in the memory of the judge, and afterwards to reclaim what we have deposited." He cites both Virgil and Ovid as his witnesses, going on to decree, "Similar or identical to this figure is one we use greatly in the present day . . . it is a figure in which we intimate, by some suspicion that we excite, that something is to be understood which we do not express, though not something contrary to what we express . . . something latent and to be discovered by the hearer's penetration."[96] We know that Quintilian was not the last to formulate such ideas, as we can find the same in Martial as well.[97] What we should understand from this is that allusion as a named praxis is not yet mature, but as a skill it already had accepted norms in existence by the time Quintilian wrote and as others have discovered, by retro-identification in Virgil.

Recently, post-structuralists have attempted to redefine allusion but a rebellion is occurring to free allusion from the liberating imposition of Kristeva and Barthes. Stephen Hinds suggests that allusion exists in the literary ether.[98] Others, even those whom Hinds seemingly attacked, have come out since against a literary tradition that has no anchor. Hinds takes an almost completely reader-centric view point where the reader is the determining factor in how a work is understood. One of those whom he called a "philological fundamentalist" is Richard Thomas who responded briefly to Hinds in a subsequent work. Knowing how problematic allusion would become, Thomas began to use the term reference.[99] Hinds would argue that allusion would better "capture

---

grander message and converts the author's story into the reader's own. As Pucci notes, the readers know "an allusion is only part of what is contained in it (44)."

96. Quint., *Inst.* 9.2.63–68.

97. Martial, *Epigrams*, 3.68.7. For a connection to Pauline rhetoric see Thiselton, *First Corinthians NIGTC*, 348–50.

98. Hinds, *Allusion*, 11.

99. The use of reference is directly tied to this present volume. It was during

the teasing play which is defined between revelation and concealment" although Thomas's rejoinder reverses the label of 'fundamentalist' upon Hinds in suggesting that Hinds has drawn too neatly a line between the overt and the covert.[100] Indeed, where Hinds suggests that any allusion deciphered by the audience is worth consideration; Thomas is more cautious and stable as a theorist due to his insistence that an allusion is not a likely understood by the audience, but one that is forced by the author upon the audience.[101] Hinds argues for zero-interpretably and thus has a range of interpretations opened up for the audience. Thomas suggests that there is hardly the casual reference, and as much, that there are indeed certain boundaries for interpretation that must make use of the author and the audience.[102] For Hinds, then, the original audience remains just out of reach, but in reality, such an audience is attainable if we pay close attention to the methodology of the author. If, as Thomas suggests, casual allusions (or references) are in reality a rarity, then we should not expect to find a random insertion here or there based only on a single word or two that does not point us to a larger intertextual structure, a structure easily identified by the audience as the intent of the author.[103]

Thomas's study of allusion in Virgil that he decided that a new term, to strengthen the connection to the author, was needed. See Thomas, "Virgil's Georgics and the Art of Reference," 172n.8.

100. Thomas, *Reading Virgil*, 1–2.

101. Language is the product of the human experience. No doubt, in hallowed antiquity, language and myth were born seconds apart. Yet, theorists today insist language is of itself its own determining factor. I see this fallacy in Hinds. Whereas Hinds allows the audience to receive the language as they so desire, Thomas and others rightly see the referent of language as existing from the external human experience. Against Barthes, we can argue that the referent is not completely consumed inside the semiotic act, but the semiotic act balances the referent. This is the gray area between the overt and the covert. The semiotic act is not consumed by the language, and neither the language by the semiotic act, but both work together because both are based on the human experience.

102. Thomas, *Reading Virgil*, 7–8n.10.

103. In 1942, Giorgio Pasquali published one of the definitive works on allusion in Augustan poetry (now reprinted in *Pages extravagant*, 2nd Edition., pp. 275–282). He wrote, "Allusions do not produce the desired effect if the hearer does not remember clearly the text to which you refer ... That process is essential." He is also noted for separating allusions from intertextuality, suggesting that Classicists had become too uncompassionate in ciphering out structures rather than pointers to the structures. For allusions and intertextuality to be considered a proper methodology, then we must have some boundaries. Pucci suggests that the synthesis of Structuralism and New

Conclusion:

This is only a brief introduction to the rhetorical tool of mimesis. In recent times, the discussion of mimesis has returned, emboldened with an interdisciplinary focus, within the work of René Girard who pushed mimesis as an anthropological concept important in understanding human storytelling and social evolution. It has also moved into the realm of science, suggesting that all of human culture and progress is built on something called the meme gene, or lately, mirror neurons. For the study of the Gospels, though, mimesis is still located within their authorial framework as a valid tool, one that is rarely used because it is generally under-applied.

Mimesis is not limited to examining patterns in the text. As I have shown, it is wrong to assume that mimesis is *merely* intertextuality or *solely* allusion; mimesis is correctly understood as the entire process at work when an author uses these tools purposely. It is only fitting to examine the new artistic endeavor in light of the audience's reception of the repurposed text while understanding how an author shapes that reception. These tools train us to be sensitive to the allusions of the text, moving slightly past the limitations of historical criticism.

All of our work must be built upon proper criteria used correctly and consistently. The premise of this author, then, is to follow Aristotle, that mimesis is the perfection of reality so while the old is readily transparent, it is the new (image, text, work) which perfects reality through the refocusing of perception. If reality needs only a retelling, a reboot or reimagination if you will, then we need not look for a deeper purpose. However, if we detect an ideological crisis, we must assume the author is suggesting a wild reversal; life imitates art, or anti-mimesis. If rhetorical criticism is a valid historical criticism, even with the limitations previously mentioned, and mimesis is a valid rhetorical device, then we should begin to examine if the authors of the Gospels imitated their

---

Criticism is Pasquali. This would allow for the author to remain fixed in his or her own time, complete with the literary methods, but with the emphasis on the author as the motivated wordsmith. (Pucci, *Full Knowing*, 13) This idea of one literary device pointing to another, and thus "actualizing" it first appears in Ben-Porat. Pucci, *Full Knowing*, 16.

A one or two word "allusion" is more probably a cultural usage, rather than the entirety of the intertextual structure.

In the last several decades, Structuralists and Post-Structuralists placed Mark within their examinations. See Telford, *Writing on the Gospel of Mark*, 304–7.

Greco-Roman counterparts with ideologically manipulated historical narratives of their own.

PART II

The Constant

3

His Kydoimois

Introduction

To PROPERLY EXAMINE A work for sources and meaning, the mimetic critic needs a narrowing of boundaries. In this chapter, I will examine Mark's history, social situation, and stylistic problems surrounding the author's literary world to provide the subsequent commentary with a historical foundation. This chapter is divided into three parts, tackling those three important areas. The first will examine Mark's reception in Christian tradition as well as date the work. The second part will establish, based on the proper date, Mark's social situation. The importance of the proper social situation is not one given to overstatement, as it provides for us specific boundaries when looking for sources. These boundaries are the chronotope.[1] Finally, we will examine proposed sources for Mark's Gospel as well as provide several possible answers to Mark's murderous use of the Greek language.

Part I: Mark as an Embarrassment to the Early Church?

The only evidences we have of Mark's reception comes third hand from later Christian tradition. While traditions and other avenues of human progression are at times developed through ideological controversy, I am not ready to banish tradition just yet. Like the Gospel, the tradition used by Papias, Irenaeus, and Eusebius developed in a time of crisis.

---

1. The concept of chronotope was developed by Bakhtin, described as "the intrinsic connectedness of temporal and spatial relationships that are artistically expressed in literature." (Bakhtin, *Dialogic*, 84.)

Mimetic Criticism and the Gospel of Mark

Both Irenaeus and Eusebius quote the early second century Papias as he relates what he has learned from his teacher, the Elder John. From the start of the Christian era (c.100 CE), the narrative flow of Mark's Gospel was judged as harsh and unlearned. One of the criteria used in Historical Jesus research is the criterion of embarrassment.[2] If the criterion of embarrassment is applied to the entirety of the Gospel of Mark what appears is less of an embarrassment to the Historical Jesus, but more of the value the early church placed on Mark's Gospel even with its serious flaws.

In closer examination of the tradition, we see a controversy over Mark's reception into the early church, but it is not over literary flaws; instead, it is related to Mark's trustworthiness as a reporter of the Petrine *kerygma*. Quotations from Papias usually relate the history of the Gospel as composed by a prefect of Peter but they are also used to defend Mark's stylistic choices. The second century historian records Mark as writing as Peter preached, but not in order. I challenge this assumption by suggesting that Papias defended Mark's Gospel against charge of fiction.[3] Papias is recorded as saying, "καὶ τοῦθ' ὁ πρεσβύτερος ἔλεγεν· Μάρκος μὲν ἑρμηνευτὴς Πέτρου γενόμενος, ὅσα ἐμνημόνευσεν, ἀκριβῶς ἔγραψεν, οὐ μέντοι τάξει, τὰ ὑπὸ τοῦ κυρίου ἢ λεχθέντα ἢ πραχθέντα. οὔτε γὰρ ἤκουσεν τοῦ κυρίου οὔτε παρηκολούθησεν αὐτῷ, ὕστερον δέ, ὡς ἔφην, Πέτρῳ· ὃς πρὸς τὰς χρείας ἐποιεῖτο τὰς διδασκαλίας, ἀλλ' οὐχ ὥσπερ σύνταξιν τῶν κυριακῶν ποιούμενος λογίων, ὥστε οὐδὲν ἥμαρτεν Μάρκος οὕτως ἔνια γράψας ὡς ἀπεμνημόνευσεν. ἑνὸς γὰρ ἐποιήσατο πρόνοιαν, τοῦ μηδὲν ὧν ἤκουσεν παραλιπεῖν ἢ ψεύσασθαί τι ἐν αὐτοῖς (*Ecclesiastical History* 3.39.1-16.)" Focusing on the phrase "'οὕτως ἔνια γράψας ὡς ἀπεμνημόνευσεν" reveals an unobstructed key to Papias's situation.[4] He defends the validity of Mark's Gospel relying upon the

---

2. The most prevalent example is Jesus and Mary's domestic dispute in John's Gospel along with a few other trinkets of quotes that just seem too human for Jesus to have said and thus provided a constant source of embarrassment to later Christians.

3. 2 Peter, a book important to this discussion, appears to counter the charge of Mark's fiction as well (2 Peter 1.16-8).

4. Papias would disagree with later Christian writers (such as Irenaeus, Clement, Origin, and Eusebius) in suggesting that Mark is responsible for the content of the work, something that should not be taken as a word for word transcript of Peter's preaching, but only making use of some of it. Zahn writes, "Papias expressly limits the dependence of Mark's Gospel upon the discourses of Peter to *some* portions of the Gospel. More than this, the discourses upon which he was dependent were not designed to give an historical survey of Jesus's life, but where intended for an entirely

statements he knew as genuine.[5] While most scholars take Papias's statements as a way to deflect Mark's stylistic choices, he is not speaking anachronistically about our concerns, but defending the Gospel solely based on the Petrine statements found therein. This is not likely to settle the controversy regarding Mark's dating or location of composition, but it does give us some breathing room to suggest that the early church questioned Mark's recording of history—a recording saved only by an association with Peter.

The Date of Mark's Gospel

A majority of scholars, following a mixture of internal and external evidences and tradition, date Mark to sometime after 66 CE, but others

---

differently purpose." (Zahn, *Introduction*, 440.) Robert Grant has noticed the same thing. He points out that Papias is defending Mark from various charges. It is not just the bad order but inaccuracies in Mark's Gospel such as omissions, the Messianic secret, and false statements as inaccuracies. Grant suggests that the canon of measurement Papias is using is Luke. (See Grant, "Papias and the gospels," 218–22.) J. Kürzinger believes Papias is suggesting that Mark follows his teacher Peter in adapting the material to the present needs of the audience. (See Kürzinger, *Papias von Hierapolis und die Evangeliem des Neuen Testaments*. For a fuller discussion of this, see Black, M. "The Use of Rhetorical Terminology in Papias on Mark and Matthew," 31–41. We have enough to establish he idea that the words of Papias are often incorrectly used to suggest that Mark was just lackluster. What is more realistic is that Papias had an exemplar Gospel in mind, but Mark did not rise to the level; however, Papias accept Mark as emendations on Peter's amendments to the story of Jesus, amendments and emendations put forth for the concerns of the audience. Papias would not need to know what those concerns were in order to know that concerns existed. It may be that we have simply not paid enough attention to Papias's view of Mark as Peter's interpreter. It is entirely plausible that Papias, in this singular word, has already told us what we have spent nearly two millennia attempting to discover, that Mark interpreted Peter's teachings about Jesus, and as we know of interpretation, it includes changes needed for the present audience. This view is a little syncretistic I admit, but it is one fitting well with rhetorical practices of the time. Regardless of culture or time, we come to understand our world by the images we identify. Thus, myth. If Christian is correct, and Peter moved to Rome, he faced a culture filled with myth so he would need to shape his *kerygma* to answer that myth. These images shaped Peter and Mark, and the Christian community there. To deny them, then, that essential part of human contextualization is to deny to them their independence from the modern reader. For the use of images in language in the early Christian community, see Wilder, *Early Christian Rhetoric*, 120–8.

5. Papias collected the sayings of Jesus, something devoid of the miracles. If any second century church historian was able to judge the words of Jesus as genuine, or near genuine, it would have been Papias.

such as Maurice Casey and James Crossley date the Gospel to the early 40's CE. Irenaeus tabulates Mark' composition as happening after Peter and Paul's ἔξοδον. He writes, "Ὁ μὲν δὴ Ματθαῖος ἐν τοῖς Ἑβραίοις τῇ ἰδίᾳ αὐτῶν διαλέκτῳ καὶ γραφὴν ἐξήνεγκεν εὐαγγελίου, τοῦ Πέτρου καὶ τοῦ Παύλου ἐν Ῥώμῃ εὐαγγελιζομένων καὶ θεμελιούντων τὴν ἐκκλησίαν. Μετὰ δὲ τὴν τούτων ἔξοδον, Μάρκος, ὁ μαθητὴς καὶ ἑρμηνευτὴς Πέτρου, καὶ αὐτὸς τὰ ὑπὸ Πέτρου κηρυσσόμενα ἐγγράφως ἡμῖν παραδέδωκεν. Καὶ Λουκᾶς δέ, ὁ ἀκόλουθος Παύλου, τὸ ὑπ' ἐκείνου κηρυσσόμενον εὐαγγέλιον ἐν βίβλῳ κατέθετο. Ἔπειτα Ἰωάννης, ὁ μαθητὴς τοῦ Κυρίου, ὁ καὶ ἐπὶ τὸ στῆθος αὐτοῦ ἀναπεσών, καὶ αὐτὸς ἐξέδωκεν τὸ εὐαγγέλιον, ἐν Ἐφέσῳ τῆς Ἀσίας διατρίβων."[6]

Convinced Mark remained in Rome to keep alive the Christian sect, Crossley argues for the translation of "departure" instead of "death."[7] Contra Crossley, however, is the traditional consensus that Mark was composed after 66 CE. Winn, in his monograph, deals expressly with the assumption that Irenaeus's statement more than likely means death, given the nature of those who died.[8] He also counters Crossley's view of a unique Christian tradition suggesting Peter and Paul left Rome before martyrdom. However, there is a canonical testament to Irenaeus's use of ἔξοδος. It is found in Luke 9.31 relating to the death of Jesus in Jerusalem and, more importantly, in 2 Peter 1.15 as well (σπουδάσω δὲ καὶ ἑκάστοτε ἔχειν ὑμᾶς μετὰ τὴν ἐμὴν ἔξοδον τὴν τούτων μνήμην ποιεῖσθαι) when Peter's death is mentioned."[9] It does not matter if these canonical texts date before or after Irenaeus—one author is sitting in the audience of the other, and thus, provides the appropriate interpretative strategy

---

6. "Matthew also issued a written Gospel among the Hebrews in their own dialect, while Peter and Paul were preaching at Rome, and laying the foundations of the church. After their departure, Mark, the disciple and interpreter of Peter, did also hand down to us in writing what had been preached by Peter. Luke also, the companion of Paul, recorded in a book the Gospel preached by him. Afterwards, John, the disciple of the Lord, who also had leaned upon His breast, did himself publish a Gospel during his residence at Ephesus in Asia." (*Against Heresies* 3.1.1.)

7. Crossley, *Insight*, 7–8; 43; Crossley is not alone in dating Mark earlier than the late sixties. See also Robinson, *Redating the New Testament*; Ellis, "The Date and Provenance of Mark's Gospel." Such a view follows a variety of Christian tradition that both Peter and Paul continued their missionary journeys, only to return sometime later to face death.

8. Winn, *Purpose*, 44–46.

9. "I make it my priority to insure that you will always remember these things after my departure." (Author's translation).

needed to understand Irenaeus as speaking about the theological view of the death of Peter and Paul.[10]

We have one final word regarding the dating of the Gospel. If the social situation is not accurate, we are left with either a false history or sources that only cloud the proper reading of the Gospel. The examination of the remaining three Gospels and the Book of Revelation reveal that key Christian concepts began to rapidly develop shortly after the destruction of the Temple, often through conflict with theological neighbors. If Mark is writing to combat an ideological crisis (to which we will arrive shortly), then we must assume his audience was such a one to have lived under a psychological siege, aimed at changing their allegiances and refocusing their loyalties. The belief-altering effects of this war require a very specific community in a very specific temporal locality. If we include other factors in our method, such as internal and external evidences of the Gospel, then we can arrive at a more approximate time.[11] Already, we have established that the date of Mark's Gospel is after 66 CE, but let me go further and suggest that Mark has a post-70 CE dating, perhaps even as late as 75 CE. Mark's mimetic sources, developed through his social situation, reveal that we are dealing with a Gospel received sometime between 71 and 75.

This section does not detail the full breadth of scholarship of the various critical insights into Mark's Gospel but seeks to solidify the date to discover the Evangelist's possible sources. The early date supposed by Maurice Casey and James Crossley simply does not make use of available historical material. A date in the 40's would prevent us from accurately finding the needed sources and create a problem for future critics, leaving us to suspect—rather, to hope for—an eyewitness account. If Mark's Gospel is not primarily an eyewitness account, then he relied on sources, and in regards to sources, a proper date and social

10. "The *fact* that, between the years 75 and 100, a book dealing with the words and deeds of Jesus, and written by a disciple of Peter, was in existence in the province of Asia," Zahn writes. Zahn stands just outside the late date according to Irenaeus in suggesting that Mark took root slowly until sometime near the turn of the century when other Gospels were used to defend his work. (Zahn, *Introduction*, 444.) Without trying to flood spoilers into our melody, one should understand the book is introduced outside of Rome and protected by non-Roman Christians.

11. One does not simply walk into Mark 13 alone. This singular chapter remains a huge factor in determining the date of Mark's Gospel. I will explain how Mark 13 points to the destruction of the Temple not as foreknowledge but as interpretation in a later chapter. Mark 11.15–17 is another hallmark of dating Mark's Gospel to a post-70 date.

location is immediately important. Going forward, the reader should remember that Mark's Gospel is commonly thought of as the first such work. The scholars referenced in this chapter all assume a Markan priority, meaning, regardless of an original source, Mark is still the first of the genre, with Matthew and Luke following sometime afterwards. The literary development of the remaining Synoptics is generally seen in the polishing of Mark's poor Greek by Matthew and Luke. Both of these Gospels date near or past 80 CE.

Part II

Introduction

After a thorough examination of Mark's purpose, Winn concludes Mark's impetus for writing was a looming Christological crisis regarding the rise of the imperial cult of Vespasian who borrowed Jewish messianic expectation to secure his throne.[12] This volume does not stand completely part from that conclusion but I attempt to give some rhyme to Winn's reasoning by building upon his work. Mark's community in Rome is faced with several deep fissures. The aftermath of a year of civil war, terrible news coming from Judea, the unlikely return of Jesus, and the coming news being marshaled out at the tip of a legionnaire's sword that Vespasian was now declared the Jewish Messiah caused the leaderless Christian community to contemplate how—or even if they should—move forward. While Winn dates Mark shortly after the destruction of the Temple, is it better to date the promulgation of the Gospel later, but not by much, given the needed time for Vespasian's divine status to become the psychological factor it did.[13] The choice for the proto-Christian community is simple—either a dead brigand or a live victorious general who became emperor of the entire world in Judea with the proclamation of a new *Pax Romana*. This is Mark's social crisis—where is Jesus?

12. Winn, *Purpose*, 199.

13. Winn maintains that Mark was written shortly after 70 CE (Winn, *Purpose*, 153); however, he notes that the causes of the crisis do not fully develop until after, at the very earliest, the Triumph (c. 71) which would have demonstrated the completion of Vespasian's rise to power and the full demonstration of his claim to the Messianic Throne. Further, he notes that the fear of persecution would have risen *after* the end of the Revolt, which would have taken place after 73 (Winn, *Purpose*, 171–72).

His Kydoimois

It is not a crisis, however, that developed in a short space, but was the result of nearly three quarters of a century worth of resistance, of which the Jesus movement was an early and small part. We have to remember socio-religious institutions as well as political constructs continued to evolve during this time and no doubt were then used to reflect on previous traditions. This is not uncommon and indeed, still occurs today. For example, the Civil Rights movement in 1960's America anchored their movement to an idea of a "check" the Founder's wrote. This check promised freedom and equality to all citizens regardless of race, creed, or color. The revised understanding of social equality among the races and sexes was then retro-redacted to suggest that the Founders somehow would have supported the Civil Rights movement. The concern was not the actual history of the Founders, but how their use supported the current cause, something that in turn allowed the Founders to be seen in a new light. Mark is doing nothing different by taking the various messianic motifs developed between the time of Jesus and the aftermath of the Jewish Revolt to recast Jesus in light of these progressions.

Social History

Not Merry Men

Before we arrive at *how* Mark wrote, we must discover *why* he wrote. The social history of Roman-occupied Judea began approximately 70 BCE, leading to a revolt that caused Roman General Pompey to invite himself into the most inner sanctum of the Temple. Sects evolved and formed new, non-temple based cults. Works such as the *Psalms of Solomon* were written to express dissatisfaction with the situation and a hope for a return of the son of David, a mortal king who would rid Israel of the wicked. An anonymous source reinterpreted *The Testament of Moses* to suggest that suicide by martyrdom was acceptable to God.[14] Rome was fused with the biblical Edom to create a ready-made polemic in Scripture. The powerful more easily adapted to the new situation, embracing the Romans and Roman practices such as coining money leading to the shrinking "limited good" of society. As power, money, and the means of production were slowly consolidated with the support

14. Horsley, *Revolt*, 160–4.

of the upper classes, unrest grew. Popular resistance movements led by messianic claimants developed apocalyptic traditions and used social banditry to fight a subtle war. Herod abated the flow of violence by his violent hand but it returned as a heated cancer eating away at Palestine and leading to a gangrenous revolt that destroyed the septic Temple. We should not dismiss the social unrest that began to really develop after the time of Jesus, as this movement developed of various theological stances.

Shortly after the death of Jesus, Gaius Caesar attempted to establish more of a foothold for Roman religious practices within the Jewish cult. Josephus records such event causing an immediate backlash against the Romans, including the rise of λῃστῶν (see *Antiquities* 18.274; 20.261–78; *B.J.* 2.184–-203).[15] Unlike the time before Jesus this social class development into revolutionaries.[16] During the time of Jesus bandits were more often than not little more than less-than-glorious highwaymen, preying on travelers, but with no overt political motivation.[17] With the rise of political banditry, however, Rome took a more active role in policing Judea. This was the reason Rome sent Pontius Pilate to Jerusalem, to deal brutally with the rising number of brigands. After the death of Jesus, more Jewish rebels attempted to become well-known brigands. Josephus records the account of Tholomaus (*Ant.* 20.5) raiding the border between Idumea and Arabia.[18] He was most likely purged when Fadus came to power.[19] The procurator Felix was also known to have expelled brigands from Judea. In the middle of the century, Tiberius Alexander began to rule Judea followed by a severe famine. Josephus records the execution of the sons of Judas the Galilean after an aborted rebellion (*Ant* 20:100–103).[20] But, in all these, there is

---

15. We see the intrusion of this social class into the Gospel of Mark in 11.15–17 and 15.27. The use of Josephus as historian is not intended. What is intended is the historiography Josephus reveals to us. I am not taking Josephus's accounts without question, but only as it applies to the constructs of the Mark's world.

16. Cf. Luke 10.30 and John 10.8.

17. Grünewald, *Bandits*, 14–17.

18. Tholomaeus may not have been a political brigand, or even Jew. (*Compendia* 1.361.)

19. Fadus was not a favorite of the Jews either. He had the priestly garments confiscated and placed under Roman control. He was soon removed to avoid any disturbances.

20. Judas the Galilean deserves more attention here. He led a rebellion in 6 CE,

one who no doubt truly pushed Judea to the brink: Eleazar bar Dineus.[21] This is not the only Eleazar to have caused trouble. Eleazar of Ananias had become the Captain of the Temple and used this power to refuse any gift or sacrifice from a foreigner. It was not just religious, but becoming political as well.[22]

The prime reason the bandits were able to secure a proper Revolt was because of their numbers and developing connections with Jewish power structures, something Eleazar bar Dineus exemplifies. Josephus writes, "ἅμα δὲ καὶ κατὰ τὸ ἱερὸν Ἐλεάζαρος υἱὸς Ἀνανία τοῦ ἀρχιερέως νεανίας θρασύτατος στρατηγῶν τότε τοὺς κατὰ τὴν λατρείαν λειτουργοῦντας ἀναπείθει μηδενὸς ἀλλοτρίου δῶρον ἢ θυσίαν προσδέχεσθαι τοῦτο δ' ἦν τοῦ πρὸς Ῥωμαίους πολέμου καταβολή τὴν γὰρ ὑπὲρ τούτων θυσίαν Καίσαρος ἀπέρριψαν καὶ πολλὰ τῶν τε ἀρχιερέων καὶ τῶν γνωρίμων παρακαλούντων μὴ παραλιπεῖν τὸ ὑπὲρ τῶν ἡγεμόνων ἔθος οὐκ ἐνέδοσαν πολὺ μὲν καὶ τῷ σφετέρῳ πλήθει πεποιθότες καὶ γὰρ τὸ ἀκμαιότατον τῶν νεωτεριζόντων συνῄργει μάλιστα δ' ἀφορῶντες εἰς τὸν Ἐλεάζαρον στρατηγοῦντα (B.J. 2:409–10)." From the end of Pilate's procuratorship

---

inaugurated when Rome, assuming direct control of Judaea, ordered a census of Palestine. His ideology was the reverse on John 19.15, with "no Lord (reference to Caesar) but God." Judas sought legitimate rule, meaning that he created a philosophy that enabled the brigands to slowly formulate a cause to resist Rome. They were not God's rulers, and Israel was not their land. Judas, and others after him, would attempt to remove Rome and establish God as the new ruler of Israel. Judas is also the founder of a line of militia fighters. He could have been the son of Judas, the son of Ezekias, but he we do know that his two sons (James and Simon) were rebel leaders as well. Menahem was either a son or grandson. Masada's Eleazar was also a descendent. While his lineage is a cell, it is unlike he established a sect. No doubt, the Zealots, Sicarri, and others came from Judas's line, but at the very beginning, he was the leader of a lost cause, but a cause that kept recurring until the end of the Jewish Revolt. Two final things are worth mentioning. Josephus calls Judas a sophist, something that has bearing on later anti-Christian apologetics (B.J. 2.118). Second, there were no reported troubles from 6–26 CE, the year Pilate arrived in Jerusalem. (Rhoads, *Revolution*, 47–61.)

21. This Eleazar was hired by the local Jewish populace to attack Rome in revenge for several months of hostilities leaving villages plundered and many Jews dead, while the Romans did nothing. He was executed in Rome at the order of Felix.

22. Josephus records several instances of religious intolerance that prompted a prophetic movement. First, Roman troops began to become insulting to the Temple (B.J. 2.223-7). During a reprisal for Jewish protest of this attitude, Roman soldiers destroyed a Torah (B.J. 2.229-30). Following this, various prophets began to lead Jews away from Jerusalem (B.J. 2.259). A prophet from Egypt led a group up the Mount of Olives while other led a group out into the wilderness. Both were brutally stopped by the Romans. (B.J. 2.61-3).

to the beginning of the revolt, the Roman governors tried desperately to put an end to the brigands. Even though they employed massive expulsions and even crucifixions, this was not enough as eventually towns and areas of Judea were abdicated to the brigands. Once the war started, it easily escalated to involve all of Judea because the brigands had infiltrated all of Judea—continuing to operate as a loose collection of gangs. It was not long after the initial volleys that Josephus assumed commanded of an army, "ὁμοίως δὲ καὶ Γίσχαλα Ἰωάννης ὁ Λήΐου καθ' ἑαυτὸν ἐτείχιζεν Ἰωσήπου κελεύσαντος τοῖς δ' ἄλλοις ἐρύμασιν ἅπασιν αὐτὸς συμπονῶν ἅμα καὶ προστάσσων παρῆν κατέλεξεν δὲ καὶ δύναμιν ἐκ τῆς Γαλιλαίας ὑπὲρ δέκα μυριάδας νέων ἀνδρῶν οὓς πάντας ἔκ τε τῶν συλλεγομένων παλαιῶν ὅπλων ἐγκατασκευαζόμενος ὥπλιζεν (B.J., 2:575–6)"[23]

Of Wars more than Jewish

In 66 CE a building project in Caesarea caused a violent outbreak after Nero granted the Greeks of the city the administrative rule. The Roman Governor withdrew seventeen talents from the treasury of the Temple leading to small skirmishes that brought swift and harsh reprisals from the Romans.[24] This caused an outright conflict forcing Florus, the Roman leader to quickly flee the city. The governor of Syria sent a military tribune to investigate. Through internal political plays, the Roman negotiations proved ineffective and led to the overthrow of the Roman governor in Jerusalem, an event ignited with the ending of patriotic sacrifice in the Temple.[25] Once this occurred, Eleazar bar Ananias (son

---

23. Josephus saw himself at the center of the world stage. In his *Life*, he suggests that as early as 14, he was well known in the Temple cult as one who knew the Law. He would go on to spend time with various Jewish sects in the meantime only to become a priest at nineteen. At 26, Josephus was sent to Neroian Rome to plead for the release of several priests. While in Rome, he met Nero's royal consort who became enamored with him and sent him back to Jerusalem laden with special gifts from the Court. His time in Rome no doubt helped to broaden his worldview.

24. This was not the first time that a Roman Governor had withdrawn money from the Temple Treasury. Pilate did the same thing (*B.J.* 2.175–7). The Jewish populace must have felt like history was repeating itself.

25. The ending of the sacrifices by and for gentiles is understood as a cultic revival and cleansing of the Temple, perhaps patterned after the Maccabean revival. This was not the only change occurring at the Temple as the High Priests were denied their duties and soon removed while one favorable to the Zealots installed. The Temple became a symbol for the religious cause of the Revolt and as such, saw the worst

of a High Priest), John of Gischala, and Simon bar Giora emerged as the leaders of the rebellion. Gischala stands out not as a common robber or otherwise lowly criminal, but as a man of some means who resisted the Revolt at first, but soon found himself embroiled in the fight.[26] These early fighters were religiously minded individuals with the goal of removing the Gentile overlords and reestablishing the Judean kingdom of the messianic age. As at Masada, Roman Guards were massacred. All of this was met with the invasion of Jerusalem by Josephus who led the takeover of the Temple. More Roman soldiers were killed along with a massacre of Jews in Caesarea as a part of an imperial reprisal.[27] The Revolt finally began.

Levick proposes that the main instigation for the deployment of the full force of Rome to take care of a self-contained regional crisis was that it risked igniting the long brewing a war between Rome and Parthia.[28] Nero appointed a proven soldier in Vespasian who likely already had longstanding connections to the upper class Jews, such as Tiberius Julius Alexander. Vespasian became the *Legatus Augusti pro praetor exercitus Iudaici* symbolizing the limited role of the General in ending the hostilities. His goal was to prevent the spread of the war and to gain control over the people, but nothing more. Vespasian arrived in Antioch on 1 March of 67, at which point he assumed command of several legions, including one the X Fretensis—a particularly important legion to Mark's Gospel. Vespasian's goal was always to retake Jerusalem, but this had to be done by first re-extending Roman control over the rest of the province, beginning in Galilee where he dispatched Placidus with 7,000 troops.

After spending two weeks organizing his troops and drafting plans, Vespasian began his march to bring Judea back under Roman control. Initially, the general became a popular figure. Levick notes that ancient historians pictured Vespasian as "a worthy successor of the commanders of old, Hannibal and most notably Marius."[29] He was a man of the people,

---

atrocities committed within its walls. Tribunals, torture, and outright murder would stain the Temple of God before the Revolt finally destroyed it.

26. Grünewald, *Bandits*, 100.

27. In an effort to keep the revolt from spreading outside of Judaea, Prefect of Alexandria, nephew of Philo, ordered his troops into the ghetto put down any hope of shared resistance, resulting in a blood massacre.

28. Levick, *Vespasian*, 96, 156, 168.

29. Levick, *Vespasian*, 31.

never above his raising, and always a soldier. His participation in the fight gave him the general appearance of a fighting man, contrary to a Legate sitting on the imperial cushion. The Legions' show of might and military prowess cowered the soldiers under Josephus's command, who fled to Tiberius. Galilee was therefore left almost defenseless, expect for small pockets of resistance confined to the towns. After a devastating attack on Jotapata by the Romans, Josephus surrendered becoming what can only be styled as an opportunist, a trait that would not leave him throughout the war or for the rest of his life. He gave the Roman legions special insight into the land of Judea, acted as translator, military recorder, and propagandist. During this time, those who had fled to Tiberius were beginning to cause more revolts. Vespasian, Titus, and Placidus would put an end to this quickly and retake Galilee. This would force the factions in Jerusalem to become apprehensive, even to the point of turning upon one another with murderous results. Within the first year of the revolt, Vespasian was nearing the final solution for Jerusalem, but tragedy struck in Rome with the death of Nero on 9 June 68 CE.

Nero's death occurred at the outset the civil war and lead to questions of succession. Upon hearing of the death of his benefactor, Vespasian ceased all military operations until he received license, or orders to depart for Rome, from the new emperor. He had no choice, although this allowed the Jews to replenish their losses and to entrench themselves in Jerusalem. War was effectively stopped until 69 CE while the struggles over succession continued. Galba was usurped by Otho who was later deposed by Vitellius. Vitellius's reign was challenged by Vespasian who had during the reigns of Otho and Vitellius made plans to be proclaimed Emperor. In July 69 CE, Vespasian was proclaimed emperor in both Egypt and Caesarea. He soon left the war front to track down Vitellius whom was no longer recognized as Emperor. Vitellius was murdered in December 69, securing Vespasian's claim to the throne. The object of this volume is not to chronicle the conspiracy of Roman politics of that age, only to state some of the historical sequence of Vespasian's quick rise to power.

Rise of Messianism[30]

That other messiahs arose before, during, and after the time of Jesus is ingrained in the Gospels and Acts; it is an underlying fear in such passages as Mark 13 and indeed, Revelation 13.[31] Jesus was not the only person to have claimed the role of messiah, and he would not be the last. During the time between Jesus and Bar Kokhba (c. 136), numerous claimants to the Messianic Throne arose and died, with none proving successful in meeting the expectations of the messiah, but oddly enough, it was not until post-70 that earnest expectations began to solidify. This brief section will examine several of the claimants leading up to Mark's second historical referent. This is not the sum of a study of messianic expectation until 70 CE, but only a means to an end. Nor is this a suggestion that messianism was a central part of Jewish belief, especially the messianic expectation of the Christian variety.[32]

It is rightly said that the while a sort of proto-genesis thought of messiah originated sometime before Jesus, it was not until after several embarrassing pretenders that the messianic ideal took a firmer shaper. Horsley notes, "For from being uniform, Jewish messianic expectations in the early Roman period were diverse and fluid. It is not even certain that the term *messiah* was used as a title in any literature of the time. There was no uniform expectation of 'the messiah' until well after the destruction of Jerusalem in 70 C.E., when it became standardized as

---

30. Dennis MacDonald has noted that he believed that Mark was in rivalry with classical Greek Myths. (MacDonald, *Homeric*, 6.) This following section has the singular intention of showing that if such a rivalry existed, and I concur that a rather significant one did exist, then it not with Homer and the dying Greek myths or with elementary education practices, but with the political cults that were his next door neighbors. However, it is not one but two rivalries that forced Mark to issue his response, and they were directed related to the end of the world.

31. See Mark 13.6, 15.7; John 18.40; Acts 5.34–7.

32. Often times, Jewish messianism is seen from the developed Christian expectation. Jews seek a messiah that is local, militaristic, and temporal, while Christianity has the universal, divine, messiah. This is hardly the case. While the term does appear in the Hebrew Bible 38 times, it is rarely in the eschatological sense. Only Daniel has a sliver of a connection to how Christians would develop the term after Jesus. Geza Vermes suggests that if "each single usage of the term in the Pseudepigrapha, Dead Sea Scrolls and early rabbinic sources is taken into account and accorded equal value" the only thing apparent is the highly inconsistent use of the term. He writes, "It would seem more appropriate to bear in mind the difference between the general Messianic *expectation* of Palestinian Jewry, and the peculiar Messianic *speculations* characteristic of certain learned and/or esoterical minorities." (Vermes, *Jesus the Jew*, 130.)

a result of scholarly rabbinical reflection. In fact, the term is relatively rare in literature prior to, or contemporary with, Jesus."[33] Horsley goes on to diminish the oversimplified view found in the Gospels that Jesus simply did not meet Jewish expectations because they were looking for a political figure rather than a messiah like Jesus.[34] The views were divergent and only truly began to be explored in a time contemporary with Jesus. While we have evidence that pre-dates the time of Jesus of a kingly figure (cf. *Psalms of Solomon* 17 and 18) who would come from God to restore Israel, this was not an expectation shared by all Jews. As with messiah and its lack of literary support, Horsley notes that the title of "son of David" is too infrequent before 70 to be considered an important as a well-structured belief. Even in the *Psalms of Solomon*, it is not "the son of David" but the return of Solomon who is expected. When the title did appear, it was not meant to be a genealogical concept, only that the new and legitimate king would imitate David and give glory to Israel, generally through warfare.[35] To further move us away from the notion that a singular individual "son of David" was to appear, we have to look only to Qumran with their fluid expectations involving not only the return of David or son of David, but the return of a Moses like figure (cf. Deuteronomy 13 and 18).[36] Horsley also suggests the educated elite were the only ones with the leisure time to reflect on such matters. None of this is to be understood as suggesting that Jews did not expect an eschatological figure, only to show that such a figure was not properly theologized until post 70 CE, leaving the time before the destruction of the Temple as a time of unbound creative imagination by the various tribes of Jewish theological reflection.

---

33. Horsley, *Bandits*, 90.

34. As with the Hebrew Bible, other Second Temple texts rarely have need for an eschatological figure. This does not mean that some do not exist, only that for the majority of Jewish reflection, a messiah is simply not in view. This section only focuses on the concept developed by communities who held to some sort of eschatological figure.

35. This concept of a non-genealogical son of David is supported as we by Burton Mack. See: Neusner, Green, and Frerichs, *Judaisms and their Messiahs*, 37–8.

36. Maccabean-era documents do not have any hope for the Davidic line, but focuses instead on the restored, and pure, priesthood. Vermes identified at least four non-Davidic eschatological figures. (Vermes, *Jesus the Jew*, 135–40.)

Josephus mentions several men who claimed kingship.³⁷ Of note is Judas, son of Ezekias.³⁸ A particular Simon, King Herod's servant, suffered defeat by the Romans as well as another claimant, Athronges.³⁹ As discussed in the previous section on the brigands, Judea was rife with such men and small armies leading up to the revolt; however, during the revolt the crescendo of claimants sped up until only one was left standing. Menahem seems to have presented himself first. He went to Masada to slaughter the Roman garrison and finding his goal easily fulfilled, returned to Jerusalem as king only to be murdered by Eleazar, the Temple Captain. Menahem is a case study in synthesizing what messiah was coming to mean. He was a sectarian scholar in the Sicarii, the roving bands of the cruelest of brigands. As part of this group, he fought against illegitimate rule of Jerusalem only to find himself murdered for making illegitimate and absolutist messianic claims.⁴⁰ He was simply not a son of David. Then there is John of Gischala who, in Jerusalem, would find himself surrounded by the Zealots, led by another claimant, Simon b. Giora. It is Simon who extracted the most of Josephus's anger, as we shall soon see.

Simon bar Giora

For nearly two years, Simon played the role of David, becoming a popular military figure and leading successful fights against Rome. According to Josephus, Simon began as an outlaw and a murderer, "Κατὰ δὲ τὴν Ἀκραβετηνὴν τοπαρχίαν ὁ Γιώρα Σίμων πολλοὺς τῶν νεωτεριζόντων συστησάμενος ἐφ' ἁρπαγὰς ἐτράπετο καὶ οὐ μόνον τὰς οἰκίας ἐσπάρασσεν τῶν πλουσίων ἀλλὰ καὶ τὰ σώματα κατῃκίζετο δῆλός τε ἦν ἤδη πόρρωθεν ἀρχόμενος τυραννεῖν (B.J. 2.652)." Josephus saw Simon as less intelligent than John but more cunning and physically stronger; however, no amount of personal qualities endeared the rebel to the traitor.⁴¹ The historian also records that Simon proclaimed familiar kingly decrees, such

---

37. See Horsley for the rise of popular kingship before 70 CE, which, no doubt, led to the demand to have a sound messianic theology.

38. Also identified as a brigand; *Ant* 17.271–72; *B.J.* 2.56.

39. *Ant.* 17.273–85.

40. Menahem is reported to have worn the royal robes while visiting the Temple.

41. *B.J.* 4.503–4. Simon was most likely, as his name betrays, born to a gentile mother and Jewish mother.

as the "freedom for the slaves and rewards for the free."⁴² This proclamation swelled his ranks with the lower classes and along with a victory at Hebron that brought in more support his army grew substantially.⁴³ During the months Vespasian awaited news from Rome, Simon was able to re-conquer Judea and Idumea free of Roman interference while sharpening his troops into an effective fighting force. His view of himself and his mission grew during this time as well. As his power grew, his equalizing message grew quiet. He was becoming the son of David not by restoring peace to Israel, but because of his military mandate to fight against the Romans and the Jews who stood in his way.

His fame and deeds of power grew to overshadow his previous reputation causing the citizens of Jerusalem to seek him to enter Jerusalem to remove John from power. According to Josephus, a priest Matthias persuaded the war council to invite Simon and his army into Jerusalem to restore order. The inhabitants of the city welcomed Simon with shouts of joy and cries of savior, but the adoration would not last. Simon ruled the city, but John and his band controlled the Temple, thus the city was divided. This did not sit well with the king of Israel who, subsumed in his paranoia began to turn on the city he was to protect. According to Josephus, the priest Matthias who had led Simon into Jerusalem was accused by that same Simon as a traitor. He and countless others were put to death for supporting Rome, something that was consistent with at least one stream of messianic expectation.⁴⁴ As Horsley points out, this cleansing of Jerusalem was well in line with the militant Messiah as expressed in the *Psalms of Solomon* (17.26–36).⁴⁵ Simon's murderous rampage eventually ended when Rome finally took Jerusa-

---

42. *B.J.* 4.507–13. While Josephus has placed Simon as an inept and lowly brigand, Simon's quick rise to power, his familiarity with military discipline, and his natural grasp of political power, the war chief exhibits signs of a higher class descent than Josephus as allowed. (Goodman, *Ruling Class*, 205–6.)

43. Grünewald, *Bandits*, 104; *B.J.* 4.529–34. The use of the proclamation follows King Zedekiah's emancipation (Jeremiah 34.8–11). Simon was issuing a royal decree in a time of eschatological crisis. He was, in this regard, claiming to be God's anointed deliver. (See Rhoads, *Revolution*, 142.)

44. *B.J.* 4:574–6. Simon executed Matthias and his three sons without a trial, denying them burial. Simon also refused the populace the right to assemble, threatening immediate execution to groups. (*B.J.* 5.533.) Simon was not completely evil, as he did imprison many more than he executed, including the parents (with their attendants) of Josephus. (*B.J.* 5.33; 544–5.)

45. Horsley, *Bandits*, 125.

lem, capturing the would-be king. His reception in Rome, however, was fitting of royalty, albeit a rebellious royalty. He was the single prisoner executed during the Triumph.[46] While we will explore more of Simon when we read Mark mimetically, for now, I want to explore the connection between Simon and the Zealots.

Within the walls of the Temple, John of Gischala is usually identified with the Zealots, but the Zealots did not start the war as a part of John's army. Simon, however, is identified with them first. When Josephus introduces Simon for the first time it follows the introduction to the Zealots: Τούτοις ὁ Ἄνανος παρακροτεῖ τὸ πλῆθος ἐπὶ τοὺς ζηλωτάς οὐκ ἀγνοῶν μὲν ὡς εἶεν ἤδη δυσκατάλυτοι πλήθει τε καὶ νεότητι καὶ παραστήματι ψυχῆς τὸ πλέον δὲ συνειδήσει τῶν εἰργασμένων οὐ γὰρ ἐνδώσειν αὐτοὺς εἰς ἐσχάτην συγγνώμην ἐφ' οἷς ἔδρασαν ἐλπίσαντας (B.J. 4.193)." It may be that at the start, Simon was among the Zealots, or it may be that Josephus is attempting to connect for his readers Simon and the Zealots—two groups he hated more than most. A third option also remains. Possibly John's Zealots were different only in leadership than Simon's Zealots. By the fall of Jerusalem, the Zealots of John would be only a small fighting force alongside that of Simon. The only other point worth mentioning here is that the Zealots, and Simon much later, would find their situation related directed to the Temple.[47]

For the Jews, the rise of messianism was a different concept than we have either in later rabbinical reflection, as in the *Shemoneh Esrei*, or even in the Gospels, especially in the developed Gospels of Luke

---

46. Goodman speculates that Simon was specifically given the honor of dying in Triumph because of Titus. An enemy needed a figurehead, but this was difficult for most of the war. The war began with a confederation of groups aimed, in one way or the other, at removing Roman control from Judaea. Titus did not simply choose Simon because he was the last one standing, but because Simon provided Titus a comparable enemy. (Goodman, *Ruling Class*, 203.)

47. B.J. 4.147. The Zealots followed Judas the Galilean's anarchist approach to governing. They elected their own leaders and even attacked the nobles of the city. The confusion surrounding not just the Zealots, but also all of the factions in the Revolt, should not worry us too much. The Zealots began with Florus attacked the Jews in another long line of abuses. The clash subsided, but briefly, when King Agrippa II almost persuaded the populace to renounce violence and become submissive to Florus until Rome could send another procurator. The Jews would have none of this. With Florus's attack on Jerusalem, Eleazar finally have the momentum to end the sacrifices for Rome and the emperor. He led the Zealots from within Jerusalem, but other groups by the name continued in the countryside. The disparate collection of Zealots explains why they are various associated with John, Simon, or independently.

and John. One particular notion did not take hold until after the destruction of the Temple. For the Jews, as 70 came and went, the idea of messiah and king become unified. He was going to be the political Übermensch. This new vision of the messiah allowed the brigand chiefs to see themselves as part of God's plan and their banditry as divinely sanctioned, much as freedom fighters/terrorists have done ever since. After all, David himself had been a bandit at one time. For Rome, the messianic expectations took on a new flair through the pen of Josephus, that of miracle worker as well as a worldwide political governor. We must not fault the historian too much for being just a little self-aggrandizing, as his entire way of life was uprooted. This would be, for him, a part of God's plan—and if Vespasian were at the center of it, then Josephus would be too.

Vespasian

In his account of the Jewish Revolt, Josephus records that he only surrendered due to God's prompting. "Ῥωμαῖοι δὲ τὸν Ἰώσηπον ἀναζητοῦντες κατά τε ὀργὴν σφετέραν καὶ σφόδρα τοῦ στρατηγοῦ φιλοτιμουμένου μεγίστη γὰρ ἦν μοῖρα τοῦ πολέμου ληφθεὶς τούς τε νεκροὺς διηρεύνων καὶ τοὺς ἀποκρύφους ὁ δὲ τῆς πόλεως ἁλισκομένης δαιμονίῳ τινὶ συνεργίᾳ χρησάμενος μέσον μὲν ἑαυτὸν ἐκκλέπτει τῶν πολεμίων καθάλλεται δὲ εἴς τινα βαθὺν λάκκον ᾧ πλατὺ σπήλαιον διέζευκτο κατὰ πλευρὰν τοῖς ἄνωθεν ἀόρατον (B.J., 3.340–1)." Josephus was not simply guided by divine favor, but saw himself as predetermined to be an interpreter of dreams, due to his priestly lineage, something no doubt connected to the biblical Joseph. This leads him to reconsider this dreams that preceded his capture and to offer a prayer. He writes, "ἦν δὲ καὶ περὶ κρίσεις ὀνείρων ἱκανὸς συμβαλεῖν τὰ ἀμφιβόλως ὑπὸ τοῦ θείου λεγόμενα τῶν γε μὴν ἱερῶν βίβλων οὐκ ἠγνόει τὰς προφητείας ὡς ἂν αὐτός τε ὢν ἱερεὺς καὶ ἱερέων ἔγγονος ὢν ἐπὶ τῆς τότε ὥρας ἔνθους γενόμενος καὶ τὰ φρικώδη τῶν προσφάτων ὀνείρων σπάσας φαντάσματα προσφέρει τῷ θεῷ λεληθυῖαν εὐχὴν κἀπειδὴ τὸ Ἰουδαίων ἔφη φῦλον ὀκλάσαι δοκεῖ σοι τῷ κτίσαντι μετέβη δὲ πρὸς Ῥωμαίους ἡ τύχη πᾶσα καὶ τὴν ἐμὴν ψυχὴν ἐπελέξω τὰ μέλλοντα εἰπεῖν δίδωμι μὲν Ῥωμαίοις τὰς χεῖρας ἑκὼν καὶ ζῶ μαρτύρομαι δὲ ὡς οὐ προδότης ἀλλὰ σὸς εἶμι διάκονος (B.J., 3.352–4)." This is all a well-crafted stage play to give Josephus narrative basis for telling Vespasian of the Roman's future rule of the empire, "Τοῦτο ἀκούσας ὁ Ἰώσηπος μόνῳ τι διαλεχθῆναι θέλειν ἔλεγεν αὐτῷ μεταστησαμένου δ' ἐκείνου πλὴν τοῦ παιδὸς Τίτου καὶ δυοῖν φίλων τοὺς ἄλλους ἅπαντας σὺ μὲν ἔφη Οὐεσπασιανέ νομίζεις αἰχμάλωτον αὐτὸ μόνον εἰληφέναι Ἰώσηπον ἐγὼ δὲ ἄγγελος ἥκω σοι μειζόνων μὴ γὰρ ὑπὸ θεοῦ προπεμπόμενος ᾔδειν τὸν Ἰουδαίων νόμον καὶ πῶς στρατηγοῖς ἀποθνήσκειν πρέπει. Νέρωνί με πέμπεις τί γάρ—οἱ μετὰ Νέρωνα μέχρι σοῦ διάδοχοι μενοῦσιν σὺ Καῖσαρ Οὐεσπασιανέ καὶ αὐτοκράτωρ σὺ καὶ παῖς ὁ σὸς οὗτος δέσμει δέ με νῦν ἀσφαλέστερον καὶ τήρει σεαυτῷ δεσπότης μὲν γὰρ οὐ μόνον ἐμοῦ σὺ Καῖσαρ ἀλλὰ καὶ γῆς καὶ θαλάττης καὶ παντὸς ἀνθρώπων γένους ἐγὼ δὲ ἐπὶ τιμωρίαν δέομαι φρουρᾶς μείζονος εἰ κατασχεδιάζω καὶ θεοῦ (B.J., 3.399–402)." Josephus is now the divine messenger for the soon to be Messiah, Vespasian. He had placed himself as Elijah. While there are not specific intertextual cues between these passages of *B.J.* and the Elijah-Elisha narratives, there are allusions presenting Josephus as an Elijah for the Messiah Vespasian.[48]

Josephus writes, "ὅπου γε Ἰουδαῖοι καὶ τὸ ἱερὸν μετὰ τὴν καθαίρεσιν τῆς Ἀντωνίας τετράγωνον ἐποίησαν ἀναγεγραμμένον ἐν τοῖς λογίοις ἔχοντες ἁλώσεσθαι τὴν πόλιν καὶ τὸν ναόν ἐπειδὰν τὸ ἱερὸν γένηται τετράγωνον τὸ δ' ἐπᾶραν αὐτοὺς μάλιστα πρὸς τὸν πόλεμον ἦν χρησμὸς ἀμφίβολος ὁμοίως ἐν τοῖς ἱεροῖς εὑρημένος γράμμασιν ὡς κατὰ τὸν καιρὸν ἐκεῖνον ἀπὸ τῆς χώρας αὐτῶν τις ἄρξει τῆς οἰκουμένης τοῦθ' οἱ μὲν ὡς οἰκεῖον ἐξέλαβον καὶ πολλοὶ τῶν σοφῶν ἐπλανήθησαν περὶ τὴν κρίσιν ἐδήλου δ' ἄρα τὴν Οὐεσπασιανοῦ τὸ λόγιον ἡγεμονίαν ἀποδειχθέντος ἐπὶ Ἰουδαίας αὐτοκράτορος (B.J. 6:311–3)"[49] Here, Josephus is somehow making use of an unidentified oracle to suggest Vespasian is the fulfillment of a promise of a future worldwide rule by God's agent. The Emperor is the σωτῆρα ("savior," *B.J.* 7:71).[50] It is in this political situation that Mark's Gospel grew and offered a confrontation.[51]

48. Specifically, see 1 Kings 20.12–14; 21.10; 2 Kings 1.16; 6.9–10; 8.7–12

49. That Josephus could do this is no surprise. First, he was a moderate and did not want the war to begin with. Second, he had visited Rome and upon his return was noticeably different. His surrender to Vespasian while proclaiming Vespasian as the next Caesar could derive from his time in Rome with Nero's consort. Further, the priest in him would understand the narrative of the Hebrew Scriptures that centered on God's use of Gentile rulers to punish (Nebuchadnezzar) and liberate (Cyrus) Israel.

50. This theme was later picked up by Suetonius (see *Vesp.* 4.5), Tacitus (see *Hist.* 5.13.1–2), and expanded, but it is Josephus who started the ideological motif.

51. Christiane Saulnier suggests the idea that Tacitus's account was independent of Josephus. See, Saulnier, "Falvius Josephe et la Propoagande Flavienne," 550.

Josephus, no doubt grappling with his priestly ancestors, used Scripture to build the notion that Vespasian exemplified the requirements of an Eastern and cosmic origin of the ruler of the world. Recognition of this reality could only occur after Vespasian had returned to Rome to claim his imperial scepter. After the destruction of the Temple, something Josephus witnessed, the historian would return to Rome at Titus's side to find that his position was less needed in the Eternal City than on the battlefield. He would also be aware of the still lingering effects of the recent civil war and the lack of royal blood in Vespasian's veins. While we are given accounts of the propaganda by later Roman historians (Suetonius (c. 72–130), Tacitus (c. 56–117, with his *Histories* written about 105 and *Annals* near his death), and Dio (c. 160–230)), it was Josephus who first proposed such measures.[52] Josephus began his work in his *B.J.* by highlighting the divine favor of the Romans in the war with God's people. Likewise, he disparaged the Jewish hopes, although he focused more on the leaders and the people of Jerusalem who he credited for the Revolt rather than the whole of the Jewish populace. But, Josephus was not alone in producing a syncretic work, making use of his native tradition to promote the Roman conqueror.

Upon arriving in Alexandria, Vespasian began to proclaim his legitimacy, or at least that is what we are told by the historians. He quickly moved to become the ritualistic head of Egypt by performing miracles and receiving portents from wise men. While the accounts of Vespasian in Alexandria are no less mythical than elements in other tales—and would have been recognized as such by the commoner—he did not shy away from such accolades but rather relished them. Vespasian was received in Alexandria by Philo's nephew and in such a way as to be presented as the new Serapis—the local Hellenistic deity synthesized from Egyptian and Greek mythology to accommodate the heirs of Alexander. Vespasian being declared the return of Serapis fits well with

---

52. This is not to suggest that the theory could not have been proposed by another source, especially given that Philo's nephew and prefect of Egypt supported Vespasian. Egypt was also the place connected to declaring Vespasian emperor as well as a place in which Vespasian received several portents directed towards the Romans that he was indeed divinely favored to be the Emperor, but this would be an argument from silence. See: Winn, *Purpose*, 154–156. The issue of dating of which I would disagree with Winn only by a small amount of time is one which may be somewhat settled by the use of mimetic criticism.

Josephus's oracle that the world ruler would come from the East.[53] Romans also feared that Nero would return from Alexandria to relocate the capitol to Egypt.[54] By going to Egypt, not only did Vespasian give credit to his supporters while gaining a military advantage, but also gained the image of Alexander and quieted the fears that Nero would return from Alexandria.[55] In one short sea trip from Caesarea on the sea to Alexandria and then to Rome, Vespasian metamorphosed into the Jewish messiah, Alexander, Serapis, and even Nero himself.

For now, however, it is enough to conclude with the idea that Vespasian, a commoner, had risen out of the sea of people to sit on the throne.[56] After crushing Vitellius's legions, Vespasian turned his attention to winning the ideological war. Like his legions who had marched before him, he sought a machine to create an image that the people would not question. Unlike Nero, fear would not build this image.

---

53. A logical reason why Josephus would not include the events of Alexandria in his account is his Jewish heritage. No doubt, pagan gods still troubles the decedent of the priests.

54. As Trevor Luke notes, "The silence of Josephus suggests that these wonders were not prominent in early Flavian propaganda. Josephus is the earliest extant source for Vespasian's sojourn in Egypt. Since he accompanied Vespasian and Titus to Alexandria, he should have been present to see or at least hear of these wonders, but he does not mention them. Others have ascribed this omission to Josephus's reticence to report events that conflicted with his religious scruples or his self-interest, but another equally viable explanation is that the wonders were not publicly emphasized in the early years of Flavian rule." (Luke, *Healing Touch*, 7.) Josephus, writing within a two year time frame of the destruction of the Temple records signs such as the star symbolizing the destruction of the Temple (*B.J.* 6.289) as well as his own prophecies. Indeed, the silence of Josephus on the supposed miracles, those that occurred in Alexandria rather than Judea may suggest that there is an alternative source.

55. Rome was fed with Egyptian grain

56. Vespasian was familiar with the already existing imperial ideology based on the emperor as divine. The new emperor quickly empowered it, however, but infusing it with both Egyptian and Jewish theological strata. The imperial cult was more than mythological stories, but an ideologically driven war machine laying siege to the populace preventing questions and outright challenges to the emperor. Rome was built not just on mythology, but the power of the proper employment of the myth. Crossan identifies four powers of Rome: military, economic, political, and ideological. This last imperium created the divine-man, the emperor, who mystically shared cohabitation with the Roman pantheon. It was advanced through poems, stories, and other forms of supported propaganda. (Crossan, "Imperial Theology," 60–73.) I have not focused on Roman imperial theology, but only where Vespasian used Jewish theology to support it. Roman imperial theology existed long before the birth of Jesus and Mark's Gospel, and continued after it; however, what is important are the changes Vespasian made.

Vespasian sought to return to the Augustan model. Like Augustus, he sought a scribe who could deliver a message. Vespasian employed lessons learned from previous imperials cults to create one using a variety of sources to ensure that the people would not see him as a usurper, or a dictator, or even one of impure blood, but as the divinely favored emperor. Between the destruction of the Jewish Temple and the building of this Temple of Peace (completed c. 75) Vespasian employ Josephus's writing talents. The Jewish historian proved more than capable of producing a far-reaching revelation that forced Mark's community to reconsider their positions. Mark assaulted the ideological legions when he began to *unwrite* the violent abuse of Rome.

Having established the social history of Mark's crisis, along with proposing his historical referents, we now turn the sources he used to stand against Rome.

Rome as the Crucial Impetus?

In reading Paul, we are left with no evidence that Rome had any real knowledge of a sect of Jews who believed the messiah had come. In fact, according to Romans 13, Paul was rather an accommodationist. The Roman Empire does not appear to trouble Paul; instead, it other Jewish teachers challenged Paul. Christianity was still an intramural sport in Early Judaism. The closest that we have to an anti-Christian stance by Rome is with Nero. Yet after an examination of the fire, one cannot be assured that Nero had purposely singled out the Christians, or had simply found them the only remaining group to blame. But, this crisis was different. The community to whom Mark was writing was facing something different. When Nero had promised persecution, they still had the Pauline hope that Jesus would return. They were loyal citizens, paying taxing, and living in peace as much as possible with all others. With the crisis of the civil war and the revolt, suddenly texts like the *Psalms of Solomon* became real.

Is it possible the chaotic aftermath of the Jewish Revolt forced a proto-Christian community to develop a theological position to defend against the megalomania gripping the world? The Jesus of Paul is not the Jesus of later Christian Tradition. He had a family and followers who he appeared to after his death. There are no miracles associated with the Pauline Jesus beyond this appearance. Jesus did not oppose the

Judaism(s) of his day. Paul says that he descended from David, but this was not yet the messianic title "Son of David." He was known to be crucified publicly, very human, and shared a meal with his band before he died. Early in his career, Paul promises that Jesus will return as a triumphant king. He did not. The Temple was destroyed and the world ended in Rome and in Jerusalem. No Jesus. No peace. But, the brutal tyrant Simon had waged war against Rome as the king of Israel only to suffer a bloodthirsty defeat by a Roman general who now reigned as the rule of the world, emperor of Rome, Serapis, Alexander—and the Jewish messiah. This is Mark's crucial impetus, his battle within and without, which impugns the community's relationship with Jesus. Mark does not surrender and proves that resistance is not futile. He finds his transcript and begins to reconstruct a reality challenging Augustan theology.[57]

With the social history established, we now turn to possible sources that are within Mark's specific temporal and ideological boundaries.

Part III: Literary Details

Stylistically, Mark's Gospel is a labyrinth of impoverished language, as if the author was original only in his desire to decimate the endowment of Homer's language. However, the gladiatorial arena of literary examination is no longer dangerous. Literary critics have identified, and still argue over, the role of the author and the audience. The author's role is that of force, felt unabashedly in the language of the text. Keeping the audience in view is essential in discovering various merisms throughout Mark, however. By remembering Mark as a first century Jew, we can surmise his linguistic strategies and possible sources while acknowledging a synthesized social context. Simply because one follows the pattern of another, we do not have to assume sources are equally obtained. In a recent work, scholars have suggested Jewish interpreters began to read their scriptures allegorically following the patterns put forth by Stoic interpreters of Homer.[58] We must be weary of assuming style means sources. Because Jewish interpreters used the same methods Stoics used in reading Homer, we should not expect to find Homer plastered in the Talmud or other Jewish documents of this time. Discovering accurate sources requires a light tread.

---

57. Crossan, "Imperial Theology," 60.
58. Niehoff, *Jewish Exegesis and Homeric Scholarship in Alexandria*.

Mimetic Criticism and the Gospel of Mark

The Antetext

The Septuagint is the locus of education for the Jew of Mark's time. If the tradition regarding Mark is near accurate, the Evangelist is a member of a diaspora family of Levites. Mark's social standing mirrors Josephus's own—that of an upper class Jew from a family of priests—a dual inheritance that gave him a wealth of educational opportunities. He would have studied his cultic writings from an early childhood as well as learned ways to interpret it. The Septuagint gave him vocabulary and important images while providing his audience with mnemonic cues which Mark could use to enlarge his story with just a few words. It is without question that Mark made use of the Septuagint as we can see from even a brief reading of his Gospel. Recognizing this allows us to begin to look for shared phrases and literary images buried in the Gospel.

Literacy is limited to knowing how to read and write sufficiently; this is not something we should expect from a first century Palestine. Yet, illiteracy does not imply an uneducated audience. Orality was important because it allowed for memorization, a tool that would retain a community's stories and interpretations as well as shape other stories. Memorization allows for audiences to supply their own material especially when the author demands audience participation. Modern examples of this are rampant in American political circles as those who seek or who hold public office often subtly bury allusions to biblical verses in their speeches to legitimize their stance. A prime example of this is the phrase "if my people. . ." that suddenly has taken the place of "We the people." Mnemonic devices are important not in simply memorizing something, but in transmitting a broader message to incite an audience to some emotion. A community drawing on the Septuagint in their daily religious observances would develop mnemonic devices that authors, sectarian or not, could have used to their advantage. The Septuagint gave Mark a literary backbone for his Gospel.

The Memetext

Would Mark have had access to Josephus? This is the most difficult source to ascertain; however, we have two sources related to the Jewish Revolt that lead us back to Josephus. First, there is the original written source of Josephus's *Wars of the Jews*. While some may find it unreasonable to consider that Mark was using Josephus as a literary source, we will see that Mark not only has found some reason for his story in Josephus's colloquy, but more than that, mines the historian's account for images to imitate. Josephus maintained that the source for his writings, especially the *B.J.*, were first and foremost an eyewitness account, and only later did he receive material about events he was not involved in from Vespasian and Titus.[59]

Josephus inked his first tales of the victories won by Vespasian after he arrived in Rome. He did not write in Greek; Josephus wrote in his native Aramaic.[60] Josephus's first writing was a small pamphlet in Aramaic and, after being presented to Vespasian, was transformed into what we know today.[61] Before that, however, Josephus's initial pamphlet was self-published to a circle of friends in Rome and in Asia.[62] Desmond Seward notes "a full-scale chronicle of the war in Judea, written in Greek, with numerous copies made by professional scribes on papyrus rolls...could command a wide circulation in the Roman world and would demonstrate that throughout the campaign the Flavians had enjoyed the favor of the gods."[63] Seward notes that Josephus, who admittedly had no Greek training, used the war memoirs of Vespasian and Titus along with assistants and his own experiences to write his account. Given the spirit of the venture, Mark would not need to wait long for either a copy of the original Aramaic or the translated pamphlet.[64] It

---

59. *Antiquities* 1.1–5.

60. *B.J.* 1.3.

61. ἄτοπον ἡγησάμενος περιιδεῖν πλαζομένην ἐπὶ τηλικούτοις πράγμασι τὴν ἀλήθειαν καὶ Πάρθους μὲν καὶ Βαβυλωνίους Ἀράβων τε τοὺς πορρωτάτω καὶ τὸ ὑπὲρ Εὐφράτην ὁμόφυλον ἡμῖν Ἀδιαβηνούς τε γνῶναι διὰ τῆς ἐμῆς ἐπιμελείας ἀκριβῶς ὅθεν τε ἤρξατο καὶ δι' ὅσων ἐχώρησεν παθῶν ὁ πόλεμος καὶ ὅπως κατέστρεψεν ἀγνοεῖν δὲ Ἕλληνας ταῦτα καὶ Ῥωμαίων τοὺς μὴ ἐπιστρατευσαμένους ἐντυγχάνοντας ἢ κολακείαις ἢ πλάσμασι (*B.J.* 1:6.)

62. The listing Josephus gives of the destinations includes those areas likely to still revolt, in case of imperial domains, or likely to attempt to invade the eastern portion of the empire, such as is the case for Parthia. An announcement of Rome's massive victory, the selection of a new emperor, and the idea that the emperor was already seen as divine would work to curtail any hopes of attacking Rome while the empire began to rebuild. (See Rajak, *Josephus*, 180–4.)

63. Seward, *Traitor*, 241.

64. The process of publication followed other ancient works, with a progression of books published consecutively. B.J. has a total of seven books in what we think is a single composition. Josephus could have published 1–6 before the dedication of the Temple of Peace (c 75) with book 7 coming shortly thereafter. Scholars have suggested

is likely that Mark found copies littering the streets. The reason for the fast promulgation of the propaganda is twofold.[65] The Jews were still fighting in Jerusalem and challenges were still presented to Vespasian's throne, both from the Roman nobility and the foreign nations.

There were more sources available to Mark. Vespasian and Titus kept journals of the war. Josephus claimed to have use of these journals, as no doubt they were accessible at least by the promulgation of decree of Vespasian's εὐαγγέλια (B.J. 4:618). It is doubtful, however, that the messianic elements would have made it into those diaries, unless Josephus somehow guided the their keeping. But, had Josephus or others started to proclaim that Vespasian was indeed the Jewish Messiah, or the Governor of the World who had come from Judea (or the King of Egypt, for that matter), before the publication of his pamphlet it would not have taken long for such local legends to become reality for the populace, especially in Rome. McCasland notes that it would have taken only five years for the legends of Vespasian to appear as reality.[66] Josephus records that others had started to compose histories, but with a sentiment that Luke the Evangelist would appreciate, Josephus found their histories lacking (B.J. 1.6–8). I recognize the journals and portent legends are arguments from silence; however, Josephus made use of them because they were accessible, something that allows us to think that they were most likely known to Mark.

However, what if Mark is not using a written source? In the introduction, we explored the concept of the memetext symbolizing the ideological crisis the author confronts, and thus remains in the social

---

that the seventh book is a later addition, but the approximate date is not decided. (See Rajak, *Josephus*, 195n.23.) This final book deals with scenes two important scenes, that of the Roman Triumph, something Mark saw firsthand, and Masada, a missing part of Mark's Gospel.

65. The historian writes that part of his goal was to deter others from continuing the revolt (B.J. 3.108). There may be another reason, as Josephus suggests. The audience of Josephus consists of both Romans and Jews, easily seen from inclusion of particular material in his prologue. The Romans get the table of contents, but for the Jews, Josephus writes to "give a precise description of the sufferings of the prisoners taken in the several towns (B.J. 1.22)." This passage is exceedingly important in dating Josephus's work due to the assignment of the slaves by Vespasian. Josephus claims to have known the slaves personally, and in such a way as to know their origin and their personal well-being. If this is true, Josephus would have need of writing quickly as well as making a quick publication. After all, the despair of the Jewish world would not have the urgency after Vespasian as it did in the aftermath of the Jewish Revolt.

66. McCasland, "Portents in Josephus and in the Gospels," 323–335.

ether. Mark's memetext is the Jewish Revolt, a visible event causing the heavens to take notice needing no written introduction. Regardless of accessibility to Josephus's pamphlet or final work Mark has access to the same history as Josephus.[67] However, in the subsequent commentary, I will refer to Josephus extensively because he is the closest historical account of the Revolt to Mark.[68] There are also literary connections shared between Josephus and Mark, something we cannot ignore. Josephus's written works could provide Mark a written source to write against, given that *B.J.* was published in various stages from early 71 to shortly after 75 CE. However even if Mark used the Greek translation of *B.J.*, the document would only remain as part of the memetext instead of its totality.

Language Barriers

Mark's Greek is not polished, even for *koine* Greek. Although Mark escapes the bewildering glances from scholars of the Apocalypse, his Greek is often considered just as rough. Maurice Casey suggests that Mark is making a translation directly from the Aramaic for some of the Gospel (2.23—3.6; 9.11–13; 10.35–45; 14.12–26). After all, the style of Mark shows remarkable inattention to normative Greek syntax as well as a high rate of Aramaisms. Might this really explain Mark's poor use of Greek, however? It is possible, but it is not certain and no longer the other option available to Markan scholars. Other less likely theories include supposing that Mark has conflated both Matthew and Luke. What I propose here is that Mark's language is purposeful and exhibits a crisis of the psyche.

---

67. We should assume that any source Josephus had access to, Mark did as well. Rhoads points to several documents such as the court historians of various Judean kings. Jewish sources could underlie Josephus's accounts of the various sects of Judaism. The fight hand accounts from Agrippa II, soldiers, prisoners, and others would help as well. This might not be accessible to Mark right away, but after the way, when stories began to spread (especially about the siege of Jerusalem) Mark would have received some similar information. Rhoads also notes the distinctively Roman narratives in B.J. that could only come from written Roman sources (the Triumph, troop locations, etc . . .) (Rhoads, *Revolution*, 14–6.) Neither Josephus nor Mark were the only authors of the period. Sources could come from Rabbinic circles, Qumran, and other places yet identified.

68. It could be that Mark draws from these journals or even other histories, but with no copy remaining, it is difficult to ascertain.

Mimetic Criticism and the Gospel of Mark

Robert H. Gundry writes, "Aramaisms do create a presumption in favor of earliness and of origin in or near Palestine (that is, in an Aramaic milieu). Therefore, unless one can conceive of wholesale fabrication and radical warping of the gospel tradition in the very places and at the very time eyewitnesses of Jesus's ministry lived, Aramaisms do increase the likelihood of historicity."[69] Gundry also argued that a reverse, or the absence of Semitisms, would not necessarily mean that the Gospels were inauthentic. He notes Greek had penetrated "all classes of Jews in Palestine."[70] Gundry also allows that the culture of Palestine at this time allowed for a variety of languages, including Hebrew, used by the general populace. We find this milieu on recovered ossuaries dating near the Jewish War. Gundry, citing Bagatti and Milik, note that archeological digs before 1958 recovered several of these boxes. Seven were inscribed with the Hebrew language, eleven with Aramaic, and the same number with Greek. These are not the only Greek-inscribed ossuaries found in Palestine. As a matter of fact, many ossuaries have several languages on one, including both Greek and Aramaic. The high rate of Semitism in the Septuagint likely gave rise to a form of Semitic Greek that sounded like a hybrid language of Greek with poorly translated Aramaisms seeping through.[71]

Casey makes several assumptions regarding Mark's sources and much like other historical critics begins by refusing to challenge the truthfulness of Mark's history. In *Aramaic Sources of Mark's Gospel*, Casey compiles an examination of recent attempts at uncovering the original language of Jesus. His assumptions begin early on, however, in suggesting that Gentiles filled Mark's audience. Like Crossley after him, Casey assigns a date of the early 40's. This has little historical validity,

---

69. Gundry, *Milieu*, 404.
70. Gundry, *Milieu*, 405.
71. Aramaisms are not the only other language to creep into Mark's vocabulary. Mark also uses Latin, which would have happened regardless of provenance. Words such as census (κῆνσος, 12.14), centurio (κεντυρίων, 15.39, 44, 45), denarius (δηνάριον, 12.15), legio (λεγιών, 5:9, 15), modius (μόδιος, 4.21), praetorium (πραιτώριον, 15.16), quadrans (κοδράντης, 12.42), sextarius (ξέστης, 7.4), speculator (σπεκουλάτωρ, 6.27), and flagellum (φραγελλόω, 15.15). There are also the Latin idioms in extremis esse (ἐσχάτως ἔχει, 5:23) and verberibus eum acceperunt (ῥαπίσμασιν αὐτὸν ἔλαβον, 14:65) in Mark. That Latinisms are included does not mean a Roman provenance, and neither do I mean to even subtly suggest it. Having established the idea that Mark's language is one of imperfection and well within the cultural milieu of the time, let us fully turn to Maurice Casey's theory that Mark made use of original Aramaic sources.

as there is no real Gentile mission at this point. Casey presupposes Mark's Greek is a result of a huge cultural shift taking place immediately after the death of Jesus. Further, in regards to the Eucharist in Mark 14.12–26, Casey feels comfortable that he has demonstrated that this was not an institution of a Christian rite, but a common Passover meal mistakenly accepted as ritual due to the cultural shift. Given that Casey believes that Mark was written c. 40 CE, then it is quite unlikely such a dramatic cultural shift occurred so as to cause Mark's community to forget all ritual observances and their Jewishness, especially since the God-fearers still practiced some Jewish cultic practices. Mark's Greek is filled with Semitic structures as well as untranslated Aramaic words, something he allows for as the translator. He notes that this is not found in Matthew and Luke who also do their best to polish Mark's Greek such as transforming the historical present into past tense while removing the loan words. There is, along with the historical present, the parataxis in Mark, and asyndeton.[72]

A return to the Aramaic becomes possible with the discoveries of the texts at Qumran. Casey notes that if Mark was fiction or if Mark's Gospel were so "heavily edited that Aramaic sources were irrecoverable" then a return to Aramaic would not be possible. While he is able to demonstrate that a retro-translation of the Gospel to the Aramaic is possible, this limits his ability to consider other possibilities for the Semitic structure in the Gospel. His conclusion is circular. Because he can identify an Aramaic structure underneath, Casey assumes that Mark had access to "substantial written Aramaic sources."[73] One possible explanation for the language issue is that Mark is a polyglot but still thinks in Aramaic and thus it comes out in his writing.

This is not the only fault in Casey's theory. He allows only a few years for the original sources to have need of "extensive editing." However, little doubt remains that Casey pushes us to examine Mark's poor Greek, calling attention to his language as something needing independent study. However, I do not agree that Mark made use of Aramaic sources, acting only as a translator; I will posit two explanations for Mark's poor use of Greek which will serve to show that the poor quality of the language is in of itself a strategy of his rhetoric.

---

72. Both John and Mark share a proclivity for parataxis and the historical present.

73. Casey, *Aramaic Sources*, 255.

Mimetic Criticism and the Gospel of Mark

While the topic of Mark's Christology will be dealt with below there are a few points here deserving attention. Casey's solution to the problem of the Son of Man title is also based on the Aramaic original, so we will cover it now. Again, this is based on the assumption that there existed an original Aramaic source concerning Jesus written by eyewitnesses, but while Casey is careful to avoid the ideological biases of other commentators, he is not so careful when he relies too heavily on his own presupposition. However, regardless of his own biases, Casey's central thesis around the phrase ὁ υἱὸς τοῦ ἀνθρώπου is vitally important to mimetic criticism. It simply means nothing more than the emphasis of the humanity of a person, an emphasis important to the crisis. Casey is correct that the Gospel writer made this into a substantive Christological title. Of course, while I do not agree that there is an underlying written source to Mark's Gospel, I do agree with Casey when he writes, "This means that our oldest Gospel was completely involved in the processes of the original production of ὁ υἱὸς τοῦ ἀνθρώπου as a major Christological title." An Aramaic title in a Greek composition points us to the Septuagint.

The Septuagint provides more than just a structuring scaffold for the Gospel. It gives Mark an ideological point of departure. Tessa Rajak notes the "superficially awkward translation" never saw correction until centuries after it have had become heavily used.[74] Yet, given the high Greek of the *Letter of Aristeas*, *Sirach*'s prologue, and the *Wisdom of Solomon*, the question remains as to why the Septuagint contains such poor examples of Hebrew into Greek? If the origin of the Septuagint is in Alexandria, then the quality of the Greek becomes more of a problem. Rajak notes the often-dismissive route taken by scholars and linguists when dealing with the language of the LXX. Noting the Semitisms in the translation that causes the noticeable rough language, scholars often see a poor attempt at translation, blaming the translators for linguistic ineptness. There are also problems with syntax and calques. Rajak follows Benjamin Wright in suggesting that the translators could adopt their styles as a matter of choice. She also mentions the possibility of an interlinear use to the translation.[75]

The translators of the Septuagint purposely created a translation language to subtly challenge the Hellenization of Judaism. Rajak notes

---

74. Rajak, *Survival*, 103.
75. Here, she follows Albert Pietersma.

that the translation style of the LXX does not meet either the requirements of translation or the noted ability to accurately move from Hebrew to Greek found in small pockets of the LXX. Pointing to the *Letter of Aristeas* and the prologue to *Sirach* as examples of high Greek, the author is able to note Greek learning and writing was of a somewhat higher level than what we find in the Septuagint. Further, we must consider the longevity of the translation, in that later translators did not attempt to correct the deficits. She suggests that the language contained therein is actually a comprise between two sociological forces for the translations, namely, that of the "pull of acculturation and the anxiety of cultural annihilation."[76] This style was "deliberately and consciously maintained."[77] This naivety of Greek is not due to the lack of skill, but is a rather ingenious way of subverting acculturation. Following several scholars, Rajak is able to show that even during Philo's time (c. 50) Hebrew was still known, if even by the educational elites. The Alexandrian Jewish community became dependent upon the text, and in some ways were created and then preserved by the text. However this, Rajak assures us, is the mission of the translators. She writes, "the very character of this special language in itself served from the beginning as a means of self-identifying with a primary ethnic indicator, the language of the patria, and self-distancing from Alexandrian society."[78] This allowed for a "kind of recalcitrance" to the full accession to Hellenism.[79] Such a language would allow a focus on the Hebrew to be maintained either through the rough style of it mirroring the original or because it would require the presence of the Hebrew text to understand. This rough style of language is also thought to contribute to the performance of the Septuagint in an oral setting; something Rajak notes was common in scribal circles. If Rajak is indeed correct, that the translators of the Septuagint were protecting their culture against Hellenism, then this

---

76. Rajak, *Survival*, 126.
77. Rajak, *Survival*, 134.
78. Rajak, *Survival*, 152.
79. This is the concept of illocution, something prevalent in apocalypses. See Hellholm, *Das Visionenbuch des Hennas als Apokalypse*.

is something Mark would have understood.[80] Mark's attraction to this form of resistance is probable.[81] But, there is another possibility as well

Josephus wrote his first pamphlet in Aramaic and then with the wealth of the Emperor behind him, had it translated to Greek all the while claiming that his Greek was poor (see above). Instead of an Aramaic original for Mark, it may be that the author of the Gospel is mimicking Josephus's false humility in such a way as to ridicule the fragile historian. As Rajak points out, imitation of other styles was a part of imitation. We see change of styles in Josephus.[82] It is quite possible that if Mark was indebted to Josephus for the crisis that finally pushed him to write his Gospel, then what is happening with the language of the Gospel is Mark's open mocking of Josephus by his language, or rather, calling attention to how a real Jew fought the Empire. Josephus had capitulated, even in accepting his work to be translated into Greek; Mark followed the Septuagint in resisting defeat and acculturation by taking the language of the invaders and butchering it.

Conclusion

Is there a possibility that Mark is using sources other than the Septuagint and the Jewish Revolt? There is always a possibility but the probability of a theological crisis greater than the one produced by the Jewish Revolt is rather low. If we are going to assume the use of mimesis in Mark,

---

80. Rajak calls the style of the Septuagint "the unremitting chime of an accumulation of phrases or clauses tied together by the connective 'and.'" (Rajak, *Survival*, 136.) Students of Mark's Greek recognize the deep connection present. Of the 88 recognized sections of Mark, 80 begin with καί, or about 64% of the sentences in the Gospel. Mark does not have the smooth transition between episodes, repeats himself, and moves the action along with an immediate presence. The lack of transition would bewilder modern readers as it does not allow for a linear cause and effect rationale to the actions of Jesus. For more on Mark's butchered style, see Holladay, *Introduction*, 153.

81. Lars Hartman has written on this subject as well, but in regards to the Gospels. See his *Viva Voca*, in the 1997 Mark seminar of Studiorum Novi Testamenti Societas at Birmingham. He acknowledges the use of the Septuagintal Greek in the Synoptics as well as the use of the Elijaha-Elisha narratives. Mark's rough style does away with the usual sense of structure in reading. Instead of the meaning applied to words by subordination, parataxis allows for juxtaposition in turn allowing for metonyms rather than metaphors (Williams, *Gospel Against Parable*, 81; Scheidau, *Sacred Discontent*, 286–93.)

82. Rajak, *Josephus*, 234–6.

then we need to equally assume the need for a crisis that forced Mark to write. We have shown in this chapter that the social crisis of Mark is a long and bloody social upheaval, beginning with simple brigands and ending with the rise of true messianic pretenders to the throne. In Mark's social situation we also find the antetext and the memetext—one as a basis for his writing and the other for cause of his writing. In examining the social history of the crisis, we find a much more likely scenario for Mark to combat and he could have done it, as other authors of the time did, by framing it with Jewish writings. Finally, we also suggest that an Aramaic original is no longer needed as both Mark's historical and contemporary literary models provide him with enough of an impetus to butcher his language. Butchering his language to mimic the Septuagint's style or mocking Josephus would provide a psychological basis for his audience. In the subsequent chapters, Mark's Gospel will be examined through the mimetic lens to identify the author's answer to the social crisis that his community is facing. Mark's sources and tools are varied, but his goal is singular—to combat Vespasian. Josephus, and no doubt Rome itself, caused the Christian community to question its tradition. Mark gave a response.

We understand genre by asking if the work we have in our hands resembles another work either in similarities or differences. The other work must have genealogical connections to our present work in order for us to find a deeper connection. The limits of genre prevent us from looking outside similar works, such as prose for prose, hexameter for hexameter. Instead, for Mark's Gospel, any examination of Markan genre should tie the Gospel to other like-minded literary works that aim to unseat established ideological control. Mark is not writing a full set piece of apocalyptic literature.[83] His writing is too clear and histori-

---

83. Apocalypticism is "not only a literary form. It also implies a particular view of the world. Life on earth is shaped by supernatural forces, which are both good and bad." (Collins, *Apocalypticism*, 7.) The apocalyptic writer appears in moments of crisis when the community is on the brink of complete collapse. Apocalypticism is often marked by crushing defeats of the Saints who are saved only at the last moment by God and his angels, or perhaps some other eschatological figure. The literary work is buried in political imagery that makes the enemies more cartoonish than real, the situation more dire than perhaps it really is, and the only hope is escape. Mark does not show signs of this. I contend that Mark 13 is not truly apocalyptic. The *Gospel of Mark* does not worry about escaping the political onslaught of the Jewish Revolt and the destruction of the Temple, but about undoing the effects. This is not apocalyptic literature, but something more hopeful; it is the anti-apocalyptic.

cally minded for that; however, he is writing in such a way as to create an answer to his social situation, similar to that of the apocalyptic literature; his chronotope is not the Jewish novel, giving space for the hero, but a rhetorical answer to a crisis.[84] That is the genre, a very loose understanding of genre, where Mark falls. This genre includes *Daniel* (a Maccabean-era book), *Enoch*, the *Psalms of Solomon* (meant to engage the Pompeian invasion of Jerusalem as well as the class of priests loyal to Rome), the *Testament of Moses* (see above), the pseudepigraphical books of *Esdras*, and the rewritten canonical books found at Qumran. This Jewish tradition of claiming the inspiration of God in writing to counter Rome or other foreign power is important. Challenging power in such a way gives Mark a living tradition and foundation for writing his Gospel; yet, we need not limit Mark's inspiration to Jewish literary rhetoric.[85] For Mark's inspiration, we look to the source of his crisis—to Rome.

---

84. Mark as a Jewish novel is the thesis of Michael E. Vines (Brill, 2002); however, as with the historical critics in the first chapter, Vines still sees something of a historical narrative underlying the Gospel.

85. Various rewritten texts are preserved in the Dead Sea Scrolls, including Deuteronomy, Isaiah, Habakkuk, and the Psalms. Not only are the texts rewritten, but also so are biblical figures such as Moses, Noah, and Melchizedec. Such a literary tradition would allow Mark to write to his eschatological community using rewritten history almost without question.

4

His Pedagogue

Introduction

THUS FAR, I HAVE attempted to dialogue with Dennis MacDonald's premise of Mark was using Homer as a literary source. I did this while maintaining a well anchored time and place for our author that included Greco-Roman styles of literary rhetoric. Not only does MacDonald miss the period's normative imitation of Homer, but he also charges Mark with using Homer to deflect a theological crisis; instead, I contend Mark would not need Homer either in style or images since the theological crisis was not Greek mythography. I maintain a more suitable theological crisis as well as a stylistic tutor for Mark is found in Mark's locus. We will now position Lucan (39–65 CE) as the literary stylist most responsible for shaping Mark's Gospel. It is not just the proximity shared between Lucan and Mark, as opposed to Mark and other Homer imitators, but also the style that is striking. It is so similar one is left to wonder in private if Mark did not know Lucan personally. It is not simply that Homer is too far distant to Mark, both temporally and culturally, that causes us distress in accepting MacDonald's premise. Rather we find Lucan provides us a rather transparent structure to follow and to test Mark's stylistic choices (something we will explore in more detail below). The Roman poet's style of imitation not only gave way to Mark's Gospel, but would also force the Roman Emperor to name an imperial position to control rhetoric within the Empire. Our premise is this: that Lucan was a herald of a new age of Roman Rhetoric. No longer does he just use imitation as a forum for ethical teaching (Plato) or tragedy and art (Aristotle, Ovid); now he moves past even Virgil (mimesis in crisis) and introduces to the Roman stage the art of political rhetoric as a way to directly challenge the Empire. In the midst of the moral decay of the Roman Empire, and perhaps nostalgia for the Roman Republic, Lucan was able to turn Virgil's poem of the ascendency of Rome on its head and give to the Roman people a direct confrontation to the Imperial Throne.[1] In doing so, he used a myriad of antetexts, imitating them to a point; but, like any good imitator, he became an innovator in the tradition, especially where the memetext is concerned. He takes from works previously glorifying Rome as a city on a hill, ordained by the gods and instead leads a charge to replace Nero.

Marcus Annaeus Lucanus was born in the reign of Caligula, lived through the reign of Claudius, and took his own life at the suggestion of his former friend Nero. He was well placed in a Roman rhetorical dynasty as the grandson of Seneca the Elder, nephew of Seneca the Younger (who tutored both Lucan and Nero), and a childhood friend of the Emperor Nero. We know little of Lucan's life, except aggressively by the hand of Suetonius, Vacca, and Tacitus (among others) and somewhat more passively by the imperial position awarded to Quintilian so soon after the end of the Roman Civil War. We know something by Statius, his friend and follower, as well as Martial, his hired lauder. Lucan was a Spaniard, born in the city of Corduba, the capitol of a wealthy province siding with Caesar during the Civil War. This ideal birth, both geographically and genealogically, well-positioned Lucan among the elite of Roman society, a position serving him well, in life and his death. During the tumultuous years leading up to the reign of Nero, Seneca the Younger moved from position to position in the affairs of State, providing a loud voice in the body politick, and carrying his nephew with him. When Nero came into power, Lucan was awarded a position in Nero's closest circle of friends. It was this position that allowed Lucan to fully develop his poetic anti-voice. However, he was not the only poet in this circle, as Nero saw himself as crowned with literary talent. Lucan's poetic competition lacked a significant grounding in reality, often burning with insanity.

Matthew Fox, in his introduction to *The Civil War*, suggests the breach between Nero and Lucan first appears when the latter's poems

---

1. Lucan is consistent in his political sympathies, never fully Republican, but more akin to the knighted imperial glory of lore. See Vessey, "Lucanus," 830–3.

were becoming a major success, even beginning to rival Virgil.[2] At first, his poems were in praise of the Emperor, but once jealousy possessed Nero, the poems shifted to ridiculing the Emperor, a dangerous game regardless of who was playing. Lucan was soon banned from publicly reciting his poems (c. 62).[3] During this time, Lucan's epic was finished and his life was made fuller when he married Polla Argentaria. In 64, Rome burned and Nero faced questions as to whether or not he was ultimately responsible. Lucan poetically fanned the flames of conspiracy, laying the arsonist's kindling in Nero's hand.[4] Indeed, during this time, Lucan began to build the Pisonian conspiracy. Lucan possibly acted out of family loyalty, as Nero imprisoned Seneca with the recommendation later for the philosopher to commit suicide.[5] Or, it is possible the Stoic Lucan viewed violence as the proper *telos*, given Nero as Emperor failed the Roman people by ignoring his solemn duty. Regardless, his poems were becoming the résistance to Nero's throne, but the conspiracy failed; Lucan was given the chance to take his own life. In a rather prophetic manner, Lucan's poems soon became emblematical of the coming Civil War. Lucan died in 65 by his own hand; the Jewish Revolt began in earnest in 66, and the Roman Civil War in 68 with Nero's death in the same year.[6] The publication of his memory was left to his widow.[7] She took great care for the remainder of her life to promote Lucan as a poet-hero. It is to her that we owe the continuation of Lucan's greatest work, his magnificent epic.

---

2. Fox, *Lucan*. See his entire introduction which most of this brief biography is summarized from.

3. This did not stop Lucan from reciting poems, however, as he purposely recited Nero's poems while relieving himself in the public toilets.

4. Statius, long after the fire, Nero, and Lucan was able to write that the fires were caused by a "guilty master" (*Silvae* 2.7.61.)

5. Suicide plays a large role both in Lucan's life and in his poem. See Hilly, *Ambitosa mors: Suicide and self in Roman Thought and Literature*, 213–36.

6. The connection between Nero's death and Lucan's work has not gone unnoticed. See Griffin, *Nero: The End of a Dynasty*.

7. See Haskins, *Annaei Lucani* Pharsalia for the earliest modern accounting of Lucan's short life. Haskins combines, along with over 100 pages of his own work, the ancient testimony.

Prototypes

Livy

Before we continue further into Lucan's sources, we must speak to the model of Livy (59 BCE.–17 CE), used by both Brodie and Winn.[8] Both quote P.G. Walsh, who has summarized succinctly the methods of Livy, "He utilizes one main source, reorganizes the structural arrangement, and introduces new material to achieve more dramatic effects. He compresses or omits the less interesting content, using as criteria the purpose of his work and the interests of his audience. Then, in addition to these literary aims of *enargeia* [graphic presentation to achieve dramatic effect] and *syntomia* [compression], he seeks to fulfill his historian's duties of *sapheneia* [clarification] and *pithanotes* [credibility in narration]."[9] Of particular interest to us is Livy's view of history. Indeed, if we are to examine Lucan, Virgil, or even modern history books, they all end with the first breath of something new; history ends with each author but begins with the reader. Livy began with his present reality and built backwards the history of Rome until the *Pax Augusta*. As historians tend to do, Livy viewed history as teleological. Thus, he was more able to use *inventio* to explore synchronisms. For instance, Livy uses Polybius in following established procedures for retelling historical events, but adds to the scenes to redirect the focus.[10] Henderson notes Livy has forever stamped himself upon the history of Rome, and for our sake we consider the stamp to have extended to Roman historians as well, with the use of rhetorical flair which Henderson defines as "creative writing."[11] This creative writing was neither uncommon nor as controversial as we consider it today.

---

8. I do not meant to suggest that Brodie, and then Winn, completed their assessment of sources based only of Livy; however, both use Livy in the same manner and seemingly see only the Elijah-Elisha narratives (or other Septuagintal images) as the sources for Mark's thought. I further do not intend to suggest that either Brodie or Winn have become settled on the use of a singular source for Mark's Gospel. Indeed, Brodie suggests that we should not merely confine ourselves to one model, such as Livy (Brodie, *Birthing*, 22.) My intention here is to suggest that Livy used one source, but Lucan used a plethora. It wasn't Livy that was a model for Mark nor imitation at the time of Mark, but Lucan.

9. As quoted in Brodie, *Birthing*, 15.

10. Walsh, *Literary Techniques*, 201.

11. Henderson, *Fighting for Rome*, 319. Henderson does not provide much, or

His Pedagogue

Virgil

Virgil acts as Lucan's muse.[12] Virgil presents himself as the teacher of all subsequent Roman poets—as the Roman Homer. Naevius and Ennius, centuries before, claimed the same thing, but Virgil accomplished his goal as a true Roman. The Roman ability to make use of another culture is as powerful as their legions. The *Odysessy* was no longer just a Greek story, but was now a Roman story, or more accurately, it was made use of by the Romans to tell their story. Virgil picks up Homer's works and uses them to build an origin myth for Rome. Writing in Augustan Rome, this was beneficial not only to himself but to Rome and the Emperor. He made use of Homer's proses, characters, and structures to build a cross time narrative that at once told of the beginning of the Roman Republic and the promise of the Empire. To do so, he borrowed from previous poets and crafted a story line by line infused with allusion and intertextuality. If we may employ an anachronistic analogy, we would compare the *Aeneid* to the *Book of Revelation*. Every line of the latter book contains allusions to many of the usual Jewish and Jewish-Christian works, and in doing so the *Book of Revelation* becomes the total of Christian textual necessity. The *Aeneid* does the same thing. It was not Virgil's first poem, as he had also produced the *Elogues* and *Georgics*, poems that served as intertextual sources for the *Aeneid*.

Virgil's poem, however, differs from Homer's in several respects. First, whereas Homer concluded his poem long after the internal crisis had passed, Virgil places the crisis at the very end of this work. The crisis is not one of characters as in Homer, but one of ethics, so that ethics is taught through voice. Virgil engages his readers through the use of crisis in text, to teach ethics by instilling the principles through audience participation (Plato versus Aristotle). The scene in Book 12 of the *Aeneid* makes use of Book 22 of the *Iliad*, presenting the idea of mercy by the powerful. The spear wounds in both Virgil and Homer appear differently; one is fatal, the other is not. Virgil makes use of this motif to beg his readers to follow more ethical guidelines. No doubt,

---

rather as much as Walsh does on Livy's sources, but he does provide a deep and profound insight into the inventing of history, something Livy gave to the Roman world.

12. Statius argues with history where. The successor to Lucan has established Lucan as the poet, even greater than Virgil. Statius's Calliope sings of Lucan's superiority to Virgil, from talent to the age of composition. Lucan is the first *Roman* poet in Sivae 2.7 (See Newlands, *First Biography*, 442–6.)

this ethical suggestion was intended for Caesar as well. The Aeneid was written at the end of a century of civil strife leading to a divine emperor of Rome. Virgil used his literary text to appeal for a merciful emperor by employing his intertextual work to shape a reality he demanded. Virgil was Rome's prophet. Homer does not just serve as the literary model, but his characters also serve as models as to what not to do. This is an example of anti-mimesis—Virgil is using previous works to configure a different reality.

Lucan and Mimesis

Lucan has heard the good news of Virgil—and becomes a believer. He understands firsthand how a poet can influence the course of human events, to shape and mold a reality, or to change an emperor. He was not only open to the power of the poet, but he was well-versed in the talent needed to repeat—to overcome—Virgil's magnum opus. Lucan turned to imitation, but like any good imitator, shaped the preexistent material, the previous lessons, and the standing rules to produce a new tool for the writing of the hidden transcript.

Every detail in Lucan's work needs an examination for the ideological intent of the author, rather than seen as mere stylistic choices. Lucan literalizes rather oddly Pompey and Caesar's prolonged and heavily involved family squabble in his *Bellum Civile*. It is filled with poorly used Latin, paradoxes, tropes, apostrophes, rhetoric, internal demons, and competing voices. It could fit well within the early Christian community since it seemingly dismissed the pantheon of gods.[13] Lucan makes use of everything at his disposal to relate to his audience his goal, even language, but in this—style, the a-theistic attitude, and language—Lucan's goal remains the same. He will destroy the boundaries between the narrator and the audience, the present and the past, Rome and Hell. His poem is fractured in voice, leaving us to wonder what his ideology is. Shadi Bartsch maintains Lucan is a storyteller, a union of the rebel and nihilist.[14] This is Lucan's paradox, she insists, at the core of *Bellum*

---

13. While Lucan makes use of the gods, he doesn't allow them the usual starring role affording to them in other epics. I note that in the early parts of his poem Lucan raises Nero to the level of a god. This dismissal of the gods would have included the dismissal of the Roman emperor too.

14. Note that this fits well with the Literary Critical Theory mentioned in the previous chapter.

Civile that makes it as philosophic as historical.¹⁵ She closely follows John Henderson and his student Jamie Masters in suggesting the very words Lucan uses are worth examining by those who really seek to understand Lucan's poem. We must examine his words, phrases, and styles in how they, unlike other epics, present certain subject matter.

For instance, the bodies of the dying are regularly torn asunder and presented inside out to allow the audience to smell the entrails of the fallen, breathing the stench of Rome's decay. Bartsch relates, "Lucan expresses the folly of civil war in a language that focuses sharply on the violation of soldierly bodies through the death-dealing wounds inflicted by their fellow Romans."¹⁶ This dissolution of boundaries defines Lucan's poem because it is the most pervasive. Caesar crosses the Rubicon, indicating a political boundary torn apart, bodies, a sacred boundary, are given to the wild animals, and the greatest boundary, that of civilization, so mutilated that heroic men seem like nothing more than barbarians.

Lucan's meticulous style is matched by his use of intertextuality, allusion, and (anti-)mimesis. As discussed above, mimesis is not merely the use of images and words to preserve a former text but contains anti-mimesis, an ideological tool meant to *effect* a reversal, a bravura transformed by Lucan, via Virgil, completed in Mark. His goal is not merely to take on the mythological beginnings of the Roman Empire, but to stand against Nero—to shape the future, by challenging the audience's acceptance of history. To do so, he steals the structure of Julius Caesar's *Civil War*, transplanting it as the backbone of *Bellum Civile*. "These events," Fox notes, "are most authoritatively related in Caesar's own brilliant three-book commentary, *Bellum Civile*, which begins on the eve of the war and breaks off suddenly in the early stages of conflict in Egypt." ¹⁷ Fox goes on to note Lucan's poem not only follows

---

15. Bartsch, *Cold Blood*, 8–9.

16. Bartsch, *Cold Blood*, 11; See also Most, *Disiecti membra poetae*: The Rhetoric of dismemberment in Neronian poetry, 391–419.

17. Fox, *Lucan*, xxii. Pichon suggested that Lucan's dilettantish style would have allowed him to use only one source, Livy. The French literary critic attempted to argue that any good historian and scholar would attempt to only use a single secondary source. This provided the new historian confidence in their work. Granted, his law is faulty because it is not absolute. The more we know about Homer, Virgil, and Lucan, the idea of a single source for the ancient writer becomes ludicrous. As Masters points out, the assumption that Lucan was attempting to tell the truth remains the driving

this rather abrupt start and stop style, but also maintains as a challenge much of the same overarching structure of Caesar's poem.[18] Lucan's rewritten historical account did not escape ideological motivation. It is used not only to remove Caesar's history, but also to challenge Nero's future. After all, if you unwrite the progenitor of the Julio-Claudian line you unwrite the current heir.

Lucan was able to use imitation to (re)present reality. He reversed Virgil's telling of the splendor of Rome's founding in the *Aeneid* to present a less clouded view of history of Rome's founding. No doubt, the pathetic emotions attached to the *Aeneid* were high, so to then directly attack it would have caused a hysterical reaction. This pathos saturates the entirety of the epic. What was once portrayed as a divinely ordained victory was now recast as a defeat of the people by the gods. In a masterful reversal, Lucan turned the gloried past into a nightmare, but with the hope the nightmare would end with the dawn of a new emperor. Lucan has mimetically borrowed from Virgil but not just in the "hope through despair" motif. His reversal of Virgil's desire for the Empire helps to call attention to the need for something new. He borrows techniques of Virgil as well, especially with the apostrophe as "the artist's attempt to craft in his work a sort of second consciousness."[19] She goes on to note Lucan rejects Homer and Virgil's gods along with their myths. This was nothing new as the Stoics had long read Homer as allegory.[20] Lucan and Virgil's central characters both examine the world around them looking for trust and hope.[21] In the end, it is not enough to merely see the

---

force for those who follow Pichon. Pichon missed the role of sources, not as facts, but as points of departure. (Masters, *Poetry and Civil War*, 15–7.) See Pichon, *Les sources de Lucain*.

18. Following other authors (Griset, Haffter, and Rambaud), Masters calls Lucan's poem a "deliberate counterpoise to Caesar's commentary of the same name." (Masters, *Poetry and Civil War*, 18–9.) The ending of Lucan is debated with intensity. The tradition position is to see Lucan as failing to complete his poem, with several scholars offering logical ending point. See Ahl, 1976; Bruére, *The scope of Lucan's historical epic*, 217–35; Due, "An essay on Lucan," 68–132; Berthe Marti suggest Lucan planned a book culminating in Caesar's death. (See Marti, *La Structure de la Pharsale*, 3–34.)

19. Behr, *Feeling History*, 105.

20. Behr, *Feeling History*, 107–110. Lucan excludes the gods and their meddlesome ways into human affairs. See also Feeny. *The Gods in Epic*.

21. Behr, *Feeling History*, 79–80. For Virgil, it is Aeneas while for Lucan, I maintain that it is the narrator. Lucan's masterstroke was getting the Romans to ignore the last 80 years of glorious Empire, long for Republicanism, realize that it will never return,

Aeneid in Lucan's work; we must see the essential role that it played in the development of Lucan's work. It indeed offers Lucan a style, but in reality it serves as something more sinister. It is the villain of the story.

Philosophy, allegorical reading, and myth—sources equal to Virgil and Caesar—appear throughout *Bellum Civile*. We can get a clear example of this as we examine the scene wherein Cato is attacked by snakes while marching across the desert of Libya. Evidence suggests the ahistorical scene has precedents in material present at Lucan's time, including the march of Ophellus in *Diodorus Siculus*, Marius's work in Africa with parallels in Sallust, as well as elements found in *Theriaca*. Warner Rutz suggests, "Lucan borrowed from various Alexander-narratives."[22] Bartsch suggests that this scene is allegory. Martha Malamud concurs, "Lucan's careful reworking of Ovid's Medusa story reveals that the spring from which Cato drinks is identical to the Pierisan spring, the source of Lucretius's inspiration as well as the site of confrontation between Ovid's battling sets of Muses. This is the tainted source of Lucan's inspiration as well."[23] Ovid's Medusa to provides structure to Cato's snakes while reworking scenes from other myths along with philosophy to provide a rather intense (re)presentation of Cato's march in such a way as to deliver a cathartic pathos that liberates his poetic ability and suggests some manner of trust in the poet. Philosophy, allegory, and myth are often Lucan's frame. Lucan's hope is to save the Empire and force change through poetry, namely his. After all, empires and city-states were built on poetry. Why not save one in the same manner?

Mimesis abuses the passions. By using sources already deeply invested with emotion, a new author can carry with him or her zealous affections, using them to the author's advantage. Lucan follows some of the same techniques Livy uses when he employs the *phantasia* (visions) and *enargeia* from a variety of sources to force his audience participate in the Civil War. Quintilian suggests the mastery of these visions will have power over the emotions of the audience.[24] Vividness comes into play when the author is seeking a representation of some sort. All art,

---

and then to present them hope at the very least that someone better would replace Nero. The apostrophe is used in emotional outbursts, especially when the narrator talks to the characters in the story. (See Bartsch, *Lucan and Historical Bias*, 309–10.)

22. As quoted in Bartsch, *Cold Blood*, 30–1. See also Morford, *The Poet Lucan: Studies in Rhetorical Epic*.

23. Malamud, "Pompey's Head and Cato's Snakes," 31–44.

24. Quint., *Inst.*, 6.2.29.

poetry, or otherwise, is indeed a mimetic representation. If an author is able to combine visions and vividness, then history is no longer about representation, but about (re)presentation as a fresh recasting of history. If the poet is successful, the represented history is truer than the representation of history in the minds of the audience. In order to do so, one must appeal to emotions. Thus the source of the imitation must have some emotion attached to it.

Lucan provides us with the earliest treatment of the battle of Massilia—a sea battle exemplifying the author's abuse of patriotic impulses. We simply do not have many historical facts about the battle, nor can we know what Lucan actually knew. What we can know, however, are some of Lucan's sources for his description of the battle. Ennius provides a line (compare fr. 218 with BC 3.453). Virgil does not offer us much help with history as his account of the tale contains only seven lines, but he does however give us some semblance to Lucan's narrative and thus acts as a source for the later poem.[25] For example, Lucan's Caesar, unlike Virgil's Augustus, is portrayed as a dishonorable tyrant who does not focus on Empire, but the spoils of war.[26] This is not uncommon in Lucan's poem, but the reader must know the sources of Lucan's thought in order to know what the author intends as a reversal. Several sources are apparent. First, Caesar's own account may provide the best structure for Lucan's narrative.[27] Livy's literary legacy could also serve as a mine for Lucan, although the historian's account of this battle is lost. Regardless, we have a regular feature of epics, the sea battle, which portrays Caesar as counter to Virgil's perception. We know that Caesar and Virgil, albeit not on the grand scale as Lucan, both wrote about Massilia, and that these two authors acted previously as sources for Lucan. Lucan's use of Caesar and Virgil would have given the battle an emotional intertextual structure.

We can show intertextual structures and allusions in Lucan's work; therefore, we should expand our view of the poet's sources to include

---

25. *Aeneid* 8.675–728. If Lucan borrows from Virgil, then Pompey takes the place of Antony.

26. Compare *Aen.* 8.720–1 with *BC* 5.154–68.

27. Anxiety over a source providing a fully account for imitation is better left to the redaction criticism. Instead, we note that structuring source allows for the mimetic author to add his or her own details. Caesar's account provided structure, but Lucan used Virgil and others to provide (perhaps even Livy) details that he later expanded with his own *inventio* to produce what we have.

what is called repetition. We will focus especially on Virgil's *Aeneid*.[28] Hardie notes that Virgil is essentially the beginning of a new cycle of epics, but this time, in the Latin language. In taking the Homeric framework, easily dovetailing into another story, Virgil "transforms the role of continuation" to include another myth altogether.[29] How does this recomposition and (re)presentation work? Generally, the poets following Virgil exploit *imitato*, or repetition. Characters in succeeding poems begin to almost recall the lives of previous characters. Sometimes this is done through inversion as we find in Lucan's inverse of Virgil's proem. This repetition is one of reversal of circumstances. Hardie submits these repetitions, expected if the poem was as it was supposed to be, included the idea the poem itself would continue through successors. Hardie gives as the example of Caesar at Troy (*BC* 9.961–79). Lucan repeats Virgil to (re)present Caesar not as the one who brings enteral life, but as the one who brings extinction. We must remember mimesis is not merely the borrowing of an intertext, but often the direct challenge one text presents to the other, even if those challenged texts are historical subjects rather than literary texts.

Other themes are shared by the successors of Virgil. One such theme, which is essential to our volume, is that of the role of sacrifice.[30] Here, sacrifice is seen as the eventual end of the destruction of the social order. As Hardie notes, "The *Aeneid* begins and ends with sacrifice."[31] It is also replete with sacrifices—attempted or completed—so that it is made to appear that the entirety of the human race is sacrificed in order to bring about the glorious Empire. Virgil's poem begins, however, when the cultic sacrifices are attacked and is only resolved when one is sacrificed to bring order. This is essentially a Girardian cycle of history where society breaks down and is restored only through a vile murder. Of interest is the use of the image of the sacrificial bull(s) found in Virgil as well as Statius and Valerius Flaccus. Silias, Hardie writes, "offers two versions of Virgil's final confrontations." Ovid follows the same pattern

---

28. What follows is a summarization of many of Hardie's points, unless otherwise noted, as found in chapters 1–2 of his work, Hardie, *The Epic Successors of Virgil*.

29. This is not far from what we see in Euripides.

30. Here, we cannot help but to follow Hardie in his reliance upon Girard. For more on Girard, see Girard, *Deceit, Desire, and the Novel*; *The Scapegoat*; and *Violence and the Sacred*.

31. Hardie, *Epic Successors*, 19.

with Turnus and the other gods. Lucan's two bulls are rather easy to see already, so that we but need barely mention Caesar and Pompey. One is the victim, the other the victor. Indeed so dependent on the image of sacrifice, Lucan's epic could almost not exist if the sacrificial scenes were removed. The inverse of devotion (or sacrifice) is seen throughout when the devoted are wasted. The sacrifice is no longer a substitute but the proposed model. Private gain and not the end of disorder is the goal of sacrifice and often times, only as mere lip service. In Lucan, the two bulls seek self-sacrifice but neither approach the actual moment of sacrifice. More inverses occur when we find the victims trading places with the victor, such as in Virgil's inverse of the death of Oilean Ajax. Palinurus is replaced by Aeneas. This is also found to occur when one character possesses or imitates another, as Lucan's Pompey is said to do on various occasions. Indeed, in one instance, Caesar, who had killed Pompey, is now saved by Pompey himself. This "substitutability of the hero" is key in Lucan and his successor, Statius. Silius uses Virgil to substitute a phantom of Scipio that eventually saves Hannibal, which has mimicked Lucan's use of the phantom of Pompey to save Caesar. Even the speeches are not spared the tool of inverse as Cato's speech regarding the destruction of Rome (*BC*, 2) includes the words "that of a father at the funeral of his sons." This is an inverse, even down to the gender of the speaker, of a mother's speech in *Aeneid* 9.481–97.

Themes were not the only mechanism borrowed, but historical personas were also pilfered. Johnson writes, "Lucan's Caesar is less a representation of a historical figure than a symbol for certain inscrutable forces that operates behind and beneath what is called history."[32] Bartsch suggests nearly the same thing for the dual Pompey. "One Pompey is more or less the narrator's creation. . . . The other Pompey emerges more naturally from the text of the poem itself."[33] Lucan's Cato is connected only to the Cato of history by the weakest of strings.[34] The

---

32. Johnson, *Momentary Monsters*, 103; Johnson's work here is detrimental to understand the grisly art Lucan paints in his poem.

33. Bartsch, *Cold Blood*, 7.

34. Seo calls Lucan's Cato a Cato-mimesis. It was not just the historical Cato that Lucan borrowed from to make his Cato, but so too other characters in the story—and other characters made use of Cato's historical details. Vulteius, Scaeva, Ahenobarbus, and even Pompey share at their death a mimetic connection to Cato's own suicide. The author also supposes that Lucan draws from Protagoras's Hercules. (Seo, *Exemplarity*, 200–1.) Ahl suggests that Cato is Lucan's Aeneas. (Ahl, *Lucan*, 241–2.)

poet has made use of the intervening period between the Civil War and his own to build the myths of his characters.[35] But myth and legend are not the only sources of Lucan's characters. The personas placed upon these historical figures are borrowed from others. Lucan's Roma is modeled on Hector's ghost in the *Aeneid,* as well as the anti-Allecto. Lucan's Caesar is almost reversed from his *real* persona, embodying at times the spirit of Hannibal and at other times "both an anti-Aeneas and a Turnus."[36] Whereas Turnus is the lion lying wounded in the Carthagian fields in Virgil's epic, Caesar is positioned by Lucan as an African lion. Hardie notes that what the character of Turnus becomes by the end of the *Aeneid,* Caesar begins as in Lucan's epic. Further, Lucan pulls our attention to viewing Caesar's portrayal as the embodiment of the powers of the Underworld, or hell, whereas the portrayal of the Roman archon Aeneas is one embodied with the powers of the gods, or heaven.[37] The poet's characters are not their historical counterparts, but the needed mythologized beings Lucan wants his audience to see. They are no less real, however, than the historical counterparts, and were born only after long reflection. After all, the suicidal Cato has now become a god.

Lucan's Mimetic Turns

I will not attempt to give a full accounting or overview of each and every line in Lucan's poem connected in some way to Virgil's work(s). In reality, there is virtually no hope of surpassing the brilliant study of Lucan's use of Virgil as done by Lynette Thompson and R. T. Bruère in their 1968 essay on the subject.[38] However, I have identified in their essay three types of these reminiscences, or intertextuality and allusions—reversal, background, and transfer. In the course of their study, they also allow that Lucan is using both the *Georgics* and the *Aeneid* to provide background through the use of phrases and settings the audience will

---

35. The sources for the characters are far too numerous to give here. For example, Cato's image is built from the *exempla* as well as, other words. Homer's Hector (*Il.* 6.321) provides support for Cato as he gives his reasons for joining the war. This scene is also one that shows the tools of the declamation schools present at the time, something that gave Lucan a structure here. (See Griffin, "Philosophy, Cato, and Roman Suicide I," 64–77.)

36. Reed, *Virgil's Gaze,* 70–1.

37. Hardie, Epic *Successors,* 60–63.

38. Thompson and Bruere, *Lucan,* 107–148.

easily understand. Transfer is not completely independent of background but it serves to allow the transference of one character's circumstances or traits to another, from the hypo- to the hypertext, as it were. Examples of reversal include Lucan's echo in Caesar's refusal to cease fighting (1.832-5) reversing the Virgilian hope in *Georgics* (1.492-506), the reversal of the plight of the Trojans unto the plight of the Romans, in which both are going to suffering destruction, and the reversal of the hope in Augustus into diminishing his line while promoting Nero. Reversal occurs most notably in the proem. Lucan also reverses Virgil's good words of Rome to cast despair. Indeed, by challenging Virgil here, Lucan is in effect challenging Jupiter.

Reversals are polemical. This is the reason for Lucan's use of Virgil's '*totum sub leges mitteret orbem*'.[39] Reversals are also accusatory stances the later author uses to challenge the premise of the former author or historical event. For instance, Lucan is not simply challenging Virgil's Rome, but Caesar's legacy as well. Lucan contrasts the destruction caused by the Civil War in his proem with various scenes from Virgil, such as the view of Capitoline Hill where what was once honored is now in dishonor and disarray. Most striking is the heavy handed reversal of the entire poem, that while Virgil sees the effects of the civil war subsiding in Caesar, Lucan reminds his audience the effects of the Empire's birth are still felt and in no small way, warns them of the coming cosmic conflagration. Lucan's reversal of the use of the gods is a matter of controversy. While Thompson and Bruère see Lucan hoping to repair the breech with Nero by elevating him to divine, I am more inclined to see Lucan's praise of Nero as a rather sarcastic diatribe to remind the audience of exactly how evil Nero really is.[40] Apollo's prophecy of peace for the line of Caesar is thwarted when Julius and his line become nothing more than willing participants in the murder of Rome. The narrator actually pursues a round of theomachy with Jupiter as evidenced by his use of signs effecting a reversal of Virgil's portents.[41] Sentiment is also reversed. The heroes of the stories are motivated in different ways. Aeneas is gallant while Caesar is plainly a murderer. Finally, Lucan presents himself as a reversal of sorts in that he challenges Virgil's place as the Roman Homer.[42]

39. Thompson and Bruère, *Lucan*, 112; see BC 1.286-93 and Aen. 4.231.

40. See Thompson and Bruère, *Lucan*, 113 and compare to Pierre Grimal's essay in the same work, 59-69.

41. Thompson and Bruère, *Lucan*, 132.

42. Thompson and Bruère, *Lucan*, 144.

Background and transference occur when texts bring to light hidden meanings by the author or symbolize a transfer of the entire *Sitz im Leben*. Images provide cues in the ongoing scene whereas transference is used to merge the scene from the hypotext completely into the hypertext. Lucan begins his poem by giving some background to it from Virgil with the use of the image of the Emathian plains (*Georgics* 1.489–92). This allusion evokes not just the storyline of *Georgics*, but also the situation of social disorder in which Virgil himself lived. The intertextuality between Lucan and Virgil's proems produce a connection to the heroic events of the *Aeneid*. Once a connection is made, transference occurs. In one particular scene, Lucan masterfully transfers the Fama of Virgil to Caesar as he marches to Rome. Another scene has Lucan moving the flood of water Virgil pours into Aeneas's ships into the river in front of Caesar.[43] Transference of imagery occurs due to geographical placement as well. Caesar visits the ruined Troy while Aeneas visits Pallanteum. This exacting scene contains all three categories of reminiscences. The scene takes place in a ruined city providing a shared background. The transference occurs when the audience is meant to take the future of Aeneas as a guide to the future of Caesar. Finally, a reversal transpires when Pallenteum is a preparation for the glory of the Republic while Troy accommodates the preparation for the rise of the Empire. Lucan is not simply sharing an inkwell with Virgil. The poet stands high upon Mount Olympus as Melpomene, Calliope, and Aiode empty into him Virgil's Mneme and Melete. Lucan is inspiration incarnate to challenge Virgil's Rome *as* Virgil's scribe, repeating the epics to the proper conclusion. Just as Virgil has continued Homer, Lucan continues Virgil.

Lucan's Language Barriers

There are two essential subjects left in our examination of Lucan bearing some significance in our approach to Mark. The first is the use of language to wage war. The second is the influence of Homer on the poet. We will first examine the use of language as a space of resistance as employed by Lucan. By the time of Nero the name of Caesar came to represent something more cosmological than we would allow for names like Washington or Bolívar. It was the center of the Roman

---

43. Thompson and Bruère, *Lucan*, 138.

universe and state, very much holding a divine status. Lucan destroys this image. He takes the patriarchal epic and destroys the manliness of history, undermining *Roma* in all of her man-made glory. Henderson writes, "The *Bellum Civile* also, least *forgivably* of all, subverts the Order of Narration, mocks all that 'literary' discourse is charged to deliver in the formation of its Culture *as* the 'cultural' values of the powerful."[44] It is not that Lucan is intent on disrupting the empire and thus seeks only to rewrite history, but he seeks to level the empire by removing its mythical foundations. The first causality is Caesar, the one who allowed Rome to become what it now was, a pox on the cosmos. Lucan's use of language undermines Caesar, Virgil, and even Homer, so that what the epic once was—that of a cultural architect—is now become death and the destroyer of worlds.

The poem is known for its poor Latin, rhetorical excesses, hidden meanings, off-putting geographical detail, and multilayered meanings. Since rhetoric is the art of persuasion, how dare a poet use such devices if he would want his audience to understand his meaning? And yet, not only did the audience enjoy Lucan's work, but also I would maintain it functioned as a catalyst for the war that brought Vespasian to the throne.[45] Henderson's article noted above has offered Lucan scholars as well as those interested in ideological linguistics and semiotics a firm foundation to suggest Lucan used his words carefully with a grand design so as to challenge everyone who came in contact with it to destroy in reality the cult of Rome. This is the power of poetry. Bartsch goes to an equal distance in supposing the poem is fractured in such a way as to allow various interpretations, on purpose, due to the power of the words selected and employed by Lucan.[46] She notes his syntax re-orientates "normative syntax" to allow for an "inversion in subject-object relations."[47] Building upon Henderson, she proposes this style is "most conspicuous in the language of wounding."[48] Examples include the bodies attacking the weapons of their death. She concludes that Lucan sees

---

44. Henderson, *Lucan*, 469.

45. No need to fully investigate the synchronicity here, only to suggest that Lucan died in 65. In under three years, civil war had once again broke out.

46. Bartsch, *Cold Blood*, 97–8.

47. Lucan has a strong favor for parataxis in his poem.

48. Bartsch, *Cold Blood*, 23.

His Pedagogue

this as the "perfect expression for the paradox of civil war."[49] To further this, Lucan's Caesarian victory is redefined as a defeat for Rome. Our former hero Caesar is nothing more than a tyrannical villain. Words, concepts, and themes are redefined along with improper syntax and other grammatical mistakes to obliterate Roman sensibilities, and perhaps as Henderson would suggest, "a fight to achieve a strong identity over against his inheritance, working through and against the traditional battery of *schemta*."[50] He has not merely reversed the story of Rome, but the fame of Virgil.

What might this mean? Was Lucan merely fighting against his literary heritage? He was a young man at the center of not just the empire, but of the empire propelled by the epic. He was a childhood friend of Nero, the nephew of Seneca the Younger, grandson of Seneca the Elder. More than that, Lucan was the heir to Virgil. What was Virgil's inheritance? It was the glory of the Roman Empire and wealth of Caesar, which Virgil helped secure. Lucan, then, was not merely fighting against the cult of Rome enshrined in his own reality, but against himself. He was a sinner, a sin that had entered the world by one man, maybe two, and in need of repentance from a name. His sacrifice and regeneration was through the epic and the ill-fated conspiracy to murder Nero. His anguish over having contributed to the empire is felt in a work filled with gore, inflicting upon his audience with unsettling appetite. The poet wages war against the ghosts of Rome's past, the present reality, and the future option. The display of literary talent in *Bellum Civile* portrays a civil war still ongoing, if nowhere else than but in the mind of the poet.

Lucan does make use of existing methods, however. He uses parataxis, keeping his subordinate clauses to a bare minimum. This separates his characters from his narrative. His verses are often long enough to have given Paul trouble, with long and involved sentences as hazardous as a mountain highway. His verbs lack finiteness, relying on participles and ablatives. During these times, he makes use of the polysyndeton as well as the hyperbaton. The use of these writing styles delivers the poem to the audience at a marathon speed, with the audience struggling to keep up. The exhaustion of the audience, as tired muscles producing lactic acid, twists the reaction. As with Euripides,

---

49. Bartsch, *Cold Blood*, 22–4. Note here that such a scene, almost as if the soldiers are throwing themselves unto the spears, plays a part in the idea of sacrifice.

50. Henderson, *Lucan*, 434.

Lucan makes use of maxims (*sententiae*, Latin). They are short, paradoxical statements allowing the narrator to speak directly to the audience. Paradox is at the heart of the poem. Caesar the victorious hero is the villain. *Sententiae* allow Lucan to give the point of the passage immediately. The poet also uses catachresis, or the incorrect use of words. While distracting, it serves best as a challenge to keep pace with the poet. Added to this distraction are the puns found in words next to each other, characters, and geography.[51]

We will cease speaking about Lucan's language with one final statement from Henderson. "When once you begin to *read* this poem, you'll find among other things, that the sort of critical talk of 'puns' or 'word-play' which you can imagine being 'applauded' and (so) deplored here for *numerus* and *locus* is a pathetic insult to the power of Lucan's disfiguring representation of the discourse of power."[52] Lucan uses titles for names, mocking Caesar. This is not just a pun, but also a calculated attack on the cult of Caesar. He uses Latin and Greek to force one another to create something new, such as at 6.14, not merely as a word play, but something telling of the geographical location in which the story takes place. Lucan allows his audience to misread words, and then, as if he is waging a guerrilla war, suddenly attacks the readers with the corrected view.[53] If humor is used in Lucan, it is little more than an attempt to disarm the audience, not to lighten the mood, in order to more easily circumcise the cult from the audience's mind. Latin was the language of the world, but Lucan destroyed it just as Caesar had destroyed the Republic.

Lucan's Homer-textual Problem

I want to turn briefly to the issue of Homer. The ancient Greek poet has presented to the West a long history of many things, not just poetry. He has given us archetypes, and while those that survive today are more often than not merely shadows of Homeric archetypes, they are still doing service to Homer. To say, however, that Lucan is making as much use of Homer as he has done with Virgil and others is not a profitable exercise in my opinion; however, in the interests of a more balanced

---

51. See Lintott, *Lucan and the history of the civil war*, 488–505.
52. Henderson, *Lucan*, 441.
53. Henderson, *Lucan*, 449.

approached, we must acknowledge that the overall cognitive environment of Lucan did include Homer, although he was more than likely educated in Latin with Virgil. No doubt, as Carin Green has suggested, there is some Homeric background Lucan is using to supplement his story, but this is expected (unlike, say, the Gospel writers).[54] Virgil used Homer to launch the Roman Empire; Lucan would have to return to Virgil's source in order to put to sail the ship of state in order to bring it back to the harbor of a suitable emperor. What makes Troy so poignant for Lucan is not that its ruins gave birth to (the) Rome (-an Empire) as a true Virgilian would say, but because it is the city of the fabled, heroic past, symbolizing the ideal Rome.[55]

One final point that Green makes that I can agree with is that "Vergil knew he was writing myth, but both Homer and Lucan believed that they were writing history." Even with the questions of the historical appearance in his epic, Lucan is attempting to rewrite history to counter the imperial myth. His (re)presentation of history is meant to change the future of Rome by recasting the past. The poet's aim was not to regurgitate facts but to defy the myth, to dare the saga of the evil Empire. Lucan's epic was as much about the history of Rome as it was about the future of Rome. Since all language is temporal, the Caesar of the *Civil Wars* is Nero. His "wars more than civil. . ." were not the Caesar-Pompey struggle, but his own internal struggle and the coming free-for-all to regain some measure of freedom.

We must note Julius Caesar had set about to write history of the great civil war, as did Livy to some extent. Virgil mythologized it. Other historians before and after Lucan had put quill to papyrus in order to tell the story of the birth of the Empire, but Lucan found these histories little more than fiction, if not as damning to the state as Plato considered Homer's plays. While we may chide him for his robust accounting of history, he would have had no doubt considered himself the (re)author of truth. Beauty is not the only thing in the eye of the beholder it seems. History is only rightly told when it is interpreted. Lucan was the historian; Caesar was the mad ideologue; and Virgil the liar.

54. Green, *Lucan*, 149–83.

55. Conte, *Saggio di Commento a Lucano Pharsalia VI 118–260; l'Aristia di Sceva*. 18.42–53

Mimetic Criticism and the Gospel of Mark

Antetext, Memetext, and Hegel

In the introduction, I set out several terms that are either new or somewhat redefined. I want to apply them to Lucan's literary strategy. The poet uses Julius Caesar's commentary on the civil war as an overall structure. We might suppose Lucan used Livy's lost historical account but we have no real way of comparing the two texts. While Livy was a major influence on later historians, as we have shown, Lucan would not have needed him to provide sources for his poem. We will consider Caesar's commentaries as the antetext. The mnemonics and merisms are drawn from a variety of sources as are the allusions. Virgil, Stoic philosophy, and other sources give Lucan the needed tropes to draw in his audience. The memetext remains as the crucial impetus. What drove Lucan to write was not so much his negative view of Empire, but his loss of an idolized Nero. Nero had become the unmerciful emperor that Virgil had deplored and needed replacing, perhaps with someone resembling the Cato of legend. Lucan's crisis is not the civil war of Caesar and Pompey, but the degrading social structures of Rome. In his work are allusions to his current situation, that of a terrible emperor and the abandonment by the gods.

Thus, we might render Lucan's social situation more Hegelian like this: Virgil's merciful emperor Augustus became enshrined in the Roman literary consciousness, predestined to act as the model for all future emperors (thesis). Nero was another in the powerful Julio-Claudian line who maltreated the people of Rome, seeking to destroy Roman *libertas* (antithesis).[56] Lucan picks up his pen to usher in a movement to topple Nero Caesar. He uses Roman verse (Virgil), Nero's vain history (Caesar's commentaries), and Stoicism to urge the people of Rome to their duty of toppling Nero (synthesis). Lucan's *Bellum Civili* changed *imitatio* as evidenced by Martial, Statius, and others who came after him. But, more important than the authors following Lucan, the most telling effect of the synthesis forever remains the civil war inaugurated barely three years after his death. That war forever impacted not just Rome, but the ideological streams of Judaism out of which flowed Christianity.

---

56. Lucan's own antithetical paradoxes come into play in Book 9.190–200. (See Braund, *Violence in Translation*, 520–1.)

Conclusion

Did Lucan's epic really matter? As noted above, twenty-five years after his death, he was still a celebrated author. His wife, then re-married, continued to promulgate his poems. But, there is something more, something more damning to the reception of his epic than the love of his wife.[57] Quintilian was made the first chair of Latin rhetoric by Vespasian. More than simply an endowment to the arts, this was an ideological move to control rhetoric in the empire. Quintilian had no small role in concealing the genre of epic during his reign in this chair. His excuse, no doubt, is one hidden with self-preservation. He comments in one place that "Lucan is fiery and spirited, sublime in sentiment, and, to say what I think, deserving to be numbered with orators rather than poets."[58] While there is nothing more said; there is nothing more needed. The impact of Lucan's poem is felt in the position created by the Emperor for Quintilian, the effort to keep epics out of vogue, and in Quintilian's slight against Lucan. Not having yet reached thirty years of age, Lucan left an indelible mark on Rome as well as, I insist, on the New Testament.

Rightly so, this chapter is bereft of anything "new" on Lucan, but serves only as an introduction to the poet who I believe bequeaths a great heritage to the author of Mark's Gospel. We turn now to reading Mark mimetically through commentary. After these two chapters, I will present a Lucan reading of Mark's Gospel that makes use of some of this material as well as other facets of Lucan's style in order to help the reader understand the central thesis, that Lucan and his style of mimesis is the lens to read Mark's Gospel.

---

57. For an overview of Lucan's reception, see von Albrecht, *A History of Roman Literature*.

58. Quint., *Inst.*, 10.1.91.

PART III

Application

5

Reading Mark Mimetically

Jesus against Vespasian

Introduction

THE FOLLOWING THREE CHAPTERS are mimetic criticism at work. Before we continue, however, I want to rehearse some facts. Thus far, we have explored why historical criticism faces limitations in searching for the various problems in Gospel criticism. In answering the critique, we (re)introduced mimetic criticism as the way forward in examining the *Gospel of Mark*. The social situation, including dating and reception history, prevails as a key in properly distinguishing sources. The date is near 75 CE. The social situation is the synthesis of Jewish theology with Roman imperial ideology in the aftermath of the Jewish Revolt. Lucan, the great Roman poet, is Mark's muse.

Mark's social history includes two Messiahs—Vespasian and Simon b. Giora. These two men presented such a social crisis that Mark was compelled to write to his community to buffet them against the psychological attacks made by false ideologies. As the following mimetic commentary is developed, it will become clear that Mark's Gospel, while a whole work, has a bifurcated purpose and as a whole is written in a chiastic structure.[1] The first half is focused on Vespasian,

---

1. Other scholars have noted Mark's concentric approach, but to the best of my ability, I believe that I am the first to give the circles historical referents. For such examples, see Fischer and von Wahlde, "The Miracles of Mark 4.35–5.43: Their Meaning and Function in the Gospel Framework," 13–6; Gardner, "Patterns that Connect: The Transfiguration, the Providence of God, and the Chiasmus," 355–91; Scott, "Chiastic Structure: A Key to the Interpretation of Mark's Gospel," 17–26. I would propose that

but contains subtle cues to the audience to wait for the appearance of another opponent. The second half deals exclusively with the rise of the Zealots and the ultimate destruction of the Temple caused by the pretender Simon. The first chapter of the commentary follows Mark's Gospel until Jesus begins his journey to Jerusalem (Mark 9.13). Before we begin we need to examine several rhetorical strategies Mark employs.[2]

Apostrophe

Mark exploits the rhetorical apostrophe throughout his Gospel. It is not to affect "the sense, but only the form of expression."[3] Mark also employs the *inclusio*.[4] Quintilian reminds us that these two rhetorical devices operate together easily, serving to highlight each other for the betterment of the audience' emotional understanding. For Quintilian, the apostrophe is a natural course of rhetoric. He points to Virgil as one who can unite both parenthesis and apostrophe together, "*Haud procul inde citae Metium in diversa quadrigae Distulerant, (at tu dictis, Albane, maneres) Raptabatque viri mendacis viscera Tullus.*"[5] The orator manipulates the apostrophe to speak directly to audience, or as in the case of Lucan, the narrator uses it to speak both to the audience and to his characters in the story. In Mark's Gospel, the apostrophe is best seen when Jesus refers to himself in the third person.

---

the entire Gospel of Mark is the 'B' in an A-B-A pattern with both 'A's' supplied by the reader. Jesus bursts on the scene without any clue as to where he has come from and just as abruptly leaves. This would have given an audience time to consider the Jesus they knew and the choice they had to make. Mark's Gospel is surrounded by the audience's intended response. Mark, as we will see, uses Daniel. A similar overarching chiastic structure is present in that book as well. (Shea, "The Prophecy of Daniel 9:24–27")

2. While some mention will be made of the Elijah-Elisha narratives as sources for Mark, the single work needed to identify those connections has already been written by Adam Winn, but where they intersect, they will be explored (For example, see 5.21–43 below). The focus on the commentary are those other sources, primarily mimetic as defined above, or, those sources Mark is uses to counter the crisis as well as to set the mnemonic scene for his audience.

3. Quint., *Inst.* 9.3.24.

4. For studies on Mark's use of *inclusio*, see Motyer, "The Rending of the Veil: A Markan Pentecost?" 155–57. Argues that the rending of the veil of the Temple "from top to bottom" (Mk 15.38) forms a significant *inclusio* with the account of Jesus's baptism in Mk 1.9–11; Ryou, PH.-Y., *Apocalyptic Opening, Eschatological 'Inclusio'*; Uhnsev, "The Heavenly Veil Torn: Mark's Cosmic *Inclusio*," 123–25.

5. Quint., *Inst.* 9.3.22–26.

Reading Mark Mimetically

In 2.10, Jesus refers to himself in the third person, but the narrator breaks in and redirects the audience's attention by pointing out that Jesus has, after speaking in the third person, now speaks to a character in the story. In Mark 8.31–38 Jesus is giving his first predication of his death and the expectation of martyrdom for his disciples when he suddenly shifts person to once again refer to himself in the third person, but in 9.1, in a parallel to 8.38, Jesus uses the first person to refer to the final time when the Son of Man and the Kingdom of God come with power. Unlike 2.10, the narrator does not break in this time. 9.12 seems to break the pattern at first glance, but given that a question was asked and Jesus barely answers it to the person who asked, we may take this as an apostrophe as well. The second time Jesus predicts his death it is again in the third person (9.31). The same is seen in the third predication in 10.33. In 10.45, 13.26, 14.21, 14.41 and 14.62, Jesus again refers to himself in the third person. This is the apostrophe. What might this do for the audience? The apostrophe allows Jesus to speak *directly* to the audience to inform them exactly who he is. The contemporaries of Jesus are not in view when Mark uses the apostrophe. The literary Jesus turns away from them to speak directly to the audience to reveal that he was/is the Son of Man.[6] This is disjointing to modern readers but we know he meant for the audience to pick up on the apostrophe by his first parenthesis. This would signal his audience that Jesus's words where directed to them at times and to the characters in the story at other times. In 13.14, which we will examine more thoroughly later, the narrator delivers a forceful demand to the audience to not accept the story as a historical record but one figuring their own reality. This is followed by a reversion to the past tense in 13.20, another clue that Mark is speaking, at times, to the audience in particular and not simply telling a story.

Intercalation

Intercalation is recognized as a key feature in Mark's storytelling; he is the first to solidify such a literary tool. Both Lucan and Josephus show some early signs of intercalation, but Mark formalizes the process. This above almost any other recognizable feature suggests Mark is writing

---

6. The temporal matrix of Mark's language is confusing, but the reader should understand that Gospel is presented in such a way as to confuse the then and now.

Mimetic Criticism and the Gospel of Mark

with a set goal of misdirection. Fowler writes, "Mark's Gospel remains fundamentally Mark's discourse and not Jesus's, and the true master of indirection in the Gospel is its implied author and narrator, not its protagonist."[7] The first recognizable intercalation is Mark 5.21–43 with Jesus interrupted by a woman with a physical condition on his way to heal Jarius's daughter.[8] Others occur in 3.20-3, 6.7-31, 11.12-19, 14.1-11, 14.53-72 and the crowning of King Jesus, 15.6-32.[9] As we will see, intercalation was useful in combining more than theological strings into composite stories, but worked Mark's sources and ideology into an accomplished ensemble. The commentary provided by the intertextual clues, such as the healing of the daughters of Israel, is easy to see but are not the only means Mark engages his audience. We must also remember that this is different from *inclusio*—a rhetorical device used to bracket episodes by repeated phrases. Intercalation is Mark's own major innovation to his received rhetoric and indeed, like paradox (which we shall explore below), permeates the entire Gospel. Intercalation is not understood simply as stories supplied by the narrator, but as Fowler would argue regarding the episodic nature of Mark, by the audience as well.[10]

Paradox/Irony

Fowler notes "irony and metaphor regularly slip into paradox."[11] This rhetorical strategy fits well with the indirection mentioned above. We find this prevalent in 9.24 when the same person believes and denies Jesus. This is mirrored by those who mock Jesus in 15.31. Another rather easy to see paradox is Jesus's question regarding the son of David

---

7. Fowler, *The Reader*, 183.

8. This is the only intercalation Matthew retains without violence. The focus of Mark 5 as the central revealer of Mark's sources as purpose will become clear shortly and later, will serve to show that Matthew knew Mark's rhetoric.

9. There is some debate whether 2.1-12 contains an intercalation as well.

10. For more on the study identifying intercalation in Mark, see Kermode, *The Genesis of Secrecy On the Interpretation of Narrative*; Telford, *The Barren Tempk and the Withered Tree*; Van Oyen, "Intercalation and Irony in the Gospel of Mark"; van Belle and J.Verheyden, *The Four Gospels 1992 (Festschrift F Neirynck)*, 949-74; von Dobschütz, E., "Zur Erzahlerkunst des Markus," 193-98; Wallis, "Mark's Goal-Oriented Plot Structure," 30-46; Wright, *Markan Intercalations*

11. Fowler, *The Reader*, 184.

in 12.35–37. Less subtly, bordering on irony (note Fowler's description of the two roads to paradox), is the initial encounter with Jesus's family in which those who knew him best believe him least. In the same intercalation, the Jewish leaders believe that he has used the powers of Beelzebub to cast out demons; Jesus's rebuke is a small paradox but calls attention to the ludicrousness of the original paradox. Fowler also points out other paradoxes embedded into the words of Jesus (8.31; 8.35).[12] Of course, were we to step back away from our involvement in Mark we could readily see the giant paradox looming before us. The messiah is one who willingly dies at the hands of the Romans. Even with all the power Jesus has on earth, he is unable to stop history from crashing down on him through the whips of the centurions. The looming paradox is the cross.

Doubling

Mark tasks us as we attempt to defend his originality from those who see him as an immature author. He doubles his passages, making use of the same story almost as if to mock my pleading that he is a competent writer doing more than collecting and organizing traditions. For example, we encounter two boat stories where Jesus proves that he has power over the winds and the sea (4.35–41; 6.45–52). Jesus feeds two multitudes (6.30–44; 8.1–10) and welcomes children twice (9.33–37; 10.13–16). This is not all, however. Frans Neirynck has shown that Mark's repetition is not limited to the repeating of scenes but found on four different levels. They are "grammatical usage," "duplicate expressions and double statements," "correspondence with one pericope," and a duality in the "structuring of the gospel."[13] These "hammer blows" drive home the point of Mark's purpose and rhetoric into his audience's mind.[14] The doubling of episodes provides framing to the intercalated episodes, as well as with irony (in the first episode) and paradox (in the repeating episode). The voyeuristic audience is dutifully reminded that not even the disciples knew who Jesus really was.

---

12. Fowler, *The Reader*, 187–188.

13. Frans Neirynck, *Duality in Mark: Contributions to the Study of the Markan Redaction*.

14. Fowler, *The Reader*, 140.

Mimetic Criticism and the Gospel of Mark

Parataxis/Aurality

The language of Mark suffers from an excess of debate, with scholars examining the problem from different angles, but rarely from the position that his language is a rhetorical tool. Language as rhetoric fits Mark's education. Next to the Hebrew Scriptures, the Greek provided for a way to preserve a middle ground between the past and the very real, and very Hellenistic, present. Mark pretends to suffer from the same grammar abuses the translators inflicted upon the Septuagint.[15] The Septuagint provides for us a reasonable answer, but not the final word, on Mark's parataxis, the abundant use of the historical present, and aurality. These tools, related to how the audience heard the Gospel, are important to the all–important premise that spoken language, and often times written, is not temporal but involves a communal act of the then-and-now viewpoint. Before we move on, we must consider the stark difference between today's readers and the first audience, the receptive audience. The words on a page are rarely anything more than symbols given meaning by our social situations.[16]

Criteria

The following criteria will serve as the basis for our utilization of mimetic criticism:

Theological Justification (Intertextuality; antetext; memetext)

Theological or ideological justification must contain a crisis presented in a text or social situation, which is historically identifiable and currently disrupting the audience's life. More than being merely accessible the audience, are the texts accessible in such as a way as to need imitation or provide a crucial bridge? In other words, it is not enough to just have a text within reach, as I have even now plenty. But one must

---

15. Mark's use of parataxis, while falling in line with both the Septuagint and Lucan, allows for an internalization of the story. Alter, Schneidau, and Williams all note the use of the paratactic language to pull the audience into the ambiguous nature of the story. It confuses the audience, helping to push the audience' acceptance of historicity. (See Williams, who cites these scholars, in *Gospel Against Parable*, 80–2).

16. Jakobson has pointed out that parataxis is the home of metonymy, with the latter helping the reader to understand the former. (Jakobson, *Fundamentals*, 56–82).

be challenged by by this outside text, or transcript, in such a way as to push for a mimetic response. This involves the purpose of the hypertext. What pushes the author to use the antetext for his audience? Is it only to preserve the textual, social, or religious tradition (Brodie) or is there a crisis (MacDonald)? If it is only to borrow a known image, or story structure, then it is doubtful that mimetic criticism—seeking to understand the hidden transcript—is identified as the purpose of the author; however we should leave room for intertextuality and allusion. There is no psychological attachment to the reception of the work by the audience if the author is only borrowing to make up a deficit in his or her originality.

We may take recent work done (in a forthcoming publication) by Dr. Vivian Johnson in regards to the story of Ehud (Judges 3.15–31) and the use the Hebrew author made of material in the Zoroastrian religious text, the *Avesta*. There is clear intertextuality, but not a crisis. On the other hand, Genesis 1 is not only intertextual, but also attempts to resolve a theological crisis; thusly, we could use mimetic criticism on that passage. Mimetic criticism goes beyond the surface text to examine the role the antetext enjoys in the audience's mind. For example, Paul speaks about the new creation in his epistles. This easily refers to Isaiah's use of that term, but Paul is not offering a reversal or improvement upon Isaiah, but using it to interpret the Christ event within the expectation offered by the Isaianic passage. Jesus is Paul's memetext. If Paul, on the other hand quotes a portion of the law in a reversed way without alluding to the fact that he had done this, then we could consider this as a form of (anti)mimesis.

MacDonald orients us to the reader, as does Rhoads before him. We must endeavor to keep the audience in mind when exploring possible sources. I would propose that for Mark, his community is not competing with the dying classical Greek culture, but engaged in a deeply ideological war, where one side has already imitated texts sacred to the community. Therefore, we must look for the antetext, the structuring literary element, and then the memetext, the situation that needs reversed.

Mimetic Criticism and the Gospel of Mark

Similar Narrative Events

Several passages in Mark mimic without deviation passages from other sources. While the characters are different, and end results are somewhat different, the episodes remain surprising intact. Narrative outlines may not always follow the A-B-C-D-E pattern, but may be A-C-E or even B-c-D/E where c is detected, but muted, and D is now merged with E. A has simply disappeared as recognizable because the mimetic author chose another image for A, perhaps an image extracted from external sources. The narrative events must be in a rather approximate closeness to one another. While there is always an allowance that the author is conflating several sources (as we will see in Mark 5.21–43), one should not try long to find in one passage of the hypertext a relationship to various passages strung throughout the hypotext. MacDonald does this with his varied and forced assemblage of what he supposes underlies Mark 5.1–20. If an audience was to have a constant and consistent connection to the hypertext, it must appear easily because the antetext gives the passage an overall structure. In regards to anti-mimesis, a reversal is not simply D-C-B-A, but D-C-B-X where X is the perfection or reversal.

Verbal Allowance (Allusion)

Here, we must go beyond both MacDonald and Winn and note the use of mnemonic and metymonic devices in play with Roman rhetoric. Merisms, short phrases leading to larger thoughts, stand for the entire passage. Therefore, to base the pass or fail of mimetic criticism on whether or not there is a coloration of *literary* texts is to, again, not take into account the role orality/aurality played in ancient audiences. This model is best expressed in our reading Mark 5.1–20, when a small phrase is first mentioned from Deuteronomy but the audience is able to import the whole of the LXX passage and provide structure for Mark's story. A good subset to this rule is to examine the entire passage where the connection phrase is found and compare the broad features of both. This is where the tool of allusion is important to mimetic criticism. While not always fully used, the ten criteria developed by Perri are impossible not to employ.[17]

17. Perri, *On Alluding*, 300; I stress the dual importance of crisis and memetext.

Mimetic criticism, as Powell writes, is a criticism that has in "view the literary work as a reflection of the outer world or of human life and evaluate it in terms of the truth or accuracy of its representation."[18] If we may wax philosophical for a moment, in mimetic criticism, we must ask ourselves how best to evaluate a product in "terms of the truth or accuracy of its representation." This is what plagued Socrates as spoken through Plato. To imitate is to tarnish the original, but Aristotle saved us from these ravings. The this finished product is received well it will enjoy imitation at some point because it becomes the basis of a new truth and reality. If Mark, as I suspect he is, is mimicking several sources to right the perception of his community and creates a new perception, is it thus wrong or somehow inaccurate? Hardly. What Mark and other literary masters accomplished was to take situations plaguing them and use what resources they had to issue a confrontation. That confrontation was their answer to the false perception, because for them, their perception and representation of reality was very much the truth. Perception *is* reality. If a writer is able to shape perception by his rhetoric, then a new reality emerges.[19]

If the critic is able to identify the crisis, then the memetext will appear. Imitation still gives way to intertextuality and intertextuality still makes use of mnemonic merisms, but if they are only used to aid the audience's memory in preserving the text and not push them to some new action, then it is not mimetic.

18. Powell, *Narrative Criticism*, 11.

19. For a modern analogy, we should look at the effects Ayn Rand (1905–1982) has had on the American populace. Her two fiction works (*The Fountainhead* (1943) and *Atlas Shrugged* (1954)) are more widely known than her newsletters of later years. These two works form the philosophical basis for the Objectivist movement in the United States, but are nothing more than poorly narrated fictional stories unable to withstand actual scrutiny. Unlike her European counterparts who invested time and effort into economic policies supported by academic papers (I do not pretend to believe that the Austrian School is a valid economic system, but those who established the philosophy did so with scholastic work), Rand used *chreia* and parables to instill in her audience her philosophy. The shaping of politicians and would-be movement leaders by these two fiction novels are, albeit anachronistically, examples of how movements are shaped through fiction.

Mimetic Criticism and the Gospel of Mark

Commentary:[20]

1.1[21] Winn notes in his examination of MacDonald's thesis that Mark lacks hypertextual clues linking the two, "But if his claim was true, one would expect to find specific and obvious clues at an early point in Mark's gospel—clues that would signal the reader to read with an eye on the episodes, characters, and themes of the Homeric epics."[22] Logic insists that if an author is burying in his text previous texts for a particular purpose, he will need to subtly inform his audience with these hypertextual clues near the beginning of the literary work. Winn finds his clue in Mark's prologue when the Evangelist quotes from the Jewish Scriptures.[23] Since Lucan opens his work up with mimetic references to Virgil's *Aeneid, Georgics,* and other poems, we should expect no less in Mark. The opening line, an incomplete sentence, gives us our first clue as to Mark's purpose and because of this announced purpose, his sources.[24] If the quotation in 1.2–3 tells us who is coming in the story, then 1.1 tells us why. Mark's social situation pushes the author to issue a line in the sand against the Roman imperial ideology, proclaiming Jesus as messiah rather than Vespasian. The first volley in the counter-offensive is found in Mark's mimicking of the Priene Inscription.[25] It reads, "ἦρξεν δὲ τῶι κόσμωι τῶν δι' αὐτὸν εὐανγελίων."[26] The connection is present, although Mark uses the singular form of εὐαγγελίου and the nominal form of ἄρχω. The imperial cult impacts Mark's community in much the same way it has affected other sects of Judaism, by suggesting that Caesar is divine keeper of the calendar.[27]

---

20. For those readers who need an immediate plausible application, please see 5.1–20.

21. Rightly, 1.1–13 is considered a special introduction, or *prologus*, to the entirety of the Gospel. It becomes Mark's chiastic structure, much like the last eight verses close it. The sudden thrust of Jesus into the historical situation is not easily overlooked. Unlike the later Evangelists, Mark has no need to establish Jesus, possibly indicating an established structure existent already. For Mark, Jesus's intrusion into history is sudden, just as his departure is, requiring no authorial examination or historical reliance.

22. Winn, *Elijah-Elisha*, 39.

23. Mark uses Malachi 3.1, pointing to the return of Elijah.

24. I will examine the textual issue present in this verse later.

25. Kim, *Anarthrous*, 222–241.

26. Evans, *Mark's Incipit*, 67–81.

27. This is likely a slight reference to Daniel 7.25. There, the eschatological gentile ruler would seek to change the calendars and customs of the Jews. No doubt

This is not the only use of this word accompanying the image of a Roman emperor. In Josephus's *Bellum Judaicum* (*B.J.*), twice the word is connected to Vespasian, καὶ ὁ μὲν πεπιστευμένος ἤδη τὰ περὶ τὴν ἀρχὴν προπαρεσκεύαζεν αὐτῷ καὶ τὰ πρὸς τὴν ἄφιξιν τάχιον δ' ἐπινοίας διήγγελλον αἱ φῆμαι τὸν ἐπὶ τῆς ἀνατολῆς αὐτοκράτορα καὶ πᾶσα μὲν πόλις ἑώρταζεν εὐαγγέλια [δὲ] καὶ θυσίας ὑπὲρ αὐτοῦ ἐπετέλει (*B.J.*, 4.618). The second instance reads, "Εἰς δὲ τὴν Ἀλεξάνδρειαν ἀφιγμένῳ τῷ Οὐεσπασιανῷ τὰ ἀπὸ τῆς Ῥώμης εὐαγγέλια ἧκε καὶ πρέσβεις ἐκ πάσης τῆς ἰδίας οἰκουμένης συνηδόμενοι μεγίστη τε οὖσα μετὰ τὴν Ῥώμην ἡ πόλις στενοτέρα τοῦ πλήθους ἠλέγχετο (*B.J.*, 4.656)." Josephus uses εὐαγγελίζεται to describe victories by Vespasian and Titus (3.143; 3.503). It is possible Mark uses εὐαγγελίου as Paul does in concert with Isaiah 40.9 (εὐαγγελιζόμενος, or adopted from Isaiah 52.7),[28] but this does not allow for the tenor of Mark's Gospel, especially given that Mark's first use of the word is clearly associated with Caesar. It is probable Mark is attempting to reclaim the word from the Roman usage, by first reacting to Vespasian and then reminding his audience what the idea entails. It is the victory of Jesus Mark announces against the Imperial cult with Paul's use of Isaiah in view,[29] namely, that Isaiah promises victory over Israel's enemies. Late Jewish polemical writings would identify Rome in this regard (see commentary on 5.1–20 below). This is the only time in the Gospel it appears in an absolute sense and is wholly different from Paul's normal usage connecting the good news to preaching. Given the incompleteness 1.1 better understood as an announcement from a herald, challenging Rome.

A possible parallel also occurs in Genesis 1.1, another heading beginning mid-thought and forming an incomplete sentence, ἐν ἀρχῇ ἐποίησεν ὁ θεὸς τὸν οὐρανὸν καὶ τὴν γῆν.[30] Mark writes for a new reality, one that is caused not so much by the death of Jesus (although it begins there), but with the destruction of the Temple (see commen-

---

representing Antiochus IV originally, a reuse of the Danielic passage could give Mark a certain edge from the start.

28. Watts, *New Exodus*, 99.

29. For a fuller discussion of the incipit as anti-imperial, see Winn, *Purpose*, 92–99.

30. Genesis 1 may also provide Mark some additional background coloring here. While a certain amount of imperial flair is seen at the baptism of Jesus, so too is a reenactment of Genesis 1.2–3 with the spirit of God, waters, and the opening of the heavens. Another scene comporting well with Mark's goal here is the use of the other creation story in Genesis 8.6–12.

tary on Mark 13 below).³¹ We have established our first hypertextual clue, linking Mark to the Roman imperial cult, not in support but in opposition.³²

1.19, 3.17 *See Mark 10.35–45*

1.21-28 Capernaum is mentioned once by Josephus and only in passing, but for Jesus, it is the start of his public ministry and base of operations in Galilee. It is the place where on the Sabbath he begins to teaching in the Synagogue causing only a small stir. This is also the first time which Jesus casts out demons. Καὶ εἰσπορεύονται εἰς Καφαρναούμ· καὶ εὐθὺς τοῖς σάββασιν εἰσελθὼν εἰς τὴν συναγωγὴν ἐδίδασκεν. καὶ ἐξεπλήσσοντο ἐπὶ τῇ διδαχῇ αὐτοῦ· ἦν γὰρ διδάσκων αὐτοὺς ὡς ἐξουσίαν ἔχων καὶ οὐχ ὡς οἱ γραμματεῖς. Καὶ εὐθὺς ἦν ἐν τῇ συναγωγῇ αὐτῶν ἄνθρωπος ἐν πνεύματι ἀκαθάρτῳ καὶ ἀνέκραξεν.³³ Capernaum has no military value for Vespasian, and indeed, serves only as a sort of an intercalation of poetic beauty describing the land between battles in Josephus's account. While Vespasian is never said to visit Capernaum, there is little doubt given his travels and summer campaigns that the Roman legions came close to it at the very least. Capernaum is on the shore of the Sea of Galilee and far from Caesarea, if one travels by map. The one time it is mentioned in Josephus is just a short distance from the mention of Caesarea (3.510 for Caesarea and 3.519 for Capernaum), the place of the initial outbreak of the Revolt (2.230–66).³⁴ It started over the issue of land. The Greeks in the city owned land preventing the synagogue's construction (*B.J.* 2.285-9). Agrippa II had already quelled the violence in the city but this reignited the flames. The ruler of the city, Florus, well aware of the sedition about

---

31. I also note the beginning of John's Gospel.

32. There have been recent books self-published which attempt to draw connections between the Gospels and the Flavians, but only as a conspiracy inaugurated by Rome to create a new religion and calm the rebellion. An honest reading of Mark's Gospel, in light of the Jewish Revolt, will show that there the Gospel is anything but conciliatory to the Roman Empire. Further, objections will be raised as to whether it could be that Josephus, and even later Imperial cults, could in fact be borrowing from the Gospels. Given that Mark's Gospel is a rout of the Empire, it is unlikely that a skilled writer like Josephus would have need to embarrass both the Emperor and himself in presenting Jesus as superior that Vespasian.

33. Mark 1:21–23.

34. Roman emperors had awarded Capernaum to Agrippa II, while appointing Florus as procurator. It is unlikely, however, Capernaum existed as a Jewish province before this time. While Mark does not expressly state Capernaum is a Jewish city, it should be assumed Mark is attempting transference.

to take place, decides to leave Caesarea for Sebaste. The Greeks took this time to instigate, "Τῆς δ' ἐπιούσης ἡμέρας ἑβδομάδος οὔσης τῶν Ἰουδαίων εἰς τὴν συναγωγὴν συναθροισθέντων στασιαστής τις Καισαρεὺς γάστραν καταστρέψας καὶ παρὰ τὴν εἴσοδον αὐτῶν θέμενος ἐπέθυεν ὄρνεις τοῦτο τοὺς Ἰουδαίους ἀνηκέστως παρώξυνεν ὡς ὑβρισμένων μὲν αὐτοῖς τῶν νόμων μεμιασμένου δὲ τοῦ χωρίου (B.J. 2.289)." Sabbath is mentioned only six times in B.J. while Josephus mentions the Seventh Day fifteen times. For the Gospel of Mark, however, it is always Sabbath. This helps to narrow down the memetext.

Capernaum is Peter's and thus Jesus's home, providing a locus of travel for Jesus and his disciples. Three Markan pericopes take place in Capernaum (Mark 1.20, 2.1, and 9.33). In two of those pericopes, Jesus performs a miracle. The first time, he casts out demons. The second time, he heals a paralytic. The last pericope is a discourse with the Twelve involving, among other things, an exception for other exorcists who are using Jesus's name to cast out demons. We find somewhat of a connection here with Vespasian and Caesarea. Vespasian and the X Legion are based in Caesarea and from there, on three different occasions, use it as a staging area for three different campaigns.[35]

A hidden mirror is buried in this text. The image we are to see is one of Jesus who lives in peace after removing the demons and healing the sick.[36] He goes out and returns three times, as does Vespasian but he does so in Caesarea. Vespasian goes out to conquer, but Jesus goes out to liberate. Caesarea is the scene of the religious provocation

---

35. The three campaigns by Vespasian are matched by Jesus's three departures from Capernaum. In 67, 68, and 69 Vespasian marches from Caesarea into the countryside to attack the Jews. In the fall of 67, Vespasian moves against Jamnia and Azotus while Titus comes to Caesarea. A year later, in a successful Spring campaign, Vespasian conquers much of Judaea, and begins to turn to Jerusalem. In the summer of 69, Vespasian finishes his campaign against the Judean countryside and nearly decides to march on Jerusalem, but as history has showed us, this was year of the Roman civil wars, which ended with Vespasian becoming emperor when his soldiers, both in Egypt and Caesarea proclaimed him as such.

36. Mark's metonymic demons are understood better in 5.1–20. Bultmann believed that this story was rather a healing, although the form of it was originally an exorcism. This prologue connects exorcisms with healings, something not dismissed too easily (See Bultmann, *History*, 209–10). Dibelius sees the story as one meant to focus on who Jesus is rather than what Jesus can do. See also Dibelius, *From Tradition to Gospel*, 43, 54–5. The binding spell Jesus uses is similar to ones existent during his time as identified in Betz (*Magical Papyri*, 106); however, the binding does not work on demons, but is meant to bind humans. (Contra Collins, *Mark*, 172–3.)

that begins the Revolt in earnest, in a synagogue on the Sabbath. If we leer into the looking glass, we see a Jesus who teaches on a Sabbath in Capernaum where others recognize his rightful authority without the need for violence.[37] This side of the mirror, however, is a frantic sea of fear and unrestrained fury—where Vespasian is the image we see—but it is the current reality. Here, the Greeks newly invested with authority from Caesar use it to torment the Jews and destroy a synagogue and leave a town supportive of Vespasian's military ventures. Then, out of the corner of our eye, we see a foreshadowing of someone who will come later in the Gospel, Pontius Pilate. The mirror, then, is complete.

Would the Jews of post-70 CE have inserted Pontius Pilate into this story? William Ong has brought to the front the idea of spatial communication.[38] Fowler goes on to suggest "in an oral cultural an utterance is never a static spatial artifact containing and univocal message or meaning."[39] Mark grows these hints in the fertile ground of his oral/aural culture, a fruit he is able to twist. Knowing that the Revolt began in Caesarea, with its history of Pontius Pilate and as the headquarters of Vespasian, Mark is folding time. Both Pilate and the recent Roman governor withdrew money from the Temple treasury, starting a violent outburst (*B.J.* 2.169–74). Pilate was governor of Caesarea where, but not when, the Revolt had started. Herein exists a connection to the historical Jesus as well; A procurator of Judaea, had he not been associated with the early Markan community, would not stir the emotions needed by the author. Thus, in the opening salvo of the prologue, we have visible allusions pointing to the Revolt, drawing the audience inward.

1.39[40] The phrase, εἰς ὅλην τὴν Γαλιλαίαν, is found nowhere else in canonical Scripture, but is found once in Josephus, "ὅπως τε τὰς περιοίκους ἐτειχίσαντο καὶ ὡς Νέρων ἐπὶ τοῖς Κεστίου πταίσμασι δείσας περὶ τῶν ὅλων Οὐεσπασιανὸν ἐφίστησι τῷ πολέμῳ καὶ ὡς οὗτος μετὰ τοῦ πρεσβυτέρου τῶν παίδων εἰς τὴν Ἰουδαίων χώραν ἐνέβαλεν ὅσῃ τε χρώμενος Ῥωμαίων στρατιᾷ καὶ ὅσοι σύμμαχοι ἐκόπησαν εἰς ὅλην τὴν

---

37. Mark's allusion to Jesus's authority (v.22) should point the reader to Daniel 7.14a, another textual clue to Mark's sources.

38. Ong, *Orality and Literacy*, 31.

39. Fowler, *The Reader*, 45.

40. The lonely prayer of Jesus broken only by those searching for him begins a concentric pattern ending in the Gethsemane, although the latter scene is one of distress rather than the pressures of fame.

Reading Mark Mimetically

Γαλιλαίαν καὶ ὡς τῶν πόλεων αὐτῆς ἃς μὲν ὁλοσχερῶς καὶ κατὰ κράτος ἃς δὲ δι' ὁμολογίας ἔλαβεν (B.J., 1.21)." Like Capernaum above, and Gerasa below, Jesus is casting out demons near what we could consider a reference to Josephus's account. Why the exorcisms of Jesus are related to the Romans and, thus, points us to looking towards (not necessarily always to) B.J will achieve meteorologically clarity.[41] I note 1.39–41 is a pericope awash in parataxis.

1.[41] Here, we see where mimetic criticism can help resolve certain textual issues. At present, the question is between ὀργισθεὶς and σπλαγχνισθεὶς. The minority MSS traditions reflect the former, while some of the better MSS reflect the latter. In Mark 1.21–28, the "demons" call Jesus the Holy One of God. The term "holy one" was used numerous times in the Hebrew Scriptures to represent, most notably, God (usually with the addition of "of Israel"), David (in the Psalms, cf. 22.4, 71.22; 78.41; 89.19; 106.16) and Aaron. One was King and one was High Priest. I do not take the use of "Holy One" to mean that Jesus is called the Son of God by the demons, but following his adoption and anointing in baptism (see Psalm 2 as well as the fact that Jesus can now heal lepers, Lev 14.), Jesus is now both King and Priest, a recognition placed in the mouths of the "demons" so as to propel the story along.[42] As Winn has identified, there is a connection between Mark and the Elisha narratives, and specifically, I think that the emotion of King Jesus is related to the emotion of the King of Israel in 2 Kings 5.1–8. The King of Israel is sent the leper first, but is unable to overcome his paranoia, believing that it is a ruse to trap him. Elisha enters and declares that there is no reason for anger, since a prophet is here. Jesus, while the text does not say, could have sensed a trap (it happens throughout the Gospel) so he ordered the leper to the priest, angrily.

2.1–13 There is a small literary connection between Mark 2.2 and Josephus, but there is a certain amount of thematic material available for consideration. 2.1–13 is a pericope featuring a paralytic with friends who dig through the roof to lower him down to Jesus, who we are supposed

---

41. Mark, in the opening lines of his work, pulls from the opening lines of Josephus's work.

42. Jesus's baptism, while not covered here, is well within Jewish tradition. See *Test. Levi* 18 (cf. 4Q213–214 and 1Q21) and *Test. Judah* 24. On the subject of Jesus's baptism, however, it is best compared with the Transfiguration in Mark 9. For now, however, the image of Jesus's baptism is meant to suggest the Roman imperial cult. See the following chapter for the discussion of "colonial mimicry."

to understand as so successful that his handlers prevented any easy approach. The same idea, that the character of the story was by now greatly celebrated, is found in Josephus, "καὶ ὁ μὲν πεπιστευμένος ἤδη τὰ περὶ τὴν ἀρχὴν προπαρεσκεύαζεν αὐτῷ καὶ τὰ πρὸς τὴν ἄφιξιν τάχιον δ' ἐπινοίας διήγγελλον αἱ φῆμαι τὸν ἐπὶ τῆς ἀνατολῆς αὐτοκράτορα καὶ πᾶσα μὲν πόλις ἑώρταζεν εὐαγγέλια [δὲ] καὶ θυσίας ὑπὲρ αὐτοῦ ἐπετέλει (B.J., 4.618)."

In this passage Josephus recounts a very important account for both Vespasian and the historian. Vespasian realizes Josephus was correct in his former pronouncements that Vespasian would reign as emperor. Remembering this, Vespasian sets Josephus free by cutting off his chains.[43] It is possible this is a primary source, but it is more likely a secondary mnemonic device to counter the four lepers proving Elisha right, "καὶ τέσσαρες ἄνδρες ἦσαν λεπροὶ παρὰ τὴν θύραν τῆς πόλεως καὶ εἶπεν ἀνὴρ πρὸς τὸν πλησίον αὐτοῦ τί ἡμεῖς καθήμεθα ὧδε ἕως ἀποθάνωμεν ἐὰν εἴπωμεν εἰσέλθωμεν εἰς τὴν πόλιν καὶ ὁ λιμὸς ἐν τῇ πόλει καὶ ἀποθανούμεθα ἐκεῖ καὶ ἐὰν καθίσωμεν ὧδε καὶ ἀποθανούμεθα καὶ νῦν δεῦτε καὶ ἐμπέσωμεν εἰς τὴν παρεμβολὴν Συρίας ἐὰν ζωογονήσωσιν ἡμᾶς καὶ ζησόμεθα καὶ ἐὰν θανατώσωσιν ἡμᾶς καὶ ἀποθανούμεθα (2 Kings 7:3-4)." If this was to provide an aural background noise, then we could see the use of this passage to speak to the idea that God was working through Jesus to send away the enemies of Israel. If we take a poetic leap forward, the four friends in Mark are the four lepers in 2 Kings, lowering down the paralytic, or Israel, to the savior. As we will see, Israel is often pictured throughout Mark as the sick and the dead. Josephus already declared the destruction of Israel happened because of her sins. She was paralyzed. Israel was made sick by the constant rise and fall of the social bandits, finally destroyed by the Romans due to the fault of the Jews, at least according to Josephus. The four men are the four lepers of the Elijah–Elisha narratives bringing the news of victory to Israel.

We should not forget the rebuttal offered to Elisha by the King's officer, "καὶ ἀπεκρίθη ὁ τριστάτης ἐφ' ὃν ὁ βασιλεὺς ἐπανεπαύετο ἐπὶ τὴν χεῖρα αὐτοῦ τῷ Ελισαιε καὶ εἶπεν ἰδοὺ ποιήσει κύριος καταρράκτας ἐν οὐρανῷ μὴ ἔσται τὸ ῥῆμα τοῦτο καὶ Ελισαιε εἶπεν ἰδοὺ σὺ ὄψῃ τοῖς ὀφθαλμοῖς σου καὶ ἐκεῖθεν οὐ φάγῃ (2 Kings 7:2)." There are likely no solid literary connections (at least seen through the eyes of the redaction critic) here, but as a mimetic source, this pericope fits Mark's

---

43. This also seems to have some resemblance to the story of Joseph and Pharaoh.

Reading Mark Mimetically

purposes well. The four lepers have brought news that Jesus is God's victory and they do so through the windows of heaven.

A less than likely comparison remains, however, but we would be remiss not to consider how such a history of false monarchs and pretenders would play into the question by the Scribes as to who Jesus actually thought he was.[44] In *B.J.* 2.100-10, Josephus tells of a man who forges his identity to fool the Jews on his way to Rome acting as the heir to Herod's throne, Alexander, whom was killed by his insane father (cf. *B.J.* 1.586-603). He bore such an uncanny resemblance to the dead noble that he was easily treated as a king all the way to Rome, until he stood before Caesar who saw through his façade. There are a few shared words (or rather, lemmas of words rather than the same words), such as διδαχθεὶς (*B.J.* 2:102) and ἐδίδασκεν (Mark 2:13) among other less important ones, but thematically, the connections are relatively important. Mark's purpose is not to position Jesus as similar to any of the host of pretenders who were dotting the community's psychological countryside but to show Jesus as the ultimate reality, casting him as the one whom the pretenders imitated, then we can find some allowance for us to consider similar stories relevant to the telling of the Gospel. After all, in the Gospel the uneducated people, the gullible masses, were following Jesus without question but it was the religious elite who increasingly demanded the proof of his identity—even doing so at the very moment the windows of heaven were opened pronouncing God's victory. Jesus's identity was always first and foremost in the author's mind.[45]

2.14-17 In 2 Kings 6.32-33 we find, as we do in Mark, the presence of the elders of the people, a location of a house, and the inclusion of a

---

44. It is commonly thought Mark's use of scribes and Pharisees indicates an editorial ignorance, rather Mark used different sources, one mentioned Scribes and another mentioned Pharisees. Collins argues that this is not necessarily the case. As we have seen, several groups during this time had little time to distinguish themselves by set names. See Collins, *Mark*, 164 n.45.

45. Dewey notes a chiastic structure in this section. See Dewey, *Markan Public Debate*, 109-16. Also noticeable in this passage is the intentional lack of God. Jesus, although in the passive voice, pronounces forgiveness of sins. Priests and prophets were still required to sacrifice to God, proclaiming God as the one who has forgiven sins. Forgiving sins without God has led Christian interpreters to allow that God is not one, to allow for the Trinity in this verse, but it is doubtful Mark was alluding to the fourth century of Christianity intentionally. Instead, following the passage closely, the Pharisees claim loyalty to God, and in fact are the more religiously honest of the two, but it is Jesus who still insists that he can forgive sins alone.

murderer into the group—best identified with the presence of Levi the tax collector. The stage presence surrounding both pericopes is a one of turmoil. For Elisha, it is the death and destruction brought on by war, while in Mark Jesus is healing the land of the strife between kinship, or rather, those who are sick. Levi was a Jew feeding off his family, just as the scenes of cannibalism mentioned in the 2 Kings 6.28-30. We can also note that the order of these particular pericopes in Mark present a natural reflection of the order of the scenes in 2 Kings.

2 Kings 5–6	Mark 2.1–18
Israel Occupied	Israel Occupied
Cannibalism	Jesus calls the tax collector
Windows of Heaven	Four men open the windows of heaven
Elisha in his house hides from the murder	Jesus welcomes sinners and tax collectors
Four Lepers announce God's victory	Jesus heals the sick

Jesus is not just one mimicking Elisha, but also outperforming him. Unlike Elisha, Jesus does not hide from the tax collectors (figurative cannibalism who feed off their fellow Jews to aid the Roman Empire) or sinners, but one who welcomes them into his house.

2.18 1 Kings 12.24 seems to play an underlying role here, as there are connections to that verse throughout Mark 2.14–18. The verse reads, "τάδε λέγει κύριος οὐκ ἀναβήσεσθε οὐδὲ πολεμήσετε μετὰ τῶν ἀδελφῶν ὑμῶν υἱῶν Ισραηλ ἀναστρεφέτω ἕκαστος εἰς τὸν οἶκον ἑαυτοῦ ὅτι παρ' ἐμοῦ γέγονεν τὸ ῥῆμα τοῦτο καὶ ἤκουσαν τοῦ λόγου κυρίου καὶ κατέπαυσαν τοῦ πορευθῆναι κατὰ τὸ ῥῆμα κυρίου." The scene with Jesus dining among those outcasts of society creates an intensity that is magnified when it is placed next to some messianic claimants. While several brigand chiefs had made a regular charge of leveling the classes, the Revolt had accomplished this better than any of them. This equalizing tendency in the life of Jesus is very plausible standing alone, but next to the shattered remnants of the Revolt, a revolt started in part by those who promised equality, it becomes rather heightened.

3.1–6 The man with the withered hand was sent to Jesus under the gaze of a group not identified until 3.6. This delay in naming the group watching Jesus is part of Mark's misdirection. The image is similar to that of 2 Kings 5.1–8 where the King believes that the request to help heal the leper is a trap. Mark, here, clearly says that a trap was intended for Jesus. However, there is also a connection to a scene in *B.J.* needing examination. This scene is important, especially for Mark's later pericope of the civil war in Satan's kingdom. In *B.J.* 4.335–41, the Zealots holding Jerusalem, decided to weed out suspected traitors. They suspected a man by the name of Zacharias who they accused of attempting to betray the Revolt to Vespasian. Josephus relates that no evidence was presented by the prosecution, so when it came time for the defense, the accused simply refuted his accusers. He was found innocent, although this did not stop his accusers from murdering him. The idea of the trap of the innocent is one found in scripture and in recent reality where during the final months of the siege, the factions turned inward and civilization became a detriment to the innocent.

In the Markan pericope, Jesus heals a man with a withered hand. Tacitus records that Vespasian upon arrival in Alexandria heals a blind man and one with a malformed hand, "*igitur Vespasianus cuncta fortunae suae patere ratus nec quicquam ultra incredibile, laeto ipse vultu, erecta quae adstabat multitudine, iussa exequitur. statim conversa ad usum manus, ac caeco reluxit dies. utrumque qui interfuere nunc quoque memorant, postquam nullum mendacio pretium* (*Hist* 4.81)." Mark's scene is a twofold reference to the historical reality. First, Jesus is the innocent man that others seek to ensnare. Second, his miracles are greater than that of Rome. This helps with the first part, because if Jesus is acting with Vespasian' power, might he then be an agent provocateur of Rome? We may also see the miracle as a sign which was meant to suggest to the Pharisees (in the story) that Jesus was indeed working for Rome, after all, the audience who received Mark's story could very well have connected the two miracles. Jesus emerges as the innocent man from the outset countering the religious leaders who are also the upper classes. These classes are convinced that Jesus is a Roman infiltrator, but Jesus denies them any way of suggesting that he is operating behind closed doors by showing his power and doing so to deny glory to Vespasian. What emerges in this scene is a greater-than-Vespasian Jesus not afraid of Rome or the priestly classes.

3.18-19 The fact that Jesus had twelve specially chosen disciples has long been recognized as a typological reference to the tribes of Israel. While no doubt many of the disciples mentioned were historical figures, it does not follow that all of them were. In Paul's letters, we are introduced to Peter, James, and John but those are the only ones mentioned by name. Paul's closest mention to Judas is in 1 Corinthians 11.23 where Paul recounts the meal of Christ, mentioning only betrayal. While we may not stray too far from consideration that some of the disciples are historical figures given the large amount of verification available to us, there are at least two problems with the list. Simon the Zealot and Judas the Sicarii are identified by their allegiances to groups that did not exist until over thirty years after the death of Jesus. Indeed, the Zealots were not known by that name until 66 CE at the beginning of the Revolt, although the knifemen, the Sicarii, had already made a name for themselves.[46]

Josephus mentions Simon the Zealot and of Judas his brother, the sons of Jairus (6.92, 6.148, and 7.215) who are related to Manahem, dead tyrant of Masada (2.447). Do not, just yet, confuse Simon the Zealot wholly with Simon b. Giora, although the latter is possibly a Zealot, or a member of a subset of the Zealots. In Josephus's list of those who fought valiantly for the Jews, there are two Judases. Throughout both Mark and Josephus, there is a heavy instance of Simon, Judas and even the name of Jesus. It is the place in both lists which call our attention that Mark creates two characters for his audience, "ἠγωνίσαντο δὲ ἐξ αὐτῶν ἐπισήμως κατὰ ταύτην τὴν μάχην Ἀλεξᾶς μέν τις καὶ Γυφθέος τοῦ Ἰωάννου τάγματος ἐκ δὲ τῶν περὶ Σίμωνα Μαλαχίας τε καὶ ὁ τοῦ Μέρτωνος Ἰούδας καὶ Σωσᾶ υἱὸς Ἰάκωβος τῶν Ἰδουμαίων ἡγεμὼν τῶν δὲ ζηλωτῶν ἀδελφοὶ δύο παῖδες Ἀρί Σίμων τε καὶ Ἰούδης (B.J., 6.92)."

Compare this to Mark's placement of Simon and Judas "Σίμωνα τὸν Καναναῖον καὶ Ἰούδαν Ἰσκαριώθ, ὃς καὶ παρέδωκεν αὐτόν." Simon's designation, Καναναῖον, is a transliterated Aramaic word meaning "zealot." Judas's supposed family name is Ἰσκαριώθ bearing some linguistic semblance to σικάριοι. Elsewhere, Judas and Simon are both mentioned as usurpers to the messianic throne (B.J., 2.56-57). In 5.534, a Judas is a subordinate officer of Simon b. Giora. Giora was the leader of the Sicarii

---

46. For a broader discussion on the use of the term Zealot, which did not appear until the middle of the Jewish Revolt, see Richard Horsley, "The Zealots," *Novum Tertamentum* XXVIII, 2 (1986).

in the final days of Jerusalem, and while we could maintain that his actions were that of a Zealot, the break off of the Sicarii, history does not permit us to align Simon with that group so permanently. However, Mark is not writing history. Mark conflates the various Simons, including Simon b. Giora, into one Simon the Zealot, a favorite technique of Lucan in BC. Given that zealots and Zealots (see Josephus's attempt at distinction, *B.J.* 2.651) were not completely separated by cause, Simon the Zealot is a signal to the audience that Mark is also going to level his rhetoric against Simon b. Giora as well. After all Simon and Judas regardless of whom they may represent, had betrayed Jesus (or at least, Mark's community) through their actions of supporting the Zealots and the Sicarii.[47] This will become more apparent as we examine 11.15–17 and chapter 13, below.

3.20–30, 4.1–34 Sitting in the aftermath of the destruction of the Temple, either in Rome or Palestine, the recent Roman civil war would still plague the minds of the audience. After all, Vespasian was trying to prevent another civil war by securing not just his throne, but the throne of his son, Titus. This passage is connected directly to 3.1–6 providing a direct answer to the snare by the priestly classes. Jesus confirms to those who insisted he had lost his mind that they were right by speaking about demons, Satan, and Beelzebub, all engaged in a civil war.[48] This is not merely a story about circles and doubting Jesus, but Jesus is speaking to the distorted social situation.

With the mentioning of Beelzebub, no doubt his audience would hear the story of the king of Israel who, when he was sick, sent to seek help from Baal (2 Kings 1.1–8). The king soon regretted his decision as his servants were met by Elijah and given a message that the king would soon suffer death. Twenty years before the Caesarean Civil War, the Jews were engaged in their own civil war. Factions sought help from Rome to bring peace to Palestine. Then the Romans under Pompey marched in, they marched directed into the Temple and revealed the Holy of Holies to the world.[49] Nothing happened, of course except for

---

47. For a short summary of the problems with the historical facts behind Judas, see Collins, *Mark*, 224 where she argues against the inclusion of Judas as a marker for the history of the Twelve.

48. "Satan" in this passage is not a proper name or singular individual, but (following Day, "Satan (I-III)," 726–30) to the accuser, an individual with a temporary status.

49. Pompey walked into the Holy of Holies, finding nothing in particular, and left. See *Psalm of Solomon* 2.

the death of thousands of Jews and the rise of non-Temple based cults. This also sparked an interest in the rise in the hope of an eschatological figure. In Mark's recent memory, another Jewish civil war had preceded another Roman civil war. Like their predecessors, both civil wars ended with a new Caesar and Rome firmly in control of Palestine, but now the Temple was destroyed.

Here, I see a satirical approach to the civil war, admitting however my own biases. Jesus who is casting out demons is now called a demon, a semiotic Roman collaborator. As we saw in Mark 3.1–6, a trap was laid for Jesus. This trap caused him to perform the same miracle Vespasian had, perhaps setting him up as a Roman conspirator. This would explain why the Pharisees would seek to conspire with their natural enemies to rid themselves of Jesus. He was not the messiah; he was another Roman impostor. When approached with this viewpoint, Jesus replies that he is not a Roman pretender; he is not about securing Roman power, but about ending it! He uses the language of the war to rebuff the suggestion that he was a Roman fighting Rome. Jesus has provided objections to two accusations. First, he is not a Roman plant. Second, Jesus is not fighting Rome from the Roman side.

There is a possibility of another hidden clue more for the author than for the audience.[50] Mark had access to Lucan's poem, so it is possible he may have sought to include a memorial to his literary master. The poem opens with paradox, of "of crimes made law we sing" and of images of a proud people now debased through constant war. Of particular are the verses which read, "Then, Rome, if you love wicked war so much,/ Once you have subjected/ all the world to Latin laws,/ *Then* attack yourself. You've not lacked yet for foes./ But now that walls are teetering under roofs half ruined/ In Italy's cities, and from crumbled structures/ Massive stones lie idle, homes are left untended." The imagery of the Jewish Revolt and the Roman Civil War is present here in the words of Jesus, words exploding with meaning in the immediate aftermath of the wars.[51]

---

50. This fits the bill of the authorial biographical note.

51. Collins has identified v.27 as an ancient fable, meant to hide a statement, or a request, from a weaker party to a more powerful one (Collins, *Mark*, 233). I would agree; Mark is hiding his statement in the form of a weaker person, both of Jesus and of the Roman Empire. Given the hidden context of "binding" (spells), Mark is relying upon the audience to understand the role of exorcisms against the temporary "satan."

The warning in 3.28–29, along with 2.7, would bring to mind several things, including the sacrilege of Antiochus who sacrificed swine on the altar of the Temple. After all, the blasphemies are what caused the Maccabean Revolt.[52] Both times, the blasphemy is said to occur only against God. In Josephus, Herod plots to kill his sons by suggesting that they are speaking evil against him (see above on how the story of the death of his sons relate to the identity of Jesus), but it also takes the usual form of blasphemy against God; however, added to this is the possibility of railing against Moses that brought the death penalty (ἐβλασφήμουν is used; see B.J. 1.603, 2.145). That reward is met by Jesus's sentence condemning those who speak evil against God's Spirit as guilty of an everlasting sin. He also, as Josephus does with Moses, connects speaking evil against him as on the same level of speaking evil against God. There is also the juxtaposition of the πνεῦμα τὸ ἅγιον with πνεῦμα ἀκάθαρτον to consider apart from earlier Pauline thoughts and later Christian doctrine. The spirit Jesus operates under is different from the spirit the Romans operate under. Here, Mark is no doubt using familiar terminology but casting it next to this ideological enemy.

Jesus, for the first time in Mark, begins to speak in παραβολαῖς (3:23). This is followed by several parables in 4.1–34. Daniel hears παραβολαὶ (Dan 12:8), but it is more likely that Mark's use is shaped by Psalm 77.2 LXX, "ἀνοίξω ἐν παραβολαῖς τὸ στόμα μου φθέγξομαι προβλήματα ἀπ' ἀρχῆς." An examination of the context of Jesus's first parables along with the Psalm 77 (LXX) reveals that there are some similarities. It is about God's ultimate victory through bringing Israel back from exile. It also promises an agent from God by reminding them of David, but ending abruptly with this mention. No doubt, this expanded the audience's aural experience while hearing that David was given to a destroyed people. Further, it allows for Mark to suggest that he was indeed speaking messages to the people in a way only they would understand. The idea is simple. The hidden sayings, rather than literary fiction, are non-temporal forms of communication allowing Mark to give his audience statements from Jesus about their situation. Indeed, his audience would have gone through persecution and watched as many became apostates, all the while the Kingdom of God

---

52. Cf. 1Ma 2.6; 2 Ma 8.4; 10.35; 15.24.

began to grow. It would also have solidified the authority of both Jesus and Mark.[53]

We should here, at least in passing, note that Mark 3 is often cited in the criterion of embarrassment. It is in this section that Jesus excludes Mary and his other family members which no doubt would have served as an embarrassment to later Christians who turned to adoring Mary; however, this is not the embarrassment that matters. Indeed, what would have mattered to Mark's audience is news that not even his family believed him. Only James is recorded to have been convinced of Jesus's claims, whatever they were, but his other brothers so enumerated here, cannot be found in Christian annuls. Further, we must consider what role the exclusion of the family plays if the main part of this section is to deal with the suggestion that Jesus is really an agent of Rome. It is possible that this section fits Mark's overall strategy in a way to deflect from those of his family who continued to avoid association with Jesus. Mark could have taken this chance in Jesus's story to co-opt it to highlight the notion of the civil war and to provide for Jesus's Jewishness, something that will come into play in the second half of Mark.

4.35–41 This particular pericope begins a series of decisive literary events matched only in Mark 13–15.[54] The storm is meant to set the scene into the middle of a chaotic event, much like the scene in Genesis 1 as well as other Jewish creation stories, but the intertextuality is not merely an allusion to creation.[55] *Psalm* 41.8 (LXX) is used by the Evangelist to draw his audience into a world filled with sea monsters blocking the promise of God's deliverance. This verse reads, "ἄβυσσος ἄβυσσον ἐπικαλεῖται εἰς φωνὴν τῶν καταρρακτῶν σου πάντες οἱ μετεωρισμοί σου

---

53. The parables are likely grown from the Jewish Scriptures. For example, compare the damnation of the wicked by Mark with Hosea 2.23–25. Mark is filled with imagery of growing things, symbolizing some part of the warnings issued by Jesus, imagery found else (likely grown as well from places like Hosea) in 1 Enoch 62.7–8 and 1QH 14.14–16. Likewise, Seneca delivers a similar fertile ground for the parable (*Ep. Mor.* 73.16). (Collins, *Mark*, 243–5).

54. Specifically, the pericopes begin in 4.35 and last until the end of chapter of 5. A smooth transition between them is not he connection that we should look for, but instead, it is the use of the Jewish Scriptures to provide a structure for Mark's story; however, the transition is noted in the continued image of crossing the sea (4.35–6; 5.1, 18, 21).

55. 4:35 begins a new section of Mark's Gospel. Thus far, we have the prologue, the introduction ending with 4.34, and now a rather large literary unit stretch until the end of chapter 8.

καὶ τὰ κύματά σου ἐπ' ἐμὲ διῆλθον." The psalm is composed by one who seeks God "ἡμέρας καὶ νυκτός." This is mirrored in 5.5 with "νυκτὸς καὶ ἡμέρας."[56]

Intertextuality is more than a word or phrase, but a scaffolding providing internal support for the author's premise. The psalmist cries out to God wounded, oppressed, and crushed, "ἐν τῷ καταθλάσαι τὰ ὀστᾶ μου ὠνείδισάν με οἱ θλίβοντές με ἐν τῷ λέγειν αὐτούς μοι καθ' ἑκάστην ἡμέραν ποῦ ἐστιν ὁ θεός σου (Psalm 41:11 LXX)." This crushed psalmist is the person who we meet in the next pericope. The sense is that God is answering the calls of his people through the chaos. The psalmist acknowledges that he is far removed from God but relies upon the promise that regardless of the current desperate situation, God will eventually bring deliverance over the oppressive enemy (41.10 LXX). This is the prologue to 5.1–20.[57]

5.1-20 This chapter is the Rosetta stone of mimetic criticism in the *Gospel of Mark*. I cannot place too much emphasis on this entire chapter since it acts as a lexicon for Mark's Gospel. This is the second pericope in the series that attempts to tackle the effects of the Revolt by un-writing history. After an intertextual examination of this section, we find that Mark uses mnemonic sources and metonymies providing the key to understand Mark's miracles stories.[58] We first need to examine some of the recent scholarship on Mark 5.1–20.

Roger Aus connects Mark 5.1-20 with Psalm 90 LXX observing that this was quoted by Jesus in other synoptic interactions with demons

---

56. This is not the only Psalm possibly used. See also Psalm 43.24-7 LXX. In regards to a national cry to God, see Psalm 105 LXX.

57. The missing boats are explained not by the roughness of the storm (Theissen, *Miracle Stories*, 102, 180) or by an allusion to Homer (MacDonald, *Homeric Epics*, 58–61), but by an allusion to Psalm 106.23-32 LXX. The storm's description is found in the LXX in several places. In Job 38.1 and Jeremiah 32.32, it describes the appearance of God while in Sirach 48.9, 12, it describes Elijah's stormy entrance into the heavens. Anyone of these is more applicable to Mark's scene here than a phrase found in the *Odyssey*. We should not cast overboard John (1.4-6) either as we search for relevant literary sources. In regards to the sleeping Jesus.

58. R. Bartsch suggests that metonymies, part of concept formation, involve "mapping of a conceptual network from a source domain into a target domain" and "a shift in perspective which makes possible the mapping from one domain to the other by selecting suitable aspects of the source network, and also source domain, which can be satisfied on the target domain." (Bartsch, *Generating polysemy*, 50-2) There is nothing similar (metaphorical) about Rome and demons, but Mark is attempting to present a contiguities mass (metonymy).

(Matt 4:6–7; Luke 4:10–11). Further, he notes that the use of Psalm 90 LXX is found in pre-Christian exorcisms suggesting a connection to the words of the Legion when it asked Jesus, "τί ἐμοὶ καὶ σοί, Ἰησοῦ υἱὲ τοῦ θεοῦ τοῦ ὑψίστου?" Aus also connects the title invoked here back to the beginning of the Psalm (τοῦ ὑψίστου).[59] He further observes that this association makes it "very probable that the madman's designation of Jesus as son of 'the Most High God' in Mark 5.7 derives from the Psalm connected closely in early Judaism with madness." Aus questions the rationale of suggesting "the Most High God," was on the tongue of a pagan. He looks to the Septuagint for literary clues and suggests the inhabitants of the story are most likely Jews.[60]

Dennis MacDonald begins his commentary on this passage with a remark on the anomalous aspect of the Gerasene Demoniac episode, recognizing that no other New Testament exorcism is this detailed.[61] Citing the "standard deviations," MacDonald applies too little weight to the use of the Septuagint opting instead for a Homeric allusion.[62] These are suspicious connections, tenuous at best, and not all fitting Mark's portraiture. For example, MacDonald connects the request of the demon's name in Mark 5.9 with a similar scene between Odysseus and the Cyclops in *Odyssey* 9.354–56 and 363–66. Names are exchanged in both scenes, but names are regularly given in stories for various reasons. In the *Odyssey*, it is an introduction whereas in the life of an exorcist, the control of the demon is directly related to the hearing the name of the demon.[63] MacDonald constructs a more solid connection between Homer and Mark is the story of Circe (*Odyssey* 10) turning soldiers into swine, but as we will see, this connection suffers problems due to the reality that the use of Homer does not fit Mark's narrative threshold.[64]

Brian Incigneri, Gerd Theissen, and Adam Winn independently elucidate the Markan tale in terms of its relevance to the historical

---

59. We find the title in Deuteronomy 32.8 and Isaiah 14.14.

60. Aus, *My Name is "Legion,"* 9–10.

61. MacDonald, *Homeric Epics*, 64–5.

62. MacDonald notes the connection of tombs, demons and sleeping in caves between Mark and Isaiah, calling it "impressive," but only in a footnote. See 222n.4.

63. In ancient times, to know a demon's name was to have power over it. If asking for a name was imitating Homer, then we must believe that the practice originated with Homer, and thence to all subsequent exorcisms, even if the scene in Homer's Odyssey has nothing to do with exorcisms when the name is sought.

64. MacDonald, *Homeric Epics*, 66–7.

situation of the author. Incigneri writes that this pericope is "the first event in the Gospel to occur in a Gentile territory."⁶⁵ He suggests that while Legion does have Roman undertones, it is more likely that the swine represent something from the Scriptural narrative, such as the image of a self-destruction army akin to Pharaoh's in the story of the Exodus. Theissen asserts a buried Gentile *parole* in the *langue* of the swine, contra Aus. An important contribution by Theissen is to draw the critic into the geographic textual error, as he sees clearly the connection to Simon bar Giora.⁶⁶ Theissen sees this as a way to head off any Gentile interference in the Jewish Revolt against Rome.⁶⁷ He argues that contrary to the way other cities treated Jewish minorities the request of the people for Jesus to leave is representative of the way Jews were treated in Gerasa. Jesus is among the select few in the ancient world who was said to exorcise demons.⁶⁸ According to Winn, this power is one Vespasian expressly lacks and in Mark's hands, nurses the "tailor-made" polemic against the Roman Emperor. This "could be read as a Markan response to Vespasian's awesome military might."⁶⁹ Winn uses this story to either suggest the divine sonship of Jesus or how a good disciple is defined.⁷⁰ However, there is a historical event attached to this story.

There exists in this account a synchronism tangible in history. Josephus records the advance by Vespasian on the Jewish rebels in and around the Sea of Galilee. In the space of about three months, Vespasian rampaged methodically over the Galilean province, finally marching against Gadara in late March 68. Seeing a perfect opportunity to secede from the confederation, the leading and wealthy men of the city sent an embassy to Vespasian for peace with a "desire. . .of peace, and for saving their effects, because many of the citizens of Gadara were

---

65. Incigneri, *Gospel to the Romans*, 190.

66. This follows the statement that Gerasa is a "geographical mistake." (Theissen, *Context*, 109). See Foley, *Immanent Art: From Structure to Meaning in Traditional Oral Epic* and Chapman, *Location the Gospel of Mark: A Model of Agrarian Biography* for recent scholarship showing that in an oral culture, a phrase or geography may represent something larger.

67. Theissen, *Context*, 110–1.

68. It should be noted that in the known recorded history of exorcisms in the ancient world, Jesus is the only one who does not have to call upon a higher power.

69. Adam Winn, *Purpose*, 111–2.

70. For the idea of divine sonship in Winn's use of Mark 5.7 see 19, 94, 101, 182–3. For his use of 5.19–20 to present the good disciple, see 10, 147, 187 in Winn, *Purpose*.

rich men (*B.J.* 4:414)." Those of the anti-Roman party were holding the city hostage, killing the pro-Roman citizens who attempted to escape; however some did and asked that Vespasian come and save them. These sympathetic citizens intended to pull down the city's walls and accept a garrison from Vespasian, a plan so angering the rebellious citizens that they decided to extract revenge before fleeing the town. To do this, they found a young man named Dolesus who, as the leader of the city's nobility, had sent the embassy to Vespasian with the intention of avoiding war.[71] Josephus reports that the anti-Roman party "slew him and treated his dead body after a barbarous manner, so very violent was their anger at him, and they ran out of the city" followed by Vespasian's lieutenant, Placidus, while he entered the town at the request of the rulers of the city. At the final battle of the Gadarenes, the Romans killed fifteen thousand, "while the number of those who were unwillingly forced to leap into the Jordan was impressive (*B.J.* 4.435)." Josephus notes that the remaining two-thousand two hundred were taken as prisoners (*B.J.* 4.437).

With some historical background established, we will now turn to the intertextual structures in this pericope. In Deuteronomy 30.13, the people are asking if they will need someone to cross over the sea (πέραν τῆς θαλάσσης) to bring back the commandment that brings an end to exile. Another connection to Psalm 41 LXX is seen as well in this allusion, providing a dual structure, along with Deuteronomy 30, to the setting of Mark 5.1–20. Mark 5.1 sounds a repercussion to Deuteronomy's echo that Jesus is the one from the πέραν τῆς θαλάσσης. Deuteronomy works to help a community maintain an identity in exile, becoming important in the Judaisms of this period.[72] The promise by God to return the Israelites from exile is stated in 30.1–5; 30.6–14 promises to turn the curses the Israelites experienced upon the enemies as well as a warning to Israel. Adherence is not required to an individual but to the commands (30.8) and the "word" of God (30.14); this acceptance

---

71. We do not have to assume that Dolesus was a Gentile, given Roger Aus's work, as well as recent works by Mark Chancey. Further, Levick (Levick, *Vespasian*, 36) notes that Dolesus was seen as a traitor and that Placidus achieved success when the Jews (much like Josephus did when faced with such a challenge) became loyalist once more. While it is, admittedly, tenuous, we are not bound to seeing Dolesus as a Gentile only.

72. The use of Deuteronomy in Pauline writings and early Judaism is important to the study of how a community used Scripture, sometimes rewriting it, to combat ideological changes in the secular world. See Lincicum, *Paul & the Early Jewish Encounter With Deuteronomy*.

of the message leads to the end of exile. The passage closes with a plea and a warning from God that they would suffer destruction in the land if they refused to obey the commandment. The use of Deuteronomy 30 in Mark 5.1–20 would allow survivors of the Revolt to remember the warning not to reject the words of God. It also leads the listeners to question their part in the recent destruction of Israel; Mark suggests a surreal possibility that the rejection of Jesus a generation prior finally was repaid with a new exile.[73] The connection to the word of God and the good news of Jesus remains in the open rather than buried in the text, but so does the hope of survival through exile to return to Israel again.[74] Having provided a visualizing narrative, Mark turns to Isaiah to provide key to his message, demanding from his readers some sort of participation. He expects them to plunge into the text in a prolonged search to discover the source of his demons.

The use of Isaiah 65.1–5 in this passage provides the mimetic critic, you and I, a moment of revelatory clarity to consider just how purposeful the Evangelist is when he carefully selects his sources. He is intentional, calculating, cold. Mark extracts the sources for his story from his audience; these sources, his motivation; these sources, their control. The central connection appears between Isaiah 65.4 and Mark 5.3–5 where we find similar phrasing (καὶ ἡμέρας ἐν τοῖς μνήμασιν καὶ ἐν). Beyond the Markan use of Isaianic phrases, there is the similarity in imagery as found in both pericopes. Both passages contain people embroiled in phenomenological dissension. In Isaiah, the people are rebelling against God (65.1–2). The city mentioned in Mark is either in rebellion against Rome (as is the case in the historical situation with the Galilean province) or in rebellion against God's agent as we see in 5.14–20 wherein the citizens of the city rejected Jesus. Another, more importantly, is the presence of demons (δαιμονίοις). The Hebrew version allows that disobedient people to burn incense in what is recognized as a pagan ritual. The Hellenistic re-author goes further to clarify that the people are sacrificing to demons, but then adds something that

---

73. This suggestion is not new. It is a motif enacted time and time again throughout the Prophets. Because the people had rejected God through his agent, they would now suffer destruction.

74. Mark quite clearly stands in the Pauline tradition of Christianity. No doubt, he was part of the Roman church and had access to Paul's Epistle to the Romans. Chapters 9—11 specifically play a part in the underlying theology of rejection of Jesus leads to exile but accepting leads to resurrection found here in Mark.

Mimetic Criticism and the Gospel of Mark

is striking. These demons do not exist (ἃ οὐκ ἔστιν).[75] The use of Isaiah 65 as a merisim calms nerves of the Markan audience, taking away the night terrors of demons and other ghouls, but encapsulates Mark's agenda. Mark's demons, rather than supernatural manifestations of evil in the Gospel, are there for another purpose. The Evangelist has borrowed the stage of the Prophet, and as such, the stage still contains the props. Divine battles against demons, demons revealed not to exist before God, are given the backdrop topographical definition (65.4). Interpersonal conflicts develop between the actors as well. Whereas in Isaiah, the unholy, but self-righteous people want nothing to do with God, the demoniac rushes to bow before Jesus demanding to know what Jesus wants. Mark's use of Deuteronomy 30 provides a structure of the cyclic pattern of return from exile. Isaiah, however, gives an interpretative machine more revealing than concealing. The ghosts simply are not there.

The lingering memories of the recent Revolt are present, however, haunting Mark's account. It contains two phantoms—Dolesus and Legion—where the demoniac is a parallel to the historical figure of Dolesus. In Mark's account, the man who lived among the tombs brutally mutilated his body. His anger and strength is such that chains are incapable of restraining his actions. Due to Dolesus's violent death, he was doomed to wonder the earth as an evil spirit, or a *biaiothanatos daimon*.[76] In the action of the exorcism, Deuteronomy 30.5 and 15 provide a needed allusion testifying to God's promise of life given as a gift after the return from Exile.[77] The healing of the demonic is not an exorcism, but a resurrection. Dolesus is alive, but the demons remain.

In 5.11, Jesus sees a herd of swine on a nearby mountain. This is an unhindered symbol of the X Legion, a troop playing a large role in the Revolt as well as one left behind to put down any other pockets of resistance. This legion was station on a hilltop top overlooking Gadara

---

75. The clause is also absent in the Isaiah Scroll found at Qumran.

76. For discussion on the *biaiothanatos* tradition of demons, see Betz, *The Greek Magical Papyri*, 333 and Ogden, *Magic,*146. I should note as well that Jesus, himself dying a brutal death, could have been considered a *biaothanatos*. What we see this pericope is likely a hint of the Resurrection as well. In chapter 8, I will use Matthew as a test for my thesis, but I must note that Matthew's version of the story uses demons instead of unclean spirits.

77. Deuteronomy 30.5, εὖ is used, and like other places in that book, is connected to the idea of a long life.

and the Sea of Galilee. Along with the obvious use of legion, we have more military terminology with Jesus's address in 5.13. When asked if they could be sent into the swine, Jesus gives permission using a military command (ἐπέτρεψεν). Once this command is given, the legion rushes down the steep bank into the sea. Here, Mark is specific about the number of them, 'about two-thousand.'[78] The audience would have received an emotional jolt by the actions in 5.13, remembering the last battle of the anti-Roman Gadarenes and the massacre that happened. The end of the battle parallels Mark's account with the leaping into the sea of about two thousand demons. The reception of Vespasian is similarly used when Mark writes about the rejection of Jesus by the town. Whereas they wanted the occupation by Vespasian, they refused Jesus's offer of liberation.

To understand the Jewish metonymy of the swine, I turn to other Jews of the era. A close pejorative use of swine in connection to Rome is found in the *Mishnah Rabbah*, a second century compilation of older sources by Rabbi Judah. During this period, Rome was referred to as Edom and swine (*hazir*).[79] Not only can we use rabbinical teaching

78. We may also see a parallel in the murder of 1000 Jews by Vespasian in Gerasa if Mark is indeed doubling to overemphasize the power of Jesus compared to Vespasian. Aus suggests that this number could have no basis in reality given the expressiveness of the native language. He cites data of the time that presents the fact that swine herds numbered nowhere near that amount. He concludes that it is connected to liturgical readings that occurred near Passover (Joshua 3.4, for one) (Aus, *My Name is Legion*, 63–67). The number "two thousand" is found in several over places, in relatively close proximity. In *B.J.* 5:44, to fill up the legions depleted by war, including the Tenth, two thousand men were chosen from among the armies of Alexandria. In *B.J.* 5:250, Simon's Zealots were said to number two thousand four hundred men, the same two thousand that defected to Simon in *B.J.* 4.353. Of particular note to the story of the demoniac is *B.J.* 5.552. This passage records "about two thousand" dead Jews were dissected by Arabians for the gold in their stomachs followed by Josephus attempting to show Titus would have punished those who had done such things had he caught them. Josephus later records over two thousand who were killed by various means by the Romans (*B.J.* 6.430).

79. R. Phinehas and R. Hilkiah, in the name of R. Simeon, said: Out of all the prophets, only two, namely Asaph and Moses, named it Asaph said: The boar out of the wood doth ravage it (Ps. 80, 14), Moses said: and the swine because it parteth the hood and is cloven footed, but cheweth not the cud, he is unclean to you (11.7). Why is it compared to a 'hazir' -To tell you this: Just as the swine when reclining puts forth its hooves as if to say: See that I am clean, so too does the empire of Edom boast as it commits violence and robbery, under the guise of establishing a judicial tribunal. This is compared to a governor who put to death the thieves, adulterers, and sorcerers. He leaned over to a counselor and said: 'I myself did these three things in one night.' (M.

to establish that Mark symbolized the Romans as swine, but there is surface evidence provided by the aforementioned 10th Legion. Their emblem was that of a wild boar. That the swine could represent Rome is not really arguable, but were demons used to represent Rome?[80]

The answer is preserved in the *Fifth Sibylline Oracle*. Collins notes that this oracle "may reflect the attitudes of Egyptian Judaism in the period leading up to the revolt." Like most of the oracles, this one has undergone redaction and interpolation, but Collins believes that the "greater part" of the oracle falls between 70 and 115 CE. With each victory by Rome, their negative image grew. Collins writes, "The most bitter words of the sibyl, however, are directed against Rome. Like Babylon in the Old Testament (which is invoked in *Sib. Or.* 5 as a type of Rome), Rome had said, 'I alone am and no one will ravage me.' This blasphemous pretension to divinity is typified by Nero and is the ultimate sin in the biblical tradition." He goes on, "More significantly, it was Rome which destroyed Jerusalem (vss. 160–161) and was thereby established as the new Babylon."[81] There exists within the more specific section of 160-171 a certain idea against Rome (including the Latinism in 171) that it was filled with an unclean spirit.[82] The same thoughts persist in John's Apocalypse as well, with the image of Babylon/Rome as the haunt of unclean spirits and vile demons (Rev. 16.13–14; 18.2).

Thus far in this section, I have ignored Mark's geographical oddity. After all, it is possible that an author writing in Rome might mistake towns. After all, Gerasa could not possibly be the central location for the story given the story has Jesus immediately stepping off the boat into a city nearly thirty miles inshore. I suggest, following Theissen, the use of Gerasa is a purposeful act to engage the memory of Simon. Mark is likewise creating a trail of breadcrumbs for the audience to follow to a climatic end. How? Gerasa is the city of Simon's birth: "Ἐπανίσταται δὲ ἄλλος τοῖς Ἱεροσολύμοις πόλεμος υἱὸς ἦν Γιώρα Σίμων τις Γερασηνὸς τὸ γένος νεανίας πανουργίᾳ μὲν ἡττώμενος Ἰωάννου τοῦ προκατέχοντος ἤδη τὴν πόλιν ἀλκῇ δὲ σώματος καὶ τόλμῃ διαφέρων (*Wars* 4:503)." By having Jesus go into Simon's home territory and vanquish the Romans, Jesus is

---

Rabbah—Leviticus 13:5).

80. At times, Josephus called various Romans inspired (δαιμόνιον; *B.J.* 4:501) along with the courage Titus is said to have (*B.J.* 7.120).

81. Collins, *Between Athens and Jerusalem*, 143–4.

82. θυμόν should be understood as a Latinism for anima, or breath/spirit.

established as the legitimate messiah. Further, as we have seen above, Mark has a habit of conflating sources. Jesus in Gerasa would have also been a way to combat the death of 1000 Gerasenes at the hands of Vespasian. It is at this geographical location, often attributed as an error on the part of the author, that the false messiahs of Mark converge.

With the establishment of Mark's allusions and intertextuality as well as historical habiliments, I want to present Mark's anti-reality to the massacre of Jews by Rome. Above, we introduced the theory of anti-mimesis, the idea of "life imitates art." There is no finer example of this in Mark's Gospel (if not, dare I say, in all literature) than in this passage. Mark's simulacrum has intentionally disparaged reality, abusing it in such a manner as the audience by now has suffered a psychological reaction. Faced with the crimes committed in the Revolt, by both Jews and Romans, the audience endures a bright-light interrogation, beckoning them to consider Jesus and what the preaching of Jesus can do. By accepting the message of Jesus, the sin of murdering Dolesus is forgiven and he lives. Furthermore, so does the town. No longer does it suffer a holocaust at the hands of Vespasian and Placidus, but it is quickened and restored. Jesus punishes the Legion who perpetrated the violence upon the defeated Jews, removing the Roman control from Judaea. Deuteronomy promises the return from exile while Isaiah assures the onlookers that the demons that torment them stand before God as if they do not exist. This is more than a mirror, but a complete reversal of the horrors of the Revolt.[83]

5.21–43 This recognizable intercalation begins the final series of pericopes that join Mark's sources and themes. They are the backbone of Mark's Gospel. Jesus is again on the seashore when he is approached to come and heal a dying girl. On his way to answer the request, Jesus comes across a woman suffering twelve years of uncontrollable bleeding. Her hemorrhage is stopped and very shortly thereafter the dead child lives. It is no accident that in these pericopes are hints at the resurrection of Jesus, but that is not the concern at the moment. Allusions,

---

83. Ched Myers has suggested a similar basis for Mark's story here (Myers, *Binding the Strong Man*, 191–2) while Collins notes that Josephus is more likely speaking about a different town than our Gerasa (Collins, *Mark*, 269n.76). While archeological evidence may suggest Geresas are confused in Josephus, and thus Mark, the Evangelist is not concerned with factual incidents, only with countering ideological incidents. After all, given Mark's propensity with alienating cartographers, accurate GPS coordinates are not Mark's primary concern.

rather than a solid intertextual structure, to an Elisha story—specifically 2 Kings 2.19-22—exist. In this story, Elisha is confronted with a city in drought. He produces a miracle to end the death and miscarriage (θάνατος καὶ ἀτεκνουμένη) endured by the women. In 4.464, Elisha is said to have used his hands, in part, to bring this about. The story also makes an appearance in Josephus's account as well.

The intertextual source comes from a historical event. Vespasian launched another campaign at the beginning of spring (69 CE) following the massacre at Gadara. The Romans make quick work of the Jewish defenses and begin to move south towards Jerusalem marching across the Great Plain. Josephus gives a botanical account of the area, attributing the fruitfulness of the area to Elisha's miracle (*B.J.* 4.459-73). He is careful to report that the fountain was the cause of death and miscarriage until Elisha arrived to make it healthy. Much of Josephus's recounting of the story from 2 Kings is additional information contributed to local oral tradition, rather than a to a written text.

The woman's medical condition is related specifically to an unhealthy foundation (πηγὴ; Mark 5.29). Josephus calls the spring πηγήν. There is also the use of hands (χειρὸς; 5.41) to accomplish the miracle; Josephus has προσχειρουργήσας (4:464). Shared images abound. There is a dead child and a woman suffering a constant miscarriage; Jesus heals them both. These two miracles follow closely Jesus's rout of Vespasian's legions in Gadara, mirroring the structure of Josephus's account. Elisha' fountain is here, or rather, Jesus restores the health of Elisha's fountain so that children will not die and women can be mothers again, a sign of peace and prosperity.[84]

Before we continue, I want to note Mark's ability to use the proper Greek. We see in these intercalations the normative Greek. Mark's use of language is demonstrated as equal to that of other Greek scribes of the time, but he simply chooses not to do so in other places, indicating madness to this method in butchering the language of the day.

6.1-6 There is little here to critique mimetically except for a slim connection to the story of Elisha and the two child-killing female bears (2 Kings 2.23-25). While Bethel was not Elisha' home, it was the House

---

84. We should skip, for the moment, consideration of the role a Jairus played in the Markan account and the role in which a Jairus figures into Josephus's story. Considering that there are at least two different Jairuses in Josephus, it was possibly a common name as well.

Reading Mark Mimetically

of El and had become the center of the Jerusalem cult recreated in Dan. Josephus mentions it once in Wars, noting that Vespasian easily overran it (*B.J.* 4.551). However, there is a possible connection to Psalm 77 LXX, "καὶ ἐποίμανεν αὐτοὺς ἐν τῇ ἀκακίᾳ τῆς καρδίας αὐτοῦ καὶ ἐν ταῖς συνέσεσι τῶν χειρῶν αὐτοῦ ὡδήγησεν αὐτούς (Psalm 77:72)."

Let us focus our attention on the suggestion that Jesus is a τέκτων (6.3). MacDonald suggests that this is, in some way, an allusion to Odysseus, although the hero is referred to as a master carpenter, given great construction feats (including the building of the Trojan Horse as well as his own palace), Jesus is a man rarely without sorrow who throughout the Gospel never builds anything.[85] When the word is used in Josephus, it is not for the vaunted builders of the future, but for those who do menial labor under the command of another (cf. *B.J.* 3.78; 171–3; 5.275).[86] However, this is not yet all that we need to put to rest the Homeric connection. Indeed, MacDonald is correct in his assumption that often times carpentry is connected to Wisdom, but he somewhat skips past the prevalent issues of Stoicism found throughout Mark's Gospel.[87] The idea of Jesus as a τέκτων is more in line with Seneca the Younger (specifically his Epistle 90) than Homer. The philosopher presents one such instance when the working of a man with his hands is considering the greatest feat of human wisdom. We will discuss Mark's Stoicism later; however, for now it is rather easy to suggest if a theological crisis was pressing Mark to try to re-create Jesus as better than Odysseus by comparing the carpentry legacy of both men, then it is left to us to decide if Mark failed or if the theory of the scholar is faulty. After all, what did Jesus ever build that is comparable to Odysseus?[88]

We need to take a moment to examine the *chreia* in v.4. These maxims are prevalent in Mark, acting to summarize the entirety of the

85. MacDonald, *Homeric Epics*, 15–9. MacDonald's first error is to take the term as a compliment. It is likely carpenter, just as "son of Mary," is an implied insult. See Collins, *Mark*, 290–1. The level of offense directed towards Jesus is controlled by the Jewish Scriptures (Collins, *Mark*, 291).

86. Carpenter is a figural understanding of poet as well (See Nagy, *Concept of Hero*, 297–300).

87. See Seneca's *Epistle 90*

88. Let us also add that there is a strong connection here to Wisdom 13.11, "εἰ δὲ καί τις ὑλοτόμος τέκτων εὐκίνητον φυτὸν ἐκπρίσας περιέξυσεν εὐμαθῶς πάντα τὸν φλοιὸν αὐτοῦ καὶ τεχνησάμενος εὐπρεπῶς κατεσκεύασεν χρήσιμον σκεῦος εἰς ὑπηρεσίαν ζωῆς." Given the work of Hugh Humphrey, this is a serious possibility. See Humphrey, *He is Risen!*; Humphrey, *From Q to Secret Mark*.

passage in a brief way. This maxim, that the prophet is not welcomed in his native land, is possibly one representing the Historical Jesus, but it does not have to be. In fact, this maxim could represent another biographical footnote for Mark, who was clearly not in Palestine, but in Rome. It might also represent Peter, who had fled to Rome and with Peter, Paul who has a similar story of rejection. This maxim is relatable not just to Jesus, but so too the disciples; yet, I have no issue with placing it in the mouth of Jesus who would expect rejection as a prophet. In this regard, such a rejection is natural and fitting to a person who viewed himself and demanded others view him as a prophet like Moses or Elijah/Elisha, or even Jeremiah. These maxims are something we see in Lucan and others of the time, developed by some teacher or another to quickly present a larger philosophical truth.[89]

6.11 The mission of the disciples is tinged with hints to the return from exile. We find an intertextual connection between 6.11 and two passages in the Old Testament. The first is, "καὶ κατέστησας αὐτὸν ἐπὶ τὰ ἔργα τῶν χειρῶν σου πάντα ὑπέταξας ὑποκάτω τῶν ποδῶν αὐτοῦ (Psalm 8:7)" while the second most likely has a closer aural meaning to Mark's point here, "ἐκτίναξαι τὸν χοῦν καὶ ἀνάστηθι κάθισον Ιερουσαλημ ἔκδυσαι τὸν δεσμὸν τοῦ τραχήλου σου ἡ αἰχμάλωτος θυγάτηρ Σιων (Isaiah 52:2)." We should remember a rejection of Jesus is a sign of who he is, something shaping the rejection of the disciple, indicating a role-reversal or paradox.

6.33-44 Winn has sufficiently covered this as a mirror of Elisha's similar miracle in 2 Kings 4.38-44.[90] Further, in his previous work, he has shown that the feeding could very well be seen as a polemic against the "ideal" Emperor—one who provided his subjects with food through his compassion.[91] This passage benefits from reading it against the famines brought on by the various factions as they wrestled over Jerusalem. Jesus supplied the people with food against the backdrop of the Roman Emperor and the Jewish leaders—one who fed and one

---

89. No doubt, I have fun afoul here of rhetorical critics, such as Witherington (*Art of Persuasion*, 30-1), who believe the *chreia* are symbolic of the Evangelists's shaping of historical events and words to fit the passage, aimed at persuasion; however, I do not deny the *chreia* a historical genesis, and will go so far as to say that for the *chreia* to have a maxim effect, some historical knowledge of their meaning is needed by the audience.

90. Winn, *Elijah-Elisha*, 82-83.

91. Jesus sees the people without a king (shepherd), putting himself in that place (v.34), pointing to Moses (Numbers 27.17).

who starved. Written it through the lens of Elisha, the story becomes more robust, and made even more so through the crisis of Mark's writing. The feeding stories may be a satirical take of Josephus's relating of Vespasian's compassion, "ὁ δὲ οἰκτείρων ἤδη τὰς συμφορὰς αὐτῶν τὸ μὲν δοκεῖν ἐκπολιορκήσων ἐφίσταται τὰ Ἱεροσόλυμα τὸ δὲ ἀληθὲς ἀπαλλάξων πολιορκίας (B.J. 4.412)."[92]

6.45–52 This is Mark's second use of the storm, beginning a pattern of recapitulating his previous pericopes. Several scholars suggest that this is a conflation of later Christian dogma into Mark's still Jewish context.[93] It is also possible to consider it a dream sequence.[94] However, there is another possible motivation for this rather odd story.

The first thing we should notice is that Mark says, for no real reason, that the incident takes place in the fourth watch of the night, a decidedly Roman phrase. The Roman military divided the night into four watches, with the fourth taking place after 3 am. There is no real reason the disciples would need someone standing guard on a boat, implied by the use of Roman military time. Further, the boat trip begins in the evening with the disciples going ahead of Jesus, but suddenly shifts scene to near the sun rise. This portrays an abnormally long boat trip. Instead of Jesus calming the seas, as he did before, he simply tries to pass by (παρελθεῖν) the disciples. These oddities force the audience to consider a Mark's mirror, especially considering that the disciples were not simply astonished, but suffered hardened hearts.

Josephus also makes use of phantoms in telling his story. During the account of the destruction of the Temple, Josephus tells of Jews inside the city who, upon seeing the destruction of the Temple, felt fear, depression, and astonishment, "τοῖς δὲ Ἰουδαίοις ὁρῶσι τὸ πῦρ ἐν κύκλῳ μετὰ τῶν σωμάτων παρείθησαν αἱ ψυχαί καὶ διὰ τὴν κατάπληξιν ἀμύνειν μὲν ἢ σβεννύειν ὥρμησεν οὐδείς αὗοι δ' ἑστῶτες ἀφεώρων (B.J. 6.233)." In 6.234, Josephus relates that instead of surrendering to the idea of a Roman victory, the Jewish rebels only found themselves more hardened to the goal of war. Josephus is bewildered because he has known all

---

92. Another slight against Vespasian is most likely in view here as well. Vespasian first went to Alexandria, the bread basket of the Roman Empire. Cutting off the grain, he was able to easily lay siege to the city and though his villainous act became the hero. See also Psalm 77.29 LXX.

93. For example see Achtemeier, *A Person in Deed*, 169–76.

94. Dio Chrysostom connects the water walker to a dream (*On Dreams*), using this to diminish Homer's poetic ability in the process.

along the inevitable ruin of the Temple. Had his fellow Jews listened to the same portents as he, they too would have defected, ending the war. Beginning in 6.285, he recounts several of these signs, including prophecies, signs in the sky, and the ghostly opening of the Temple's heavy brass gate (6.293). Following this, Josephus mentions a sign related to those who kept watch at the Temple, "δραμόντες δὲ οἱ τοῦ ἱεροῦ φύλακες ἤγγειλαν τῷ στρατηγῷ κἀκεῖνος ἀναβὰς μόλις αὐτὴν ἴσχυσεν κλεῖσαι (B.J. 6.294)." This sign was followed by an apparition in the sky of chariots and troops of soldiers. This sign, unlike the watch of the Temple at night, was seen at the evening of the day (6.294–298). The paradoxes of the story, including the reaction of the people, in the story point us to looking to something more. Jesus stayed behind, with the disciples moving on (or better yet, fleeing). The next time they saw him, he was as a ghost. Following Combs, it is most likely that the ghost of Jesus served a double purpose, that of relating to the audience that Jesus was not the messiah they expected.[95]

There are some literary connections between the Markan pericope and the larger of the destruction of the Temple. For instance, Jesus is said to force (ἠνάγκασεν, 6:45) his disciples into the boat while Josephus records that Titus was forced (ἀναγκασάντων, B.J., 6:240) by the Jews to destroy the Temple. Equally, Jesus is said to have attempted to pass by (παρελθεῖν, Mark 6:4) his disciples while Caesar went into (παρελθὼν, B.J., 6:260) the holy place of the Temple.[96] Mark is drawing from the same postwar inducing portent searching others did. Everything was a portent that the Jews were going to lose. The story of walking on water, or rather, the ghost of Jesus, serves as a harbinger of things to come. Along these lines, we should mention that a similar construction found in 6.48 is also found in Amos, with the emphasis that the time has come for judgment.[97]

---

95. Combs, *A Ghost on the Water*, 345–58

96. An allusion to Elijah is likely as well. (2 Kings 19.11 LXX). Mark may intend a Mosaic encounter also (Exodus 34.5–6 LXX). If Moses is intended, 6.49–50 contains an allusion to Exodus 20.18–20 LXX. However, Mark's allusion likely points to Daniel 10.12 LXX.

97. παρελθεῖν αὐτόν (Amos 8.2) compare to παρελθεῖν αὐτούς (Mark 6.48), with the subject as the change. Josephus saw the failure of the Revolt was judgment. Jesus prophesied that the destruction of the Temple would be destroyed by judgment. Further, given the way the pericope ends, a judgment akin to the judgment of Pharaoh in Exodus could be in view here.

7.24-37 While Gerasa and Gadara are commonly thought of as Gentile territory similar to Tyre, the belief in a purely Gentile Galilee is under current reexamination. No doubt, Gentiles were of a concern to Mark's community, but as of yet, the Gentile mission in Mark has not appeared as central to the story. The central character in this story is a Gentile woman from a territory of mixed ethnicities at violent odds. In *B.J.*, Gentiles from Tyre attack and kill many Jews (2.478-479). However, this is also the area from his John of Gischala sprang.[98] He gained both notoriety and credibility when he attacked the Gentiles in revenge. If we step back and consider what the Syrophoenician may represent, then we must note Syria was a stronghold for Vespasian, not just militarily, but also, diplomatically. It was the place where Vespasian first took command (*B.J.* 3.7). It was also one of the places the Jews fled to after the fall of Jerusalem (7.43). Further, this is the third well-described exorcism (following 1.24-27 and 5.1-20). No doubt the attacks before and during the Revolt which included atrocities on both sides still figured heavily into the minds of Mark's community, especially the role John played. This is another reversal, albeit one less detailed than 5.1-20, that involves Jesus driving out demons. Here John's crimes are reversed by Jesus's acceptance and healing of the Gentile woman.

We may interpret this passage, along with the next, through the lens of Isaiah, as with the clue Mark left us in his prologue.[99] In one portion in particular, the idea of a virgin daughter arising (from death?) and passing over to Kittim is found, "καὶ ἐροῦσιν οὐκέτι μὴ προσθῆτε τοῦ ὑβρίζειν καὶ ἀδικεῖν τὴν θυγατέρα Σιδῶνος καὶ ἐὰν ἀπέλθῃς εἰς Κιτιεῖς οὐδὲ ἐκεῖ σοι ἀνάπαυσις ἔσται (Isaiah 23:12)." Throughout this section

---

98. Διοικοῦντι δ' οὕτως τῷ Ἰωσήπῳ τὰ κατὰ τὴν Γαλιλαίαν παρανίσταταί τις ἐπίβουλος ἀνὴρ ἀπὸ Γισχάλων υἱὸς Ληΐου Ἰωάννης ὄνομα πανουργότατος μὲν καὶ δολιώτατος τῶν ἐπισήμων ἐν τοῖσδε τοῖς πονηρεύμασιν ἁπάντων πένης δὲ τὰ πρῶτα καὶ μέχρι πολλοῦ κώλυμα σχὼν τῆς κακίας τὴν ἀπορίαν ἕτοιμος μὲν ψεύσασθαι δεινὸς δ' ἐπιθεῖναι πίστιν τοῖς ἐψευσμένοις ἀρετὴν ἡγούμενος τὴν ἀπάτην καὶ ταύτῃ κατὰ τῶν φιλτάτων χρώμενος ὑποκριτὴς φιλανθρωπίας καὶ δι' ἐλπίδα κέρδους φονικώτατος ἀεὶ μὲν ἐπιθυμήσας μεγάλων τρέφων δὲ τὰς ἐλπίδας ἐκ τῶν ταπεινῶν κακουργημάτων λῃστὴς γὰρ ἦν μονότροπος ἔπειτα καὶ συνοδίαν εὗρεν τῆς τόλμης τὸ μὲν πρῶτον ὀλίγην προκόπτων δ' ἀεὶ πλείονα. φροντὶς δ' ἦν αὐτῷ μηδένα προσλαμβάνειν εὐάλωτον ἀλλὰ τοὺς εὐεξίᾳ σώματος καὶ ψυχῆς παραστήματι καὶ πολέμων ἐμπειρίᾳ διαφέροντας ἐξελέγετο μέχρι καὶ τετρακοσίων ἀνδρῶν στῖφος συνεκρότησεν οἳ τὸ πλέον ἐκ τῆς Τυρίων χώρας καὶ τῶν ἐν αὐτῇ κωμῶν φυγάδες ἦσαν (*B.J.* 2.585-8)

99. Winn identifies an imitation of 1 Kings 17.7-6 in this pericope. See, *Elijah-Elisha*, 84-7.

are the twin cities of Tyre and Sidon to whom YHWH will visit at the end of an exile, but what is more important is the inclusion into Mark's mnemonic world of Kittim, mentioned in Isaiah only in this oracle. [100]

Kittim, by the time of Mark's composition, have come to firmly represent the Romans. At Qumran, the sects who rewrote Scripture rewrote them, to include references to modern realities. In the *War Scroll*, Kittim comes to represent not just the Greeks, but so too, and then only, the Romans. No doubt, between 1 Maccabees 1.1 and Mark's time, the change is traced through apocalyptic and eschatological groups so that Kittim now represents the heaviest of Israel's pagan enemies. The *Third Sibyl* shows that Kittim had come to represent the Romans by using Scripture. Further, there is the matter of Daniel 11.30 in the LXX that interprets Kittim as the Romans, "καὶ ἥξουσι Ῥωμαῖοι καὶ ἐξώσουσιν αὐτὸν καὶ ἐμβριμήσονται αὐτῷ καὶ ἐπιστρέψει καὶ ὀργισθήσεται ἐπὶ τὴν διαθήκην τοῦ ἁγίου καὶ ποιήσει καὶ ἐπιστρέψει καὶ διανοηθήσεται ἐπ' αὐτούς ἀνθ' ὧν ἐγκατέλιπον τὴν διαθήκην τοῦ ἁγίου." This is not the only connection to the Romans, however.

Twice in Mark's Gospel, Jesus is said to heal with spit.[101] Given the power shown by Jesus already, it is surprising that he would turn to a folk remedy understood as magic. We have one record of Vespasian healing with the same method, but only for a blind man.[102] While a separate tradition involving the Emperor and the healing of a deaf man may exist, it is not necessary. Indeed, Isaiah provides us with the doubling of the miracle by suggesting blinded eyes will be open and deaf ears will hear (Isaiah 7.37; 35.5). Considering the often allegorical approach to blindness and deafness in Isaiah, it is fitting that Mark would use these miracles to reach his crowd so that they would finally see and hear Jesus. Adding deafness to blindness would also follow Mark's program of doubling miracles over Vespasian. If we allow for Mark to have insured that each pericope would interpret a close one, usually

---

100. In describing the peoples who joined the civil war, Lucan names the people of what would be Syrophoenica (3.225–36), mentioning their ability to navigate according to the "Dog's Tail polestar." This is possible, but the likelihood Mark is using "dog" to refer to the polemical description of Gentiles is too great to overcome fully.

101. Here, with the deaf man and in 8.23. The second half of the pericope should not be separated from the first. The geography in Mark, especially when it seems in error, is always important to the story. Here, Jesus is said to go north, and then south with the story of deaf man allowed to remain outside of a designated geographical area.

102. See Tacitus, *Hist* ,4.81.

Reading Mark Mimetically

the present one, then the combination of miracles in a heavily Roman occupied area produced another challenge to the throne with the rebuttal to Vespasian's spittle. As he does with other exorcisms, Mark was offering Jesus as a challenge to Rome.[103]

8.1–26 These miracles, the feeding of the multitudes and the healing of the deaf man are mirrored from the previous grouping of miracles. Indeed, Mark doesn't leave us any guessing room as to why he is using the doubling technique. In one short passage, Mark combines the stories of the feedings, walking on water, and the healing of the blind and deaf, "καὶ γνοὺς λέγει αὐτοῖς· τί διαλογίζεσθε ὅτι ἄρτους οὐκ ἔχετε; οὔπω νοεῖτε οὐδὲ συνίετε; πεπωρωμένην ἔχετε τὴν καρδίαν ὑμῶν; ὀφθαλμοὺς ἔχοντες οὐ βλέπετε καὶ ὦτα ἔχοντες οὐκ ἀκούετε; καὶ οὐ μνημονεύετε, (Mark 8:17)." This passage is another of Mark's concentric circles, and another of Mark's geographical errors.

Only Matthew seems to have a reasonable answer to Mark's geographical error in 8.10, giving the name of the city as Magadan (Matthew 15.39), leaving the rest of us to wonder if Mark writes about a town since vanished or simply has erred again in geography. The clue Matthew gives us helps us to see the map clearly—to see that Dalmanutha/Magadan has an ugly history and another name. We must examine the military history of the city which Josephus called Taricheae. It was here Josephus began his military career (2.596), promptly suffering a mutiny (2.598–99). After some contention, and some self-aggrandizement, Josephus began to build a defense for the city (2.606–608). During the Revolt, it became a haven for those retreating from Vespasian, such as a particular Jesus (3.457), and for a while became the pseudo-capitol of the North (3.462-5). Josephus's defenses forced Vespasian to mount a sea-born attack (3.512–531), leading to the Roman victory and a massacre of the Jews. At a sham war crimes trial, Vespasian decided to save many, but ordered that the old men and other useless members of society murdered in the city's arena. He sent six thousand young slaves to Nero to build the canal in Corinth, selling more for personal gain. This pattern of murder and enslavement was repeated by Vespasian and Titus. The Jewish slaves amassed in Rome to specifically build the Flavian Amphitheatre, the Roman Coliseum (3.532–42). This was not the only Jewish sources used to build the Flavian Amphitheatre, as according to

---

103. Hadas-Lebel, *Jerusalem Against Rome*, 23–25, 30–31.

recent archeological finds, it was financed by funds captured from the Jewish Revolt.[104]

The monument to Vespasian was built on an old monument to Nero. The so-called Golden House was built after the great fire on three of Rome's seven hills. It was a monument to Nero's ego, resembling a modern day Central Park, including a statue of Sol with whom Nero would later become identified. When Nero died, however, it was left vacant until Vespasian began to reconstruct it. The land was reclaimed in late 70; however, Vespasian would not begin the construction proper until sometime in 72–73 CE. Before that, the Jewish slaves brought to Rome by Titus after the destruction of the Temple began to lay the foundation. Nero's Golden House is more infamously named *Domus Aurea* presenting a linguistic parallel to Dalmanutha. If Mark was writing in Rome, he witnessed the destruction of Nero's image and the work of the Jewish slaves, images perhaps inspiring the name of this town by the hometown of some of the slaves. A poor satirical joke on the name of Nero's Golden House is not the only connection the Jewish rebels-cum-slaves could hear to the use of Dalmanutha.

John Lightfoot (1602–1675) suggests several meanings of the word "Dalmanutha" based on the Talmud. He writes, "But now from some such house of more note than ordinary, built for some eminent widow; or from many such houses standing thick together, this place, perhaps, might be called Dalmanutha, that is, 'The place of widowhood.'"[105] ראלמוןרתא would help explain Dalmanutha especially considering the widows no doubt produced due to Vespasian's massacre and enslavement of the town's men. If this is the case, then we may look again to the Elijah-Elisha narratives. Elijah is said to move to the widow's house in the country of Sidon (1 Kings 17.1–9). In the same house, Elijah revives a dead son (1 Kings 17.20–23). This last miracle assures the faith of the woman, something that in the story, the disciples lack, although they have seen several miracles, including the raising of the dead.

A third reasonable suggestion is that the term *dalmanutha* is an unrecognized Latinism becoming a sort of common name in Mark's hands, meaning *away* (See Mark 8.9). These two suggestions are not separate, given that widowhood is connected to death, or going away. Dalmanutha then becomes more closely associated with the Roman

---

104. See Barnes, *Flavius Josephus and Flavian Rome*.
105. Lightfoot, *From the Talmud and Hebraica*, 242.

Reading Mark Mimetically

atrocities at Magdala, specifically those by Vespasian than it does as a now lost town. Various formations of Dalmanutha (ex, *da manut ha*; *de manut ha*) produce a variety of significant results in Latin. *De manus* (of the hand), for example, or *de manus ta* (of the hands of such). This possibility provides a link to the author, as if *dalmanutha* is connected to a variety of Latinisms meaning *away*, this may in fact allow that Mark does hail from this region. Or perhaps the link is stronger if the word is meant to conceal *"of the hand."* The implications are tremendous, if indeed this is Mark's method of revealing himself in his story. Indeed, if this is Mark's signature, then it is Mark's way of speaking to his involvement in Magdala, perhaps as a bystander, or even, perhaps, as a rebel.[106] This, regardless of his position in the war, would have given him a certain amount of authority in producing the history of Jesus and the Gospel as a counter to the Roman Victory. Might these meanings coexist? As we have seen, Mark is able to blend several sources into his telling and produce a multilayered story. The possibility remains that Mark could use both Aramaic and Latin to create similar words to veil a reference to Elijah-Elisha as well as himself into the story. This third possibility remains the most speculative.

9.1 This verse does not necessarily lend itself to the support of an earlier dating. Given the temporality of language, the audience would hear the narrator proclaiming himself as the one who was the one left standing. It is quite possible that Mark was a young man (or *the* young man found throughout the Gospel) in the time of Jesus.[107] Based on census records of Roman occupied Egypt, while the average lifespan lasted into the upper thirty's, nearly ten percent reached over 70.[108] The extrapolation of date from this volume pushes Mark into the upper classes, affording perhaps a longer life span than others in the rural districts. However, we need not make such a conjecture of 70 years old. The Fourth Evangelist is often recorded as a rather young man. The literary tradition of John Mark is that he is rather young as well. If John Mark was indeed but an adolescent, he is then barely above fifty when

---

106. Research must continue on this, examining various ancient place names in Rome, especially in light of Mark's social crisis and supposed place of composition as well as a variety of ways Latin can be wrested from Mark's butchering of it. While my preferred position is that this is Mark's signature, so to speak, it could still very well be something of a smash up of Latin such as *domusaurea*.

107. Oden, *The African Memory of Mark: Reassessing Early Church Tradition*, 2011.

108. Bagnall and Frier, *The Demography of Roman Egypt.*, 1994.

he writes his Gospel. Given that city dwellers out lasted those in the fields, Mark would have easily reached this age in Rome. This is possibly a biographical footnote of the author, that is if Mark intends to present himself as the one remaining between the two advents of Jesus.

9.2–13[109] Instead of going south to Jerusalem, which is what Vespasian is doing in Mark's mirror, Jesus and the disciples head north. Why are they going to Philip's Caesarea (8.27)?[110] It is far enough away from Bethsaida to question Mark's geography, especially since it serves no other purpose in the Gospel except to give a place for the Transfiguration.[111] The only importance to this city is found in the Gospels. In the times of the great rabbinical חנאים (between the destruction of the Temple and the Second Jewish Revolt) Rabbi b. Kisma believed the fall of this Caesarea would signal the arrival of the Messiah due to it serving as likely path for the supposed Parthian invasion.[112] Caesar Philippi was an important city to Roman imperial ideology as well. During the reign of Augustus, Herod and his son were given additional territory to govern. As a celebratory honor, the kings erected a temple to Augustus on a hill, declaring Caesar as the Son of God.[113] This symbolic city provides us an image to consider alongside the strategic importance of the city. Jesus aims to invade Jerusalem and attack the ideological Son of God.

The geographic sign begins with Vespasian who marched from his base in Caesarea on the Sea to Philip's Caesarea to feast with King Agrippa II. From there he marched against Tiberias and Tarichaea. After the destruction of the Temple, Titus marched to Caesarea and from there to Caesarea Philippi to put down any other unrest in the area. Josephus reports that Titus took prisoners of war to entertain the troops with inhumane games. During this encampment, Simon b. Giora was reported captured in Jerusalem, effectively ending the major part of the resistant in Judaea. When Simon arrived in chains to the port, Titus and his prisoner sailed to Rome to prepare for the Triumph taking with him

---

109. 9.2 begins another section of Mark's Gospel.

110. Earlier, I noted Shea's structuring of Daniel to include two parts, arranged in a concentric pattern. For him, the pivot is 9.24–7, the C in the A-B-B-A pattern. The Transfiguration is Mark's pivot, the C. It contains references to both Vespasian and Simon and acts as the beginning of a second part of Mark.

111. The revelation in Mark 8.27–9.1 is replicated in the Transfiguration.

112. Hadas-Lebel, *Jerusalem*, 485–486.

113. Peppard, *Political Context*, 230.

the accumulated war spoils including artifacts from the Temple. In Josephus's account, Caesarea Philippi is not mentioned without Caesarea, with the two cities becoming almost an extension of one another. Here, we must examine the role of Caesarea in the life of Vespasian and it will become clear why Jesus went to a Caesarea for Peter's confession and the Transfiguration.

Caesarea was the start of the Revolt and winter camp for Vespasian. It was the place that he returned to after the major battles, including Gadara. During one encampment Vespasian received the news of Nero's death, leading the General to suspend his campaign. Josephus records that Titus would, by δαιμόνιον ὁρμὴν (*Wars* 4:501), join him there shortly after Otho became Emperor. It was during this that we are introduced fully to Simon b. Giora, a story interspersed throughout the year of the four emperors. After another short campaign, Vespasian returned to Caesarea to discover that Vitellius was now Emperor. Vespasian finally began to express his discontent with the situation in Rome (4.588). Josephus reports the great love that Vespasian had for Rome, a love so great that it hindered him from any future campaigns. His commanders in the field were informed of the change in command, again, and that the war was suspended. The soldiers started to whisper that a real soldier should sit at the head of the empire (4.592). In a spite of rhetorical flair, Josephus begins with the soldiers consulting with one another and then turning to the Emperor, shouting, "Ῥώμης στρατιῶται τρυφῶντες καὶ μηδ' ἀκούειν πολέμου φήμην ὑπομένοντες διαχειροτονοῦσιν οἷς βούλονται τὴν ἡγεμονίαν καὶ πρὸς ἐλπίδα λημμάτων ἀποδεικνύουσιν αὐτοκράτορας αὐτοὶ δὲ διὰ τοσούτων κεχωρηκότες πόνων καὶ γηρῶντες ὑπὸ τοῖς κράνεσιν ἑτέροις χαρίζονται τὴν ἐξουσίαν καὶ ταῦτα τὸν ἀξιώτερον ἄρχειν παρ' αὐτοῖς ἔχοντες (*B.J.* 4:592-3)," The soldiers turn back to themselves in the dialog and begin to compare Vespasian with Vitellius and decide in a deliberative manner that Vespasian must embrace his destiny for the good of Rome (4.594-600). Vespasian, of course, tried to stay away from such talk, as his goal was never Emperor. Only when he was completely exhausted did he reluctantly surrender his head to the crown, much to the adoration of his soldiers (4.601-4). This happened on 3 July, two days after the Prefect in Egypt recognized the general as Emperor. Vespasian gathered his staff, left Titus in command to finish the war, and made his way to Rome where he would eventually be crowned Emperor.

As we have seen in 1.40 and 6.49, Jesus overturns the usual messianic expectations. We see this in 8.31–33 when Jesus teaches about a suffering messiah and finds that Peter has taken an affront to this, immediately after his declaration of who Jesus is. Peter gives an understanding of the messiah differing from Jesus (and thus Mark). In the same geographical location, Jesus takes Peter, James and John up on a mountain where his clothes change color and suddenly, Moses and Elijah appear. This is another episode attempting to reverse reality. In Caesarea, his commanders recognize Vespasian as Emperor. Peter serves this role to Jesus. Vespasian receives embassies (albeit in Berytus) as does Jesus. However, more than that, this resembles the baptismal scene in Mark 1.

The Evangelist is borrowing his own intertextual structures to begin anew the story, pivoting on this mountain. The baptism of Jesus began Mark's message against Vespasian while the Transfiguration begins the story anew, but now focused on Simon. In the baptismal scene, God delights in Jesus; on the mountain, God orders that the disciples (and through the disciples, the audience) to listen to Jesus. The cloud/spirit is also present and so is Elijah (John the Baptizer). Moses is mentioned in 1.44 after Jesus heals the leper. Further, both are pictured in or near vision like states. After the baptism, Jesus is given the vision of the forty days in the wilderness; the Transfiguration takes place in a vision. Finally, the first miracle after the baptism was the casting out of an unclean spirit; the first miracle after the Transfiguration is, likewise, a casting out of a demon. This is the beginning of Jesus's journey to Jerusalem, following a rather more orderly path than he does between the baptism and the Transfiguration. Unlike Vespasian who goes back to Rome, Jesus turns and begins his decent into Jerusalem. This is Mark's trifold mirror. Through this vision, the audience sees both Vespasian and Simon as mocked and made inferior by Jesus. The first half of Mark's Gospel is dedicated to the rebuttal of Vespasian, but along the way, he has introduced to his audience key clues to his ultimate villain, Simon b. Giora. It is to this villain to whom we now turn.

6

Reading Mark Mimetically

Jesus against Simon Bar Giora

Introduction

IN THE LAST CHAPTER, we arrived at a pivot on the Mount of Transfiguration. This pivot, like all good pivots, contains elements of the story preceding it and following it. Mark, as a well versed theo-poet, makes good use of this fulcrum to pivot us to a dominating force in the waning years of the Jewish Revolt. Simon became one of Josephus's most hated enemies, with his life becoming bile in the historian's mouth. As we have seen, Mark provides his audience with clues about his second act. Simon was a would-be King, acting the part in defeating both Romans and Jews. As the Transfiguration approached, Mark began to deny normative messianic expectations. He would have to do so, especially considering Vespasian's victory and Simon's subsequent death and execution as King of the Jews.

Is Simon the Zealot a stand-in for Simon b. Giora? If so, how did b. Giora, someone who lived and died well after Jesus, come to shape Jesus's identity? As we develop Mark's literary goal in this chapter we will see Mark's idea of messiah and of whom Jesus is develop through conflict with Simon, as with Vespasian, and the social crises surrounding Mark's tiny post-Peter, Roman community. It is impossible, to separate the historical Jesus from the Christ of faith. It is through the phenomenon of war and the biographies of Jesus delivered through oral tradition that the Christian community came to abide in a more consistent set of beliefs regarding Jesus as messiah, so that even they did not differentiate. This pattern is seen throughout the Christian church as doctrines and dogmas were usually developed in reaction to crisis. This is a very human trait examined throughout the social sciences and even largely in the physical sciences. As we continue with the remainder of Mark's Gospel, we'll leave Vespasian behind and discover that while Rome was at the heart of the crisis, it was Simon who so enraged Mark, pushing his community to the brink, that the Gospel, and thus Jesus's story, was finally written.

9.17 There seems to be a literary connection with Psalm 37 (LXX), specifically verse 14, ἐγὼ δὲ ὡσεὶ κωφὸς οὐκ ἤκουον καὶ ὡσεὶ ἄλαλος οὐκ ἀνοίγων τὸ στόμα αὐτοῦ. The psalm would fit the remainder of the story of Jesus given it seems to have the author encompassed with enemies who seek to do him violence. It also seems to be a fulfillment of Mark's foreshadowing in 7.37, but the voice of the Psalmist is not specifically that of Jesus, but of Israel, whom Jesus is coming to represent.

9.18–29 Do not let mimetic criticism blind you to plausible tradition buried in the composition. What looks apparently as a pre-modern medical condition of epileptic seizures is now cast as an exorcism; and yet, if we chose to, we could understand the boy as something different, something more in line with other exorcisms in Mark's Gospel. For example, while no real literary connections exist, the description of the behavior of the boy are connected to various descriptions related to Simon such as the seizing of his wife, the actions of the people during the siege of Jerusalem, the capture of Temple by the Zealots as well as Simon's capture by Rome. Further, the attempts by the demon to either burn the boy or drown him (9.22) could represent the war effort of Vespasian and Titus. After all, throughout *B.J.*, Vespasian is said to use drowning, or in various ways use the sea, as a way to punish enemies. Likewise, grain was burnt and the Temple came crashing down in a fire Mark could still see from his literary portico. Therefore, it is entirely possible the symptoms of the boy, although they bear a striking resemblance to seizures as understood by modern science, are a stand in for the destruction caused by Rome and Simon. However, without direct literary connections or verbal overtures, we may run the risk of parallelomania to advocate for too much of a connection. Allowing that some exorcisms are based on a preexistent tradition, especially given the way this one lines up with known medical conditions, does not hurt the thesis of this volume.¹ Indeed, this is the exception that proves the rule. Mark is using the tradition of his community that of an exorcist named Jesus, as the basis of his story.²

9.30-10.31³ Simon b. Giora engaged in class warfare to suit his ego, becoming a bane to the upper classes.⁴ His goal was not so much Robin Hood style banditry, but retribution against the ruling classes who allied themselves with the Romans. His first followers were peasants, social outcasts who first rebelled against Rome. Going first to Jerusalem, he was soon exiled and forced to go to Masada due to his constant power plays. There, aligning himself with the Sicarii, he became involved in their inner ranks until the knifemen refused to push to Masada and bring more of the war to the Romans. Once the Zealots took over Jerusalem, Simon left, forming his own army and continued his peasant revolt against the ruling classes, acting as king (4.510). With his army, he began to attack Idumea, but was held back until he found a kindred spirit—a nameless traitor—who betrayed the Idumean army. This victory no doubt frightened the Zealots in Jerusalem who then decided to kidnap Simon's wife, a fatal mistake. Simon reacted in a vile and vicious way, marching to Jerusalem and laying a siege of despotic terror until they returned her.

After her return, Simon returned to further prey on the Idumeans, killing even the wounded. In the meantime, Zealot control in Jerusalem had turned the city into a modern Sodom with rampant reports of rape and murder forcing citizens to cower in fear. John of Gischala had taken control of the city for a time, but he was not able to keep the factions from engaging in a constant civil war within the city walls. The high priest, Matthias, led the charge of inviting Simon into Jerusalem to keep the peace. The real reason for the invitation was to protect the property of the elite, something explicitly stated by Jospehus, "ἐπεραίνετο δ' ἡ

---

1. Matthew (4.24) understands the difference between the epileptic and the possessed, although in this passage, he removes the naturalistic descriptions to supplant them with demonic ones. Epilepsy is connected to demon possession in the ancient world, providing a genesis to create more stories.

2. There is a familiar connection to Deuteronomy (32.20) found in v.19 in the remark of the "faithless generation." Continuing the chiastic structure, Mark repeats the scene in 1.25, the exorcism immediately following the baptism, with an exorcism immediately following the transfiguration.

3. Note the return to Capernaum (1.21) and the mention of John (1.29).

4. Seward, *Traitor*, 117-8.

βουλή καὶ τὸν ἀρχιερέα Ματθίαν πέμψαντες ἐδέοντο Σίμωνι εἰσελθεῖν ὃν πολλὰ ἔδεισαν συμπαρεκάλουν δὲ οἱ ἐκ τῶν Ἱεροσολύμων τοὺς ζηλωτὰς φεύγοντες πόθῳ τῶν οἴκων καὶ τῶν κτημάτων (B.J. 4:574)."[5]

Simon rode into Jerusalem as a conquering king, no doubt leaving his mark on the later author of the Gospel, "ὁ δ' αὐτοῖς ὑπερηφάνως κατανεύσας τὸ δεσπόζειν εἰσέρχεται μὲν ὡς ἀπαλλάξων τῶν ζηλωτῶν τὴν πόλιν σωτὴρ ὑπὸ τοῦ δήμου καὶ κηδεμὼν εὐφημούμενος παρελθὼν δὲ μετὰ τῆς δυνάμεως ἐσκόπει τὰ περὶ τῆς ἑαυτοῦ δυναστείας καὶ τοὺς καλέσαντας οὐχ ἧττον ἐχθροὺς ἐνόμιζεν ἢ καθ' ὧν ἐκέκλητο (B.J. 4.575-6)." It is in this light we may look at this broad section of Mark.

The social teachings are more prevalent in the second part of Mark, positioned in this section to focus more squarely on Simon.[6] In the first part of Mark's Gospel, there are parables and some teaching, but they are usually surrounded by miracles. In this second part, however, the teachings and other narratives of Jesus play the larger role. The bandit king, Simon, no doubt saw himself as a liberator of the masses (note B.J. 4.508, where he declares liberty for the enslaved), but his motivations were always in question. He was, after all, part Gentile. His patriotism, he promised, is what drove him to break the bonds of the Romans and seek to free his people. Later, as he ruled Jerusalem, he minted coins proclaiming his redemption.[7] He positioned himself as a new David, especially in his war against Idumea (2 Sam 8.13–18 LXX). His goal was not simply a political victory, but a messianic victory. To do so, he tried to equalize the classes; instead he maintained a tyrannical rule. He did not take prisoners, but regularly slew his opponents. At this juncture in the story, Mark is no doubt casting with reinforcements the teachings of Jesus against those of Simon. One proclaimed equality and a new social order, living out this message; while the other proclaimed liberty to the slaves, but lived differently, enslaving and killing anyone who opposed him.

In a rather long list of sins against a highly religious group, Josephus reports the inside of Jerusalem was nothing more than a bad caricature of Las Vegas—filled with homosexuality, cross-dressing, murder,

---

5. A connection to the reception of Jesus in Mark 5.1–20 is possibly found here as well.

6. The teachings of Jesus in these passages reflect the new Moses motif building throughout the Gospel, although never really reaching a thunderclap like we see with Elijah.

7. Evans, *Jesus and his Contemporaries*, 66, 66n.24.

rape, looting and more. Those inside Jerusalem—regardless of faction or neutrality—faced heinous crimes. Josephus reports that between the two men—John inside Jerusalem and Simon outside the gates—people had no hope of survival, "τοὺς ἀποδιδράσκοντας δὲ Ἰωάννην Σίμων φονικώτερον ἐξεδέχετο καὶ διαφυγών τις τὸν ἐντὸς τείχους τύραννον ὑπὸ τοῦ πρὸ πυλῶν διεφθείρετο πᾶσα δὲ φυγῆς ὁδὸς τοῖς αὐτομολεῖν πρὸς Ῥωμαίους βουλομένοις ἀπεκέκοπτο (B.J. 4.564-5)." In another scene, Josephus reports of those who were attempting to escape, but could not because of the loss of their families, "ἦσαν δέ τινες καὶ τῶν μαχίμων οὐκέτι διαρκούμενοι ταῖς ἁρπαγαῖς τὸ δὲ πλέον ἐκ τοῦ δήμου πένητες οὓς αὐτομολεῖν ἀπέτρεπε τὸ περὶ τῶν οἰκείων δέος οὔτε γὰρ λήσεσθαι τοὺς στασιαστὰς ἤλπιζον μετὰ γυναικῶν καὶ παιδίων διαδιδράσκοντες καὶ καταλιπεῖν τοῖς λῃσταῖς ταῦτα οὐχ ὑπέμενον ὑπὲρ αὐτῶν σφαγησόμενα (B.J. 5.447-8)." If we take all of these reports, even if they are subject to the same ideological program Josephus employs elsewhere, we see a community unsafe from their liberators. They had lost brothers, fathers, sisters, mothers, and houses—even if they remained neutral.[8]

10.32-4 We may find a similar scene, based on a literary connection to παραδώσουσιν (10.33), in Josephus, where we meet several familiar characters, "Ταῦτα ὁρῶν Ἰούδης τις υἱὸς Ἰούδου τῶν ὑπάρχων τοῦ Σίμωνος εἷς ὢν καὶ πεπιστευμένος ὑπ' αὐτοῦ πύργον φυλάττειν τάχα μέν τι καὶ οἴκτῳ τῶν ὠμῶς ἀπολλυμένων τὸ δὲ πλέον αὐτοῦ προνοίᾳ συγκαλέσας τοὺς πιστοτάτους τῶν ὑπ' αὐτὸν δέκα μέχρι τίνος ἀνθέξομεν ἔφη τοῖς κακοῖς ἢ τίνα σωτηρίας ἔχομεν ἐλπίδα πιστοὶ πονηρῷ μένοντες οὐχ ὁ μὲν λιμὸς ἤδη καθ' ἡμῶν Ῥωμαῖοι δὲ παρὰ μικρὸν ἔνδον Σίμων δὲ καὶ πρὸς εὐεργέτας ἄπιστος καὶ δέος μὲν ἤδη παρ' αὐτοῦ κολάσεως ἡ δὲ παρὰ Ῥωμαίοις δεξιὰ βέβαιος φέρε παραδόντες τὸ τεῖχος σώσωμεν ἑαυτοὺς καὶ τὴν πόλιν πείσεται δὲ οὐδὲν δεινὸν Σίμων ἐὰν ἀπεγνωκὼς ἑαυτὸν τάχιον δῷ (B.J. 5.534-7)." Judas, Simon's betrayer, did not meet a happy end. When Simon found out what was happening, he had Judas murdered in front of the Romans (5.540). Contrast this with the Judas who betrayed Jesus and we begin to see the image emerging in the minds of the audience as they connected Judas to Judas and then Simon to Jesus. Literary connections exist to both words preceding the above-mentioned passage. For γραμματεῦσιν, see 5.532 while for κατακρινοῦσιν see 5.530 for Simon's murder of Matthias, the chief priest.

---

8. It is not completely unnatural for such a scene to take place in the middle of factious infighting.

Unlike Vespasian, Simon would not go on to begin a dynasty, but was taken prisoner and taken to Rome where he would become a sacrifice to the Roman gods.[9]

10.35-45 Here we may be seeing the conflation of an earlier tradition with Mark's purpose, but it is difficult to prove absolutely. Hugh Humphrey does recognize and suggest the *Wisdom of Solomon* plays a part in building Mark's narrative.[10] Here, it becomes rather clear. The first layer of the tradition is the book of Wisdom.[11] The parataxis is immediately present in Wisdom's scene. Jesus seemingly rebukes the request, suggesting the only ones who can reign with him are those who suffer with him.[12] The idea of messiah is facing a Markan constriction solely to Jesus. The second tradition is the conviction of Simon and other messianic pretenders who came to power through war or might. Various messianic pretenders, including several Simons or sons of Simon, would come proclaim themselves king, lead an insurrection, and finally enjoy an execution, leaving their groups to disband rather quickly either by volunteer or because they were massacred. Jesus repudiates the tradition, suggesting a messianic warrior dies for his people and not the people for the messiah.

If an Aramaic original is hidden here it is buried under the Hellenistic book. In other words, contra Casey, a Greek original provides the tradition. As demonstrated in 5.21-43, Mark can use proper Greek, but as Casey demonstrates, his language here is poor. Then, there is the use of the word λύτρον that led to later Christian atonement theories. To

---

9. There is no secret here. For a Lucan connection to the three predictions of the death of the Son of Man.

10. Humphrey, *He is Risen!*; This work also includes a discussion of various chiastic structures in the *Gospel of Mark*.

11. δικαίων δὲ ψυχαὶ ἐν χειρὶ θεοῦ καὶ οὐ μὴ ἄψηται αὐτῶν βάσανος ἔδοξαν ἐν ὀφθαλμοῖς ἀφρόνων τεθνάναι καὶ ἐλογίσθη κάκωσις ἡ ἔξοδος αὐτῶν καὶ ἡ ἀφ' ἡμῶν πορεία σύντριμμα οἱ δέ εἰσιν ἐν εἰρήνῃ καὶ γὰρ ἐν ὄψει ἀνθρώπων ἐὰν κολασθῶσιν ἡ ἐλπὶς αὐτῶν ἀθανασίας πλήρης καὶ ὀλίγα παιδευθέντες μεγάλα εὐεργετηθήσονται ὅτι ὁ θεὸς ἐπείρασεν αὐτοὺς καὶ εὗρεν αὐτοὺς ἀξίους ἑαυτοῦ ὡς χρυσὸν ἐν χωνευτηρίῳ ἐδοκίμασεν αὐτοὺς καὶ ὡς ὁλοκάρπωμα θυσίας προσεδέξατο αὐτοὺς καὶ ἐν καιρῷ ἐπισκοπῆς αὐτῶν ἀναλάμψουσιν καὶ ὡς σπινθῆρες ἐν καλάμῃ διαδραμοῦνταικρινοῦσιν ἔθνη καὶ κρατήσουσιν λαῶν καὶ βασιλεύσει αὐτῶν κύριος εἰς τοὺς αἰῶνας οἱ πεποιθότες ἐπ' αὐτῷ συνήσουσιν ἀλήθειαν καὶ οἱ πιστοὶ ἐν ἀγάπῃ προσμενοῦσιν αὐτῷ ὅτι χάρις καὶ ἔλεος τοῖς ἐκλεκτοῖς αὐτοῦ (Wisdom 3:1-9).

12. We should note that Luke may disagree with Jesus, or perhaps with Mark, as he allows that Jesus is indeed the Righteous Man of Solomon's Wisdom. See Doble, *The Paradox of Salvation*.

this, Casey gives us the idea Jesus was not talking about the sins of the world as later Christians would have it, but about Israel.[13] I must agree, but come at it in a different manner. Turning again to the *Fifth Sibylline Oracle*, we find a literary connection that may offer us an interpretation to this verse in particular, "εἵνεκα γὰρ τῆς σῆς ἀρχῆς, ἧς ἔσχες, ὅμηρα εἰς Ῥώμην πέμψασα καὶ Ἀσίδι θητεύοντας, τοιγάρτοι καὐτὴ βασιλὶς φρονέους᾽ εἰς κρίσιν ἀντιδίκων ἥξεις, ὧν εἵνεκα λύτρα πέπομφας· δώσεις δ᾽ ἀντὶ λόγων σκολιῶν πικρὸν λόγον ἐχθροῖς (Sib 5.442–446)." It is pointless to suggest the Oracles led the Gospels in any shape or form, but they do offer us a shared history of interpretation, as we saw above with demons and unclean spirits. While the final redaction of the *Oracles* date later than Mark, we can allow one text to help define the other. The ransom Jesus intended to pay was not to the devil for the sins of all of humanity but to Rome for the sins of Israel. For the author of the *Fifth Oracle*, Rome was criticized for using people as ransom and would one day answer the call herself. Jesus preempts Rome's murderous spree by offering himself. No doubt, this is a foreshadowing of the death of Jesus, but it is a rather strong allusion to the death of Simon at the head of a Triumph, a play in which Jesus finds himself as the lead role.

The allusion to the Triumph, also points us to a greater understanding of James and John. According to Josephus, three men rode at the head of the Triumph, "μεθ᾽ ἃ Οὐεσπασιανὸς ἤλαυνε πρῶτος καὶ Τίτος εἵπετο Δομετιανὸς δὲ παρίππευεν αὐτός τε διαπρεπῶς κεκοσμημένος καὶ τὸν ἵππον παρέχων θέας ἄξιον."[14] Vespasian 'came into his glory', surrounded by Titus and Domitian, his sons. This is where we find the more suitable solution to the Sons of Thunder. Domitian, never at a loss for overstatement, saw himself as a son of Zeus and developed this mythology later in his own reign; Domitian coined images of himself with thunderbolts. Several Roman poets, such as Statius (and later, Martial), would mock the imperial brothers: "Awesome and vast is the edifice, distinguished not by a hundred columns but by as many fishermen could shoulder the gods and the sky if Atlas were let off. The

---

13. Casey, *Aramaic Sources*, 202–3.

14. *B.J.* 7.152; See above for a fuller discussion of the use of Book 7 as a mimetic source. As Mark's provenance is Roman, he likely saw the Triumph for himself. Book 7 is used here only as a historical record, not as a source.

Thunderer's palace next door gapes at it and the gods rejoice that you are lodged in a like abode."[15]

Also consider Vespasian coined his image as Jupiter. The public propaganda of the Roman Sons of Thunder becomes Mark's memetext for the Gospel Sons of Thunder rather than the Homeric Castor and Polydeuces. Given the overall tenor of Mark's Gospel, I would also point to 1 Maccabees with its tales of Jewish war heroes (καὶ δέξασθε δόξαν μεγάλην καὶ ὄνομα αἰώνιον, 1 Macc 2.51). The dying father tells his son of the promise of a heavenly reward, "νῦν τέκνα ζηλώσατε τῷ νόμῳ καὶ δότε τὰς ψυχὰς ὑμῶν ὑπὲρ διαθήκης πατέρων ἡμῶν (1 Macc. 2.50)." The intertextual source for Mark's tradition is derived from Wisdom and 1 Maccabees, books considerably closer to Mark than Homer. MacDonald goes on to list several qualifications of the analogy between James and John and Castor and Polydeuces. Two, we will take up now that we have arrived at the final scene of James and John.

He lists the qualification of the brothers being fishermen, ignoring the likelihood that many in the time of Jesus and later, Mark, were fishermen. A better antetext to the persons of James and John is found in Jeremiah and Ezekiel, texts filled with God's promise to send out fishermen (and hunters) to bring home the children of Israel in the former whereas in the latter, a miracle of fish is promised to occur. Jeremiah 16:16 reads, "ἰδοὺ ἐγὼ ἀποστέλλω τοὺς ἁλεεῖς τοὺς πολλούς λέγει κύριος καὶ ἁλιεύσουσιν αὐτούς καὶ μετὰ ταῦτα ἀποστελῶ τοὺς πολλοὺς θηρευτάς καὶ θηρεύσουσιν αὐτοὺς ἐπάνω παντὸς ὄρους καὶ ἐπάνω παντὸς βουνοῦ καὶ ἐκ τῶν τρυμαλιῶν τῶν πετρῶν." No doubt, the verbal cue of "*petron*" (or, Peter), in Jeremiah 16 with the tie in to ἁλεεῖς (the plural is in Mark), would be more likely to be the case for suggesting the Sons of Zebedee were fishermen.[16]

MacDonald infuses into Mark a tradition, something not original to the text of James, a violent death and John's prolonged life until the coming of the Kingdom. This only works if we take the Gospel stories as historically based in monologic communities. This comes from a misunderstanding of Jesus's supposedly final words to Peter in the *Gospel of John* (20.20–23), words the Fourth Evangelist clarifies, acknowledging the myths existence. In Acts 12.2, Luke records James's death, but

---

15. *Silvae IV.* 4.18–31 trans. K.M. Coleman.

16. That James and John were the Sons of Zebedee is also mentioned as an allusion to Homer, leaving the critical reader to wonder if all sons are related to Homer.

MacDonald adds an interpretation from the Old Syriac (dating to the third century), that John died many times. If one is not limited to an original text, but employs later interpretation, the argument becomes too relative to engage. One should not misunderstand later interpretations or later emendations to the text as the intent of the original authors and thus use them to understand authorial intent.[17]

The image is set, but it is not the image we suspect. In the mind of the audience, the end is already achieved, they know Jesus is crucified. The image presented here is not so much of the impending Roman Triumph. As Jesus often does, he changes what is expected of the messiah. Yes, no doubt, the author has in his mind the role Vespasian, Titus and Domitian would play in the image of the audience; yet, Jesus upends this. No one will share in his glory, because no one can do what he must. This is not so much an apologetic argument as it is a fatalistic move by the author to suggest Jesus is bound to the cross in a willing and dutiful way. It is not about exaltation, but about enforcing the idea Jesus will die and will die alone. It is not a victory that is expected, but a defeat. The messiah Jesus is promising is a vanquished one.

10.46–52 This pericope begins a large section bracketed by the mention of the son of David motif, ending in 12.40. In the middle of these episodes, we find abundant allusions pointing the audience to Simon. We begin in Jericho where the intertextual rostrum comes from 2 Kings 2. There are two different pericopes that help us define this passage in Mark. First, we find Jericho is the setting for the translation of Elijah. In 2 Kings 2.1–25, there are three 'prophecies' regarding the soon removal of Elijah from Elisha's sight. This mimics Jesus's three statements regarding his soon departure.[18] The irony of a blind man throwing off his clothing and running directly to Jesus is easy to see, given Elijah leaves a similar article of clothing behind. The second pericope begins in 2 Kings 6.1 where we meet a group of Arameans (or Syrians, LXX) who are after Elisha, meaning to take him as prisoner for his loudly abusing the king. Finding the prophet, they surround him, scaring Elisha's servant. Elisha prays that his servant's eyes would

---

17. The allowance for MacDonald's use of a later Syrian tradition does not derive from the Septuagint. The Septuagint was the bible for Mark and many of the Jews, especially in the Diaspora. The Septuagint predates Mark, but MacDonald takes a tradition postdating the proto-Christian community. This is a small fallacy.

18. Note that this passage also involves the aforementioned spring which Elisha makes whole.

be opened to the angels and—in a reversal—for the blinding of the opposing army's eyes. The army is guided to Samaria and allowed to go free.[19] Immediately after this victory is the story of the four lepers, a story we have already seen used in Mark.

X Legion is hibernating. The great symphony of Mark's Gospel is starting to reach its sonata, much as the revolt is doing in the audience's mind. The last leg of the end begins in Jericho for both Jesus and the Revolt as Jesus goes to Jericho before he leaves for Jerusalem. Titus takes several legions, including the X, through Jericho to Jerusalem (*B.J.* 5.42, 69). The X finally finds its way to just east of the great city, camping on the Mount of Olives, under the command of Titus. This is the same direction of travel Jesus will take as we see in 11.1. Do not miss the use of 10.35–11.11 as an important set of events taken in quick succession. Mark is beginning to move faster than he did before. This is because he is compressing details into the story of Jesus's story that otherwise would require a longer performance. Jerusalem, for all parties, in or out of the story, is important. There is little time to devote to other literary subterfuge for Mark, so he begins to compress details and sources on top of each other.[20]

Mark 11.1–11 Sadly, later Gospels, and especially later Christian Tradition, have inflated the entrance of Jesus into Jerusalem so much so that we expect to see a triumphant entry with the masses surrounding Jesus.[21] Mark does not relate the account this way. Jesus quietly slips

---

19. Jericho is the southern boundary of Samaria.

20. The Bartimaeus pericope is one several form critics take as having a real underpinning, but is garbled because Mark cannot decide if it is a calling story or a miracle. (See Collins, *Mark*, 505–9.) It stands out from the other miracles stories because of the differences. There is no account of the actual miracle, no reaction from the crowd, and the main character is not Jesus, but the blind man. Dibelius suggested that it is "less pure" from other miracle stories, but Bultmann sees it as a miracle story combining several Markan elements. Taylor and Jeremias independently see an older tradition at work here. Achtemeier notes the suppression of the event in favor off the other outstanding characteristics, but does not clarify the hidden intention. Telford suggests that this story is modeled after call narratives in the Jewish Scriptures, but cites Moses and Gideon as examples. See Taylor, *The Gospel according to St. Mark*, 447; Jeremias, *Neutestamentliche Theologie. Erster Teil. Die VerkUndio jesVerundigung Jesu*, 93–5; Achtemeier, "'And he followed him'. Miracles and Discipleship in Mark 10:46–52," 121; Telford, *Writing on the Gospel of Mark*, 53–5.

21. The entire account of Jesus entering Jerusalem is conflicting and without a firm basis in reality. It does, however, give Rome license to see Jesus as a rebel. See Duff, "The March of the Divine Warrior and the Advent of the Greco-Roman King: Mark's

a donkey away from its master and follows a celebratory crowd into Jerusalem only to then leave after catching a glimpse of the Temple. True to Mark, the story contains geographical locations, Bethany and Bethphage, unknown to us with any certainty.

We have already established Mark's geography is not in error, but a purposeful part of his historical strategy. For Bethphage, we need not go far to find it is no more than a transliteration of the word for "house of figs;" however, Bethany has garnered considerable scholarly discussion. It is assumed that it is a place outside the city to care for lepers. We must consider Matthew (and as we will see, Matthew is Mark's measurer) and his continued correction of Mark's geography. Here, Matthew, Luke and even John continue with Bethany. Indeed, a hidden agenda is not necessary but we must consider Bethany alongside Josephus's account. A similar structure exists between Mark and Josephus. We find a House (*beth*) we must consider, especially since the house occupies the same geographic place as Bethany.[22] Bethany is a placeholder for the mimetic imagination.

The entry of Jesus reverses the entry of Simon b. Giora. Hearing of Simon's invitation into the city, the Zealots retreated to the Temple, where they would remain until it was destroyed (*B.J.* 4.570–78). Josephus's account of Simon entering the city is important, as is his account of Herod's funeral procession.[23] We should remember Jesus is pictured as quietly arriving amongst a celebratory crowd, while Simon welcomes the invitation and the city welcomes him. The superposition, however, is the meeting of both saviors by the masses celebrating their arrival. The first thing Simon does, after securing his authority is to attempt to assault the Temple. It failed, horribly. Jesus goes to the Temple in 11.11 but does not go back to the Temple to rid it of the brigands until the following day.[24]

11.15–17 This section has been recognized by various scholars as being more appropriate to the time of Mark's composition rather than

---

Account of Jesus's Entry into Jerusalem," 55–71.

22. καὶ προελθὼν μέχρι κώμης τινός Ἐρεβίνθων οἶκος καλεῖται καὶ μετ' ἐκείνην τὸ Ἡρώδου μνημεῖον περισχὼν κατὰ ἀνατολὴν τῷ ἰδίῳ στρατοπέδῳ συνῆπτεν ὅθεν ἤρξατο (*B.J.* 5:507.)

23. ὁ δ' αὐτοῖς ὑπερηφάνως κατανεύσας τὸ δεσπόζειν εἰσέρχεται μὲν ὡς ἀπαλλάξων τῶν ζηλωτῶν τὴν πόλιν σωτὴρ ὑπὸ τοῦ δήμου καὶ κηδεμὼν εὐφημούμενος παρελθὼν δὲ μετὰ τῆς δυνάμεως ἐσκόπει τὰ περὶ τῆς ἑαυτοῦ δυναστείας καὶ τοὺς καλέσαντας οὐχ ἧττον ἐχθροὺς ἐνόμιζεν ἢ καθ' ὧν ἐκέκλητο (*B.J.* 4:575–6); for Herod, see *B.J.* 1.673.

24. Matthew has the Temple event on the same day that Jesus enters Jerusalem.

the time of Jesus. Joel Marcus sees 11.17 as a redacted allusion to Isaiah 56.7 and Jeremiah 7.11.[25] As we see in Mark 5.1–20, the author employs an allusion to the LXX to frame the current situation. The ληστῶν figure heavily into Josephus's account, but this is the first time we run into them in Mark's account by name (the next will be at the crucifixion). The scene is impossible to fully soak in if we do not consider this is another of Mark's mimetic references. Hooker notes for this detail to be correct, the story had to take place two to three weeks before Passover.[26] The literary transition time of just a few passages points to a hidden meaning unless we ignore the manifold chronological issues. This meaning was pressing on the minds of the audience.

Much like the redacted allusion, this passage comes from two different scenes. Josephus records that Eleazar, the son of the High Priest Ananias, persuaded the lower class of priests of the Temple to refuse the sacrifices of the Romans (*B.J.* 2.409–17). This began the short journey to outright sedition, which would eventually lead to the destruction of Jerusalem. This is only the first inference of the passage and the first part of Mark's redacted allusion. The second inference is from the final days of Jerusalem, when John's Zealots barricaded the Temple to hide from Simon (*B.J.* 4.575–7). The Zealots were able to hide in the Temple, surviving the siege (*B.J.* 5.3–7). It was not until the situation was desperate that John and Simon began to work together (*B.J.* 5.278). We will get to the end of Simon and the Temple in Mark 13, but for now, we must note the Zealots, or ληστῶν, occupied the Temple, committing atrocities as the city fell.

Josephus does not treat them with any respect, even blaming them for the destruction of the Temple, "ἀλλὰ γὰρ οὔθ' ἑρμηνεῦσαι δυνατὸν ἀξίως τὰ βασίλεια καὶ φέρει βάσανον ἡ μνήμη τὰς τοῦ ληστρικοῦ πυρὸς δαπάνας ἀναφέρουσα (*B.J.* 5:182)." Previously, Josephus gives an account of the Zealots, whom he aligns with ληστῶν, as an enemy of the people defiling the Temple with blood, "καὶ τοὺς μὲν ἀπὸ τοῦ δήμου διεκόμιζον εἰς τὰς οἰκίας οἱ προσήκοντες ὁ δὲ βληθεὶς τῶν ζηλωτῶν εἰς τὸ ἱερὸν ἀνῄει καθαιμάσσων τὸ θεῖον ἔδαφος καὶ μόνον ἄν τις εἴποι τὸ ἐκείνων αἷμα

---

25. εἰσάξω αὐτοὺς εἰς τὸ ὄρος τὸ ἅγιόν μου καὶ εὐφρανῶ αὐτοὺς ἐν τῷ οἴκῳ τῆς προσευχῆς μου τὰ ὁλοκαυτώματα αὐτῶν καὶ αἱ θυσίαι αὐτῶν ἔσονται δεκταὶ ἐπὶ τοῦ θυσιαστηρίου μου ὁ γὰρ οἶκός μου οἶκος προσευχῆς κληθήσεται πᾶσιν τοῖς ἔθνεσιν (Isa 56:7). μὴ σπήλαιον λῃστῶν ὁ οἶκός μου οὗ ἐπικέκληται τὸ ὄνομά μου ἐπ' αὐτῷ ἐκεῖ ἐνώπιον ὑμῶν καὶ ἐγὼ ἰδοὺ ἑώρακα λέγει κύριος (Jer 7:11).

26. Hooker, *Mark*, 267–8.

Reading Mark Mimetically

μιᾶναι τὰ ἅγια (*B.J.* 4:201)." The focus on the cleansing of the Temple here is based on the bifurcated plan of Mark wherein the final portion of Mark is devoted to tackling the character of Simon. The Temple is not so much cleansed as it is condemned and readied for demolition.

11.22–25 There are several meanings attached to this section, 11.22–25. There is in the very least a thematic connection existing between this saying of Jesus and Psalm 45 LXX, especially between 11.23 and 45.3 LXX. There is a thematic overture in this Psalm Mark replays, but literary connections hardly exist except for the images of the "mountains" and "seas." If these images triggered the connectivity, it is quite possible Mark means for his readers to understand Jesus as claiming a divine relation. This allows the audience to take into account Isaiah 11.9, "καὶ οὐ μὴ κακοποιήσωσιν οὐδὲ μὴ δύνωνται ἀπολέσαι οὐδένα ἐπὶ τὸ ὄρος τὸ ἅγιόν μου ὅτι ἐνεπλήσθη ἡ σύμπασα τοῦ γνῶναι τὸν κύριον ὡς ὕδωρ πολὺ κατακαλύψαι θαλάσσας." It is possible as well to connect this to the Revolt. Given mountains and seas are apocalyptic language (representing Jerusalem and the Gentiles respectively), this is another reference to the Gentile mission, but this is secondary. The other possible connection is that the mountain could represent the Temple and the seas either Gentiles or perhaps the actual sea. It is unlikely however, the allegories would be mixed. To that end, we can see some sort of parallel with Titus's return to Rome after the destruction of the Temple. Once the city was leveled and surrounded by Gentiles, Titus left, bringing with him the treasures of the Temple including the Menorah to Rome, the heart of the Gentile sea, via sea travel (*B.J.* 7.20–37). Any of these scenarios are possible, as is the conflation.

Not mentioned above is a connection to συκῆ. We find a mnemonic connection between 11.21 and several passages from the LXX, including Haggai 2.19, "εἰ ἔτι ἐπιγνωσθήσεται ἐπὶ τῆς ἅλω καὶ εἰ ἔτι ἡ ἄμπελος καὶ ἡ συκῆ καὶ ἡ ῥόα καὶ τὰ ξύλα τῆς ἐλαίας τὰ οὐ φέροντα καρπόν ἀπὸ τῆς ἡμέρας ταύτης εὐλογήσω." We see something similar in Hosea 9.10, "ὡς σταφυλὴν ἐν ἐρήμῳ εὗρον τὸν Ισραηλ καὶ ὡς σκοπὸν ἐν συκῆ πρόιμον εἶδον πατέρας αὐτῶν αὐτοὶ εἰσῆλθον πρὸς τὸν Βεελφεγωρ καὶ ἀπηλλοτριώθησαν εἰς αἰσχύνην καὶ ἐγένοντο οἱ ἠγαπημένοι ὡς οἱ ἐβδελυγμένοι." Habakkuk 3.17 reads, "διότι συκῆ οὐ καρποφορήσει καὶ οὐκ ἔσται γενήματα ἐν ταῖς ἀμπέλοις ψεύσεται ἔργον ἐλαίας καὶ τὰ πεδία οὐ ποιήσει βρῶσιν ἐξέλιπον ἀπὸ βρώσεως πρόβατα καὶ οὐχ ὑπάρχουσιν βόες ἐπὶ φάτναις." If the surrounding passages of the above verses are taken in context, they all promise a time of fulfillment after the destruction of Israel, and at least one (Habakkuk) includes references to the mountains and the sea as well as to the anointed (Christ). If we consider this with other language (for example, Isaiah 25.6-8), we find mountains, seas, and fig trees symbolized the Messianic Age when Gentiles would come to Jerusalem. If we set Mark 11.22-25 into the proper mnemonic context, we can begin to understand what the audience would have heard at point. This is understood as a prophecy of the destruction of the Temple that will cause the Gentile mission.[27]

12.13-17 It is almost pointless to recount the varied interpretations leveled at this passage, and so we will not. Instead, we will follow with the program of this volume and point to various instances from the history of the Jewish Revolt prevalent in the mind of the audience as they heard the account.[28]

Josephus reports of a Galilean named Judas who urged a revolt during the administration of Herod Archelaus. The historian writes, "ἐπὶ τούτου τις ἀνὴρ Γαλιλαῖος Ἰούδας ὄνομα εἰς ἀπόστασιν ἐνῆγε τοὺς ἐπιχωρίους κακίζων εἰ φόρον τε Ῥωμαίοις τελεῖν ὑπομενοῦσιν καὶ μετὰ τὸν θεὸν οἴσουσι θνητοὺς δεσπότας ἦν δ' οὗτος σοφιστὴς ἰδίας αἱρέσεως οὐδὲν τοῖς ἄλλοις προσεοικώς (B.J. 2:118)." It is not difficult to see the mimetic reversal of Judas and his peculiar sect Mark is targeting with work. Jesus was not urging a revolt and cared little about coins or who, more specifically, was on the coins; whereas Judas sought to make the issue of who gets the money the central issue of his promised rebellion.

Something else is requiring our attention here, namely, Markan irony. Coins were powerful symbols of nations and national rulers. One would not expect a king, or even a messiah, to proclaim himself as such without the issuance of coins. As well, the right to coin money was seen as a measure of independence, something we see in 1 Maccabees 15.7

---

27. If the use of this section (and it has long been recognized that the fig tree does denote the destruction of the Temple) is meant to be another push towards the Gentile mission, then we cannot date Mark any later than the destruction of the Temple. I would conclude that the cause of the Revolt, that of the exclusion of the Gentiles from the Temple, could have led the Markan community to reconsider the Gentiles in light of the Historical Jesus.

28. The historical likelihood of such an event is rather high, given Judas's revolt two decades before. Bultmann is most likely correct that this passage has some basis in the life of Jesus (Bultmann, *History*, 26), but it with Papias's Petrine allowance, Mark reshaped the narrative to fit a post-70 world.

when Antiochus promises the Jews that right after he had reconquered his ancestral land. During the revolt, numerous coins were struck and reminted—with the latter more likely the preferred method given that a war was going on, and eventually a siege as well. The leaders of Jerusalem issued their own coins, often calling for the freedom of Zion, but it was not until Simon b. Giora became the local king that the coins were stuck to read "for the redemption of Zion"—no doubt a messianic reference. We should apply the coinage of Simon to this story to give us the scene— it is a scene not of some grandiose statement about taxes, but more of a statement against Simon's reminted coins and by this attack, of the despot Simon. They are still Caesar's. Simon, having no doubt restruck coins from the time of Roman control, used these coins to proclaim his independence from Rome and his messianic rule of Zion. Mark laughs at this stance and points out the image of Caesar is still be seen on the coins, or at the very least, the coins are still Caesar's, the one who first had them made. This would again put Jesus out of the mainstream of messianic expectation. Jesus has no need to start a revolt and the coins, as symbols of anything, were nothing more than Caesar's. Through the words of Jesus, we find Mark ridiculing Simon's attempt at independence.[29]

12.35–37 Mark never misses an opportunity to destroy militaristic messianic expectation. Here, he is pointedly answering the claim made earlier that Jesus was the son of David, a phrase covered over with Christian patina.[30] If we remove this we understand the son of David theme is not about the lineage of Jesus (although Matthew and Luke certainly play this up considerably), but about the prowess of David, specifically, the military capability of the messiah. Jesus takes this moment to point out that if the messiah is also the Lord of David in any divine sense, then he has no need of military might. We first encounter the term when Jesus is approaching Jerusalem, but now, as the audience is brought inside Jerusalem, Jesus refutes the idea of his march as one of conquest.

12.41–44 The disparity between rich and poor is a well-known talking point for Jesus in the Gospels, and it was no doubt a significant cause of the rise of the social bandits between the death of Jesus and

---

29. For further discussion of coinage from the Persian period to the Second Jewish Revolt, see Kanael, "*Ancient Jewish Coins and Their Historical Importance,*" 37–62.

30. See Tannehill, "Varieties," 117n.5, where the author suggests that this is a correction to the normative view of the messiah as David's son.

the start of the Revolt; however, the disparity of the rich and poor was highlighted during the Jewish Revolt in a way not unfamiliar to our point of view. Josephus records the Jews who could pay for their lives were allowed to do so, so that in the end it was the rich who survived the Revolt, leaving the poor to die, (ὅ γε μὴν χρήματα δοὺς ἐξηφίετο καὶ μόνος ἦν ὁ μὴ διδοὺς προδότης ὥστε κατελείπετο τῶν εὐπόρων τὴν φυγὴν ὠνουμένων μόνους ἐναποσφάττεσθαι τοὺς πένητας (B.J. 4.379).

It is possible with the placement of this passage between the denial of the military role of the messiah and the destruction of the Temple that Mark is trying to highlight, again, the differences of Jesus. Simon amassed a fortune in the war and positioned himself as king, using the poor first as his army and then, in the end, as human shields against Rome. The historical teachings of Jesus are more than likely embedded here and germane to the time of Jesus. Further, the characters in this passage—from the scribes and the priests to the widows—make their way into the cataclysmic scene of the Revolt; while the elite were the cause those who suffered the most were the poor. This passage may suffer too much from its placement between the looming passages, but it is equally possible the audience, knowing their own teachings of Jesus, would have understood them in a rather powerful way, especially in light of the disaster of the Revolt.

13.1–37 It is necessary and proper that we, before delving headlong into the mimetic sources of this particular chapter, first examine the more surface level intertextual sources from the LXX—as the Septuagint should always be the first place to look for sources of Mark's Gospel. To that end, we will list the more recognizable connections and then suggest why such statements are not the sum of Mark's argument. It is best to list it as a chart:

Septuagint	Mark
Zech 14:4	13:3
Zech 14:2–3	13:7–8
Micah 7:5–6	13:12
Daniel 9.26–27 1 Mac 1:54–61 Eze 7.16 Zech 2.6–8	13:14–16
Hosea 14.1	13:17
Isaiah 65.8	13:20
Jeremiah 16.13–15	13:22
Isa 13.9–11	13:24–25
Daniel 7.13	13:26
Isaiah 11.11	13:27

No doubt, it is more than plausible the rather apocalyptic verses supplied Mark with a certain ambiance.[31] As we have seen before, allowing the LXX to supply the mnemonic source does not create a fulfillment of the LXX scenerio, but instead, allows us to see how the LXX was used as an interpretive measure of the author's *Sitz im Leben*. From the angle of the LXX and an undefined source, however, we must examine the destruction of the Temple and it acts as the historical basis for Mark 13.

We will not need to state the date of Mark, having done that before, but will find upon the conclusion of this examination, we are again faced with the only reasonable conclusion, namely, that Mark 13 does speak with the words of an apocalyptic prophet concerning the destruction of the Temple. Mark was not the first to see it this way, as the historian who witnessed the destruction of the Temple could only use the same type of narrative to describe the destruction of the city and the eradication of the Temple. I want to focus on Josephus's accounts of the final days of the Temple and then, after this, develop some of the specific rhetorical strategies Mark works into the account, including the intended theological implications of the episode.

31. I have purposely left off much of the discussion regarding the connection between Joel 2 and Mark 13, but it is recommended to read the two side by side for certain clarity.

Mimetic Criticism and the Gospel of Mark

Mark	Josephus
13.2	6:6–8; 6.217; 6.222
13.3	5.70
13.8	1.1; 4.286–7; 5:536; 6.1, 40, 299
3.14	5.412–3; 6.285–6
3.15	5.542
13.19	4.238; 5.442
13.22	6.287–8
13.24–5	5.471–2; 6.289
13.26	5.272; 6.298
13.27	6.301

Before we move into a deeper discussion of Mark 13 as the destruction of the Temple, the end of the world, and what role the Son of Man plays within this, we need to point out a few things. First, the encampment of Jesus and the four disciples on the Mount of Olives is essential to the chapter. This is, according to various reports in Josephus, the site of the infamous X Legion and a final desperate attack from the Jews against that Legion (or what was left of it). It was the main headquarters of Titus. It is also, most telling, the place the Romans sat to watch the Temple burn. Second, Jesus mentions pretenders to the throne twice. In 13.6, Jesus mentions those who would come in his name (cf. 13.21–2).[32] The Revolt and the possible invasion from Parthia is found in the following verse.[33] The governors and kings of 13.9

---

32. There are several ways to take this mimetically. First, the name of Jesus, like Simon and Judas, was a common, appearing in Josephus and other historical records numerous times. Second, Paul uses Christ as a proper name. This derives from and explains messiah, a title others claimed. Finally, the idea of "coming in a name" may symbolize authority. Mark has deployed his defenses against all of these possibilities, no doubt. It is possible as well in these lines to see a Markan defense against the abuse of oral tradition. The constant refrain of true discipleship is heard throughout Mark. Whether it is about suffering or about following the real Jesus, Mark is warning his audience against believing just anyone who claims to speak for Jesus. See Williams, *Gospel Against Parable*, 32–3.

33. The X Legion remained behind to continue the fight, attempting to finish what was left of the Jewish resistance.

Reading Mark Mimetically

are Roman magistrates; however, do not discount Simon, who is said to have acted as a king, from this picture (*B.J.* 2.652). The warning to the mothers in 13.17 is a horrific reminder of the cannibalism during the siege. The winter reference is ironic given the destruction of the Temple occurred in late summer.

Concerning the false Jesuses, false messiahs, and false prophets, one needs only to look at the various Jesuses mentioned by Josephus. One person named Jesus was a son of the high priest and became a general (*B.J.* 2.566). This Jesus would later clash with Josephus near Taricheae (2.599). Another Jesus was a leader of brigands (3.450) who led many into disaster. Jesus the son of Gamala preached against the Zealots (4.160–163) as well as made prophecies about the destruction of the Temple while spewing insults at the Idumeans during the early stages of the siege of Jerusalem (4.238–69; 83). He was later executed whom he tried to calm (4.314–6). Another priestly Jesus defected to the Romans (6.114). A Jesus prophesied the Temple would face ruin and was scourged for his claims, but set free as an example (6.300–304). The final Jesus mentioned by Josephus was another traitor, but not just any traitor. This Jesus secreted away important artifacts of the Temple to Caesar for the return trip to Rome (6.387–9). Given the popularity of the name of Jesus during this time (a hopeful stand in for Joshua, no doubt), it is no surprise Mark highlights the Jesus of whom he was speaking was in no way one of those Jesuses. The many who came in the name of Jesus more often than not did mislead many, pointing to themselves. The false messiahs (Vespasian and Simon) had their false prophets (Josephus and Simon's council, perhaps even the High Priest Matthias for a time) to point crowds and potential followers to them. Mark is not merely using the name of Jesus or an amalgamation of Jesuses to create his Jesus, but setting his Jesus apart from those who led Jerusalem into Revolt, into death, and murder—even betraying the Temple.[34]

---

34. Note the discussion by Wright on the "criterion of dissimilarity" in *Jesus and the Victory of God*. The issue of a historical critical study of the person of Jesus is important to scholars and theologians alike, else we arrive with a distinctly Aryan Jesus once more. Several important works are present now which tackle various issues of the historical criteria. Two of them are recommended: Stein, "The 'Criteria' for Authenticity;" France and Wenham, *Studies of History and Tradition in the Four Gospels*, 225–263; and Keith and Le Donne, *Jesus, Criteria, and the Demise of Authenticity*. The essential issue here, on whether or not we can trust the historical figure of Jesus in Mark's Gospel or not is not the topic of this present volume; however, an additional criterion to the discussion of the Historical Jesus will be proposed below, at which time

Mimetic Criticism and the Gospel of Mark

Thom Stark boldly declares, "Jesus was wrong."[35] He goes on to ask if Jesus is a failed apocalyptic prophet. Such a question is rather pointless given one must first take the words of Jesus in Mark as historical record to reach a conclusion instead of taking the words of Mark about Jesus as a literary function and then fail miserably at understanding the role of the Temple in ancient cosmology as well as Mark's overall purpose for his Gospel. That is a feat as breathless as the previous sentence. He tackles Wright's suggestions regarding this chapter, something only a bit more palatable to an accurate reading of Mark 13. We will examine Wright, and by way of Wright, Stark's objections to him, as well as other scholars and their understanding of this chapter. We will then highlight several of Mark's rhetorical tools found herein and given the mimetic meaning to 13.10, 13.14, and 13.26 firmly planting this chapter, and the book of Mark, in a post-70 world.[36]

The grave errors Wright and Stark both make is to take the Synoptics as presenting a composite of an original tradition, when in fact Mark 13 is the originator of the later Synoptic tradition. We will forgo any material included by Matthew and Luke, as to include it would suggest they are working from independent sources, something we cannot verify. Further, my goal here is not to prove or disprove the legitimacy of Jesus's prophetic mantle, only to draw attention to Mark's mimetic meaning. Finally, we should consider the temporality of language. If Mark was presenting this prophecy to hearers for the first time, they still heard it as if Jesus stood speaking c33 CE, regardless if Mark had

---

we will discuss further the various Jesuses and Mark's Jesus.

35. Stark, *The Human Faces of God*, 160. No doubt, Stark's book is not meant as an academic entry into Mark 13, but it is important to note Stark's work here because it, like others scholars above, removes Mark's context and instead follows the traditional reading of Mark as a historical narrative. I have had the pleasure of meeting Thom as well as providing support for one of his massive projects. Nothing personal is meant with my remarks regarding his conclusions.

36. Collins calls it an acute problem to position Mark past the destruction of the Temple, noting Marcus's date (Collins, *Mark*, 610; cf. Marcus, *Jewish War*, 460) noting the commandment to flee is antithetical to the situation in the post-70 world, but mimetically the command is relevant. In *B.J.* 6.286, Josephus decries the false prophets who, bribed by the rulers of the city, told the people to wait for God's deliverance. Here, Mark is setting Jesus a part from those by pre-commanding the people to flee. No doubt this gives added authority to Jesus; however, it is not out of the Scriptural narrative to order a flight in distress. For example, Lot's escape from Sodom, Jeremiah's flight to Egypt, and Noah's Ark. Or, the entire Qumran community who built a community in the desert to await the destruction of Jerusalem.

just invented it.³⁷ We should not assume that simply because we hear it in the past tense it occurred in the past tense, especially when much of Mark is told in the historically present, a rhetorical tool to preserve the past-future-present sense.

Mark 13 relates the end of the world, something many have erroneously assumed was meant to be the end of the physical world. The ancient audience did not hear it as we who are informed by at least two centuries of dispensationalism and sensationalist fears of asteroids, droughts, and dead birds. Rightly, Wright suggests it is the end of the age and wrongly it is the "end of Israel's period of mourning and exile and the beginning of her freedom and vindication."³⁸ Stark suggests Wright is wrong in the latter half of his interpretation because he is still focused too much on the idea of the new age, or rather; simply a highpoint in a continuing age, as Mark's intended meaning.³⁹ Indeed, Wright is more concerned with the end of the exile than with facing the reality that no such exile ended. Indeed, if the end of an exile brings the Israelites home, then the Temple, and the subsequent events at Masada and the Bar Kochba revolt, destroys such notions as Israel was dispersed and left for dead. The better understanding of what is going on, and why the destruction of the Temple is needed, is not found so much in the end of the exile (which is far better seen in Acts 2 than Mark 13) but the beginning of the Gentile mission. I also suspect Deutero-Isaiah would find it difficult to believe Wright as well, but that is another matter.

The Gentile mission is alluded to throughout Mark as well as in Acts, Ephesians and Revelation. Paul mentions it in Acts 28.28 where he tires of the Jewish rejection of Jesus and sets about to turn to the Gentiles. In Ephesians 2, the author, viewing the destruction of the Temple as a motivation, moves to create a new community of both Jew and Gentile. In Revelation 16, the Gentiles finally repent leading to the point in Revelation 20–21 when all nations finally worship God in Jerusalem. Mark already mentioned the importance of the Gentiles in 11.15–17 and 11.23. In 13.10, the Gentile mission, although not in the light it is commonly shown, is again present.⁴⁰ If we take that a cer-

---

37. Regarding the Evangelists's definition of prophecy see Mark 14.65, cf. Matthew 26.68.

38. Wright, *Jesus and The Victory of God*, 345.

39. Stark, *Human Faces*, 189–190.

40. Collins sees 13.10 (*Mark*, 591; 606) not as a signpost on the way to the

tain amount of developing Jewish-Christian theology contemplated the future of Gentile converts especially when Gentiles were not allowed to worship in the Temple, we can see how the destruction of the Temple would prompt a major leap forward in the universalism as expressed by the author of Ephesians 2. If we remember that the Revolt started in part due to the exclusion of Gentile sacrifices from the Temple, then the emphasis on the mission to the Gentiles becomes more important. It was not the end of the exile Mark is concerned with, but the throwing of the mountain into the sea, that of the Gentile mission.

Wright's second interpretative measure of the destruction of the Temple involves the vindication of Jesus. Vindication is important in the Hellenistic Jewish *Wisdom of Solomon*, as well as in the story of Stephen in Acts 8. Wright argues the coming of the Son of Man is the same event as the destruction of the Temple.[41] This is mixed somewhat with the clouds and the Son of Man when Wright suggests the idea of coming could include an idea of simply being present.[42] Stark pointedly expresses the fault in Wright's logic here, the text is not concerned with the vindication of Jesus.[43] Indeed, as I've already shown, it is not uncommon for anyone to have predicted the destruction of the Temple. Mark was not using this text in particular to do what Wright thinks he was doing, as the entire Gospel is not so much about vindication, but about identification. Stark goes on to argue the coming of the Son of Man must happen after the suffering of the war (13.24).[44] Much to Stark's chagrin, Wright also argues the coming of the Son of Man is metaphorical and understood as ongoing, again pointing to a vindication.[45]

What Stark fails to realize in his assessment of 13.24 is that Mark 13 is written in a chiastic structure, a technique the Evangelist implies elsewhere. Both sections begin with the announcement of pretenders. When 13.24–33 is read alongside 13.6–23, we find points of

---

destruction of the Temple, but as a means of expressing the mission of the community, that of during the midst of persecution, they must turn to preaching to the nations. That is their first concern.

41. Wright, *Jesus and The Victory of God*, 342, 360, 362.
42. Wright, *Jesus and The Victory of God*, 346.
43. Stark, *Human Faces*, 190.
44. Stark, *Human Faces*, 191.
45. Stark, *Human Faces*, 195–6.

interconnectivity.[46] Most prevalent is Mark's connection of the coming of the Son of with the destruction of the Temple. I would also agree with Wright that the coming of the Son of Man is not a physical arrival, despite Paul's best hope; neither is it a metaphor for vindication. What Mark presents is a Son of Man coming in the clouds seen with his angels after various signs.[47] More than likely Mark is pulling directly from Danielic passages for his imagery, although it would be interesting to know what, if anything, hearing the Gospel in the aftermath of the destruction would have produced mnemonically at the mention of the coming Son. Further, Josephus records a scene in which everyone seemed to see, after the setting of the sun, of an army of heavenly beings racing among the clouds. The timing of the actual vision may be of debate, but it is a lesser one given Mark is writing in circles, as evidenced by the beginning and ending of the two passages of Mark.

The angels hold a variety of meaning, but one should not expect a supernatural, or extranatural, set of beings traipsing over the earth in final judgment (13.27). Considering Mark 13 contains a great deal of allusions to Daniel, we might find some similarity with that work then, but of the several instances messengers from God in Daniel (7.2; 8.8; 11.4), two of them are inconsequential focusing rather on the metaphor for God's control of the earth. Daniel 7.2 refers to a foreign king challenging God who is no doubt Antiochus IV Epiphanes. These instances give us only the idea that the imagery of the four winds is prevalent in Mark's communal readings. However, it does not directly come from Daniel, the usual suspect. Ezekiel 37.9 provides us a rather more interesting place of origin. In the familiar scene of the valley of dry bones, YHWH tells Ezekiel, the son of man, to speak to the spirits to resurrect Israel after the exile. If we add to this Zechariah, we find a budding eschatological hope that those who were scattered to the four winds would return. Two visions in Zechariah are relevant (2; 6). The first vision deals with a vision of a future Jerusalem without walls that welcomes all and is protected by God. In 2.11, a Gentile mission for Jerusalem is expressly stated. The second vision of Zechariah 6 acts

46. This is not uncommon in apocalyptic writings as evidenced by Revelation, but it is a prevalent literary method Mark employs across his entire work; this chapter is no different.

47. This vision is possibly satirical; after all, when the Roman engines of war are lobbing stones into Jerusalem, the watchers on the wall warned the populace, shouting "the son is coming!"

more as a source for Mark with visions of chariots in the sky coming from the mountains. These chariots contained beings going out into the four winds to present themselves to God. They did so not in judgment, however, but in order to patrol in peace (6.7–8). This vision is important as it contains the high priest Joshua/Jesus who will rebuild the Temple and serve as God's vice-regent. Beginning not in Daniel but in Ezekiel and following through with Zechariah, we find an allusion to the resurrection of Israel, the Gentile Mission, and angels who guard a kingdom ruled by Jesus.[48]

Mark was not writing with the same social context and theological *eschaton* as Paul who expected a physical return of Jesus. Instead, Mark is interpreting the accounts of the siege – perhaps as reported by Josephus or legends that placated a defeated people—as the presence of Jesus, signifying the long hoped for kingdom. It is important to understand the Christian community of Mark reinterpreted the expected Pauline *eschaton* and his attempted universal intention of the Gospel to meet the demands of the age.[49] Even Paul, coming close to the end of his life with no sign of Jesus returning, modified his views. It not unexpected to have the surviving Christian community now leaderless with the deaths of Peter on Paul immediately followed by the massive destruction of both the Roman Civil War and the Jewish Revolt to modify their views the *eschaton*. For Mark, it became the new age, finalized by the destruction of the Temple and the beginning of the Gentile mission in earnest. Having identified various mimetic referents to the scenes described in Mark 13, we are now left with having to identify the infamous τὸ βδέλυγμα τῆς ἐρημώσεως. The identity of which has been attributed to several different historical referents, most notably Caligula. But as the astute reader will have no doubt surmised, Mark's more accurate historical referent is Simon b. Giora. It does not matter if Jesus spoke of a coming Gentile overlord; what matters is Mark was writing this after the destruction caused by Simon. In this following section, I will examine historical referents suggested by biblical scholars

---

48. There is also the possibility that the angels mentioned here could be human messengers, namely the disciples themselves. We need but look to Revelation 2–3 for allowance of such an interpretation; however, this is not preferred at the moment.

49. It is not clear that Paul was successful in reaching the Gentiles. After all, his letters to the Galatians and the Romans were both written to Jews.

and then conclude with the reasons Simon must be considered as the ideal candidate for such a position.

James Crossly, following Maurice Casey, identifies τὸ βδέλυγμα τῆς ἐρημώσεως as Caligula based on his early dating of the book and the idea that this is more in line with Daniel who envisioned a statue rather than a person as the desolating abomination. Like Antiochus IV, Caligula attempted to establish a foreign cultic statue inside the Jewish Temple. Like Antiochus IV, Caligula met with stern Jewish resistance—but unlike Antiochus IV, the Roman Emperor retreated and allowed the statue placed elsewhere. Crossley, following Casey, refers to the long lost "Syrian tradition."[50] He does allow, however, that the abominable language could very well mean something that brings desolation but easily, too easily in my opinion, dismisses this interpretation for something he is unable prove. The Markan audience knew and was invested enough with the Syrian knowledge of Daniel to pick up what Mark implied beyond the rather obvious Greek.[51] This is possible, but only if we discount what we have already shown, namely, that Mark 13 is more aligned with the Jewish War and the final siege of Jerusalem than with any other time in Jewish history from the death of Jesus to the Revolt.

While arguing for a date closer to 70 than Crossley, Winn does not allow Mark 13 to relate to the Jewish War. He bases this on the idea the Jewish War did not inflict harm upon the Christian church, at least not as much persecution as was experienced by the Jews. He is indeed correct in one point, the destruction of the Temple did not begin a long series of persecutions of Christians. Yet, I would counter there is no such thing as *the* Christian church at this time (c. 70 CE), but "Christians" were rather better identified as Jews who followed the teachings of Jesus of Nazareth. There is no real need to find a persecution of Christians to supplant Mark 13.[52] Winn ultimately does conclude Mark is writing after 70, but for Winn Mark 13 is still a future reality. In doing so, Winn has cut off the connection between Mark 13.14 and an identifiable historical referent.[53] Indeed, he goes to great lengths to counter the meme-

---

50. Casey and Crossley are not the first to suggest a connection to Caligula. See Hölscher, "Der Ursprung der Apokalypse Mrk 13," 193–202.

51. Crossely, *Dating*, 27–32.

52. We must not discount the value of Pauline eschatology on shaping our understanding of the early Christian community's view of the return of Jesus.

53. "Let the reader understand" is interpreted different. Hooker suggests it refers

text of Mark 13.14 and suggests Mark is speaking rather about a future of pagan worship, even ignoring the rather obvious links to Daniel and 1 Maccabees which connects this phrase only to the Temple.[54]

Gerd Theissen suggests Mark co-opted and adapted a preexisting prophecy to fit the actual destruction of the Temple.[55] This is neither impossible nor unknown; after all, Deuteronomy and other books were rewritten to correlate with the times, acting as both validation of the community and interpretations of the present events. Theissen suggests that for Mark, the destruction of the Temple was a historical event, but there was still something yet to come—after all, the world had not ended. The future event, for Theissen's Mark, is the construction of a pagan temple upon the site of the now destroyed Jewish Temple. Furthermore, Theissen allows the abomination to "stand" on the grounds of the destroyed Temple.[56] Concerning a possible gender of τὸ βδέλυγμα τῆς ἐρημώσεως, we find the genitive ἑστηκότα modifying the action of the abomination is masculine indicating a rather odd construction if the abomination is an altar, unless it was a *male* altar. It is not merely in place, but *he is standing*. Winn allows, briefly, "If Theissen's theory is accepted, Mark would then be referring to an idolatrous object/person standing where the temple had *once* stood."[57] I suggest we take Winn with Theissen and language dismissed by Crossley together and in doing so, arrive at the idea that τὸ βδέλυγμα τῆς ἐρημώσεως is a male figure standing upon the ruins of the Temple.

W.A. Such notes the language barriers to τὸ βδέλυγμα τῆς ἐρημώσεως as an object clearly identifying it is a person. However, Such goes further noting the importance of Mark's rhetorical use of the language here.[58] He writes, "Mark's achievement lay in coalescing together

---

to the actual reading of Daniel (Hooker, *Mark*, 314) but this is unlike. Instead, it is a literary device aimed at the audience (Collins, *Mark*, 596).

54. Winn, *Purpose*, 69–74.

55. Hartman concludes the main source of this prophecy comes from Jesus as a surviving midrash on various portions of Daniel (Hartman, *Prophecy Interpreted: The Formation of Some Jewish Apocalyptic Texts and of the Eschatological Discourse Mark 13 Par*, 235). Murray is closer to my thesis in suggesting this prophecy is molded to react to the Jewish Revolt (Murray, "Second Thoughts on the Composition of Mark 13," 414–20).

56. Theissen, *Context*, 258–64.

57. Winn, *Purpose*, 75n.79.

58. This is the importance of properly understanding the parenthetical in 13.14.

two essential ideas in the same perspective: the fact of abomination and the action of an individual committing the profane act." As Such points out, Mark is the first Greek author to do this. In doing so, Mark has the acts of blasphemy and devastation now birthed in this singular individual. After struggling with the various scholarly proposed sources, Such falls to Titus as τὸ βδέλυγμα τῆς ἐρημώσεως.[59] Titus is naturally accredited with destroying the Temple, although Josephus goes to great lengths to suggest Titus did everything in his power not to destroy the Temple. Further, in the smoldering ruins of the Temple, Titus marched in his standards and raised them, no doubt creating a stir as these emblems where symbolic of the pagan worship in Rome. It was at this site Titus was declared co-emperor by his troops. On the surface this is as much plausible as Simon b. Giora, but as we will soon discover, Titus's claim to the throne is dismissed in an array of white.

We have demonstrated mimetic plot lines throughout the Gospel uniting the bifurcated story. In the first half, Mark is pitting Jesus against Vespasian, but only in the sense Jesus is undoing Vespasian's victorious holocaust. In the second half of his book, beginning with the Transfiguration, Mark begins to pit Jesus against Simon bar Giora, not as a subtle reversal of sorts, but as a direct attack. Jesus rails against the exclusion of the Gentiles in the Temple and suggests he will save Israel by freely giving his life to the Romans. Vespasian is not the only culprit of Mark's Gospel, although his attempt to claim the messianic throne is no less troubling, but he is not the nightmarish figure lurking in the shadows of Mark 13. While Titus has appeared, he does so only when the X marches across the story. No other figure is presented in Mark as qualifying for this wrath except Simon.

Simon was not a Jew but the child of a mixed marriage. It is not uncommon to see a Gentile usurper to the throne vilified. Recently, scholars have contentiously debated the meaning of the Son of God in 4Q24, scholars such as J.T. Milik who cite Antiochus IV's defeat by the people of God.[60] To add to this is the attempted usurpation by the Gentile king found throughout Daniel, the Maccabees, and the *Psalms of Solomon*.

Best suggests that it is a pause of reflection, to draw attention to the person contained in the saying. See Best, "The Gospel of Mark: Who Was the Reader?" 124–132.

59. Such, *The Abomination of the Desolation*, 81–102.

60. Milik, "Les modeles aramaeens du livre d'Esther dans la grotte 4 de Qumran," 321–406.

There are plenty of other examples to cite, but given Mark uses this strain of thought, Simon is the likely candidate for contextualization as the Gentile king claiming the Throne of David, especially given the historical circumstances surrounding Simon's final days in Jerusalem.

As we have already identified, τὸ βδέλυγμα τῆς ἐρημώσεως is a person standing upon the ruins of the Temple. While Titus did this, surrounded by pagan emblems, he did not do so in the manner required by a strict reading of the text. First, while Josephus's account is recognizable propaganda, his acquittal of Titus is something not categorically dismissed by Jews. Throughout the meticulous account of the final hours of the Temple, Titus is constantly forced to take a series of actions, each action more severe than the former, by the insolent Jews led by Simon. Josephus even records the Jews were the ones who set the final fire to the Temple (*B.J.* 6.249–51) and Titus tried to *save* it (6.253–5, 261). Regardless of the political pen of the propagandist, we might easily surmise that had Simon given up at the start of the siege, or perhaps when the cannibalism happened, the Temple would still stand, rendering Simon the true guilty party and Titus only the instrument of God's will.[61]

The allowance that Simon is in fact τὸ βδέλυγμα τῆς ἐρημώσεως is not yet secure. Once Titus had captured the Temple Mount, he left for Caesarea, leaving some troops to find Simon and bring him to Rome for the Triumph. Before the end of the siege, Simon had started to mint coins proclaiming the *Redemption of Zion*—a slogan with messianic allusions. Yet, it was his capture that speaks more to his altered ego than the coins. Simon's capture is one that is missed by most, if not all scholars, in the search for the historical referent in Mark 13.14. To overlook it as a key identifier both to Mark 13.14 and to the Transfiguration is to miss Mark's coded message altogether. When the Romans had breached the walls, Simon and his remaining close compatriots descended into the caverns below the city to seek out an escape. Their goal was to mine a safe distance out of the city and thus escape capture, but they ran into serious issues with the geology of the area. After many failed attempts to proceed forward, their provisions began to disappear along with any hopes of actual escape. Simon, the mastermind, attempted to surprise the Romans by putting on a white and a purple coat.[62] He then appeared

---

61. Josephus may share some intertextuality here with 2 Chronicles 33.11–21.

62. λευκοὺς *B.J.* 7.29, cf. Mark 9.3. The white robe would symbolize martyrdom. Otto Michael previously reported the connection between Simon and Jesus, but only

out of the ground where the Temple once stood.⁶³ Josephus records that only for a short time did this action bewilder the Romans who, upon coming to their senses, took immediate custody of Simon.⁶⁴ In these actions of Simon, the vision of the Transfiguration achieves some clarity. The cast of characters are the same; Simon's vestments are matched by Jesus; the disciples's surprise, however, is the mirror of Simon's hopeful display. Whereas the disciples at that moment recognized Jesus for who he was, the Roman soldiers were only stunned for just a moment—then promptly repudiated the supposed notions that he was the messiah. Thusly, with such a highly polished mirror where we finally see who the monster is lurking in the shadows, we can no longer allow Caligula, nor Titus, to meet the demands of the passage. Instead, it is clearly Simon who is Mark's τὸ βδέλυγμα τῆς ἐρημώσεως ἑστηκότα ὅπου οὐ δεῖ; underneath the vision on the Mount of Transfiguration, we see Vespasian and the recognition of his imperial status by his troops as well as the mocking of Simon, white robes and all, by the one true messiah.

Mark uses several rhetorical tools in this chapter. In several places, he speaks directly to the audience, as in 13.14. There is also the present command, through the present suffering, to turn to the Gentiles to preach the Gospel (13.10). Mark also suggests that the entire prophecy has already occurred (13.20). The fully knowing reader would not miss Mark's chiastic structure in this passage. Finally, on the question of whether the destruction of the Temple was really the end, which all recent commentators and our own good sense tells us it was not, I will leave it until the next chapter when we read Mark with Lucan's eyes.

14.10, 43–45 As noted above, Simon had his own betrayer named Judas. While Matthew (and Acts) adds a death narrative for Judas, Mark has Judas only as a literary vehicle, without justice or condemnation. This should lead us to believe that Judas Iscariot, if not a complete literary invention, is at the very least a compilation of those figures from around Jesus who would leave him, or perhaps, representative of

---

in the use of white robes to symbolize the needed death to lighten the load of the Jews. (Michel, *Studien*, 404.) It is not, however, something I believe is in view here. The white robe of Simon may symbolize martyrdom, but following Simon's usual ego, it is doubtful that he did it out of altruistic compassion. As far as the white robe of Jesus at the Transfiguration, Mark is undoing the abuse of martyrdom by Simon.

63. Josephus never gives a full account of where Simon emerged, but I estimate it near the Holy of Holies.

64. *B.J.* 7.25–31.

the larger community, betraying Jesus. Much of this segment of Mark's Gospel is barren of mimetic sources in relation to the Jewish War suggesting an original tradition.

14.53-72 This is a rather odd intercalation.[65] There is a double introduction, as if Mark is drawing concentric patterns within a chiastic structure (v.53, 55). Mark begins the passage by first referring to Peter, and as expected, he ends it the same way. The testimony is of the false witnesses and are said to be as much, but this provides a quandary. The reader just heard Jesus talking about the Temple, a figure dominating the discussion in this section of Mark. Mark even finds something wrong with a statement containing a clear reference to the Resurrection combined with the destruction of the Temple (v.58).[66] Added to this is the close placement of the return of Jesus with the destruction of the Temple (v.62). The Temple is the central figure here. Its destruction is expressly tied to Jesus's death, his exaltation, and return. Mark warns the readers, however, to tread lightly in accepting the testimony of the witnesses, or perhaps, in accepting any common interpretation. I take this as a way to separate the death of Jesus away from the destruction of the Temple while allowing for a connection between that event and Jesus's return.

It is possible Mark decided to use Hezekiah rather than Elijah-Elisha for this narrative. In 2 Kings 18.28–37, Jerusalem is under siege. The Assyrian prophet, Rabshakeh, attempts some psychological attacks when he promises the Jews peace and prosperity if they surrendered. In doing so, challenged not just Hezekiah (Immanuel), but so too YHWH, the King's divine Father. Rabshakeh rehearses how the other gods failed to protect their people from Assyria's pantheon, removing the hope YHWH would come to their rescue. Instead of surrendering, the people obeyed Hezekiah's command of remaining silent. Isaiah (36–7) contains the same scene. The image is of a people under siege, forced into starvation, with only a remnant left alive (Isaiah 37.4). If this is the intertextual structure for the trial narrative, the allusion is silent. Jesus twice refuses to answer his accusers who hurl liars and condemnation

---

65. A necessary work to read when digesting the Trial Narrative is John R. Donahue's *Are You the Christ*.

66. The references to Jesus rebuilding the Temple are one that arrogates the divine role of God. The constant refrain of the "divine passive" is important as we develop the ideology of excluding God in the Gospel.

against him (Mark 14.61; 15.5).[67] Silence is heard in *B.J.* at several crucial points. First, Jews, while welcoming Vespasian as conquer, requested the execution of Josephus. Vespasian passed over their petition with silence (3.411). Second, during the siege, the people in the city, mired in cannibalism, death, and debauchery, were captured by silence (5.515). Finally, in the latter stages of the siege, the people responded with silence to Josephus's pleas to surrender (6.98). The episodes fit neatly with the siege of Jerusalem in 2 Kings and Isaiah, as well as the mimetic scene in Mark.

If Mark uses the accusations by the Assyrians, he is doing more than just borrowing an intertextual framework; he is accusing God of absence. Throughout the rest of the Passion, God is suspiciously absent, even when Jesus laments his situation from the cross. While God's presence is later seen in Hezekiah's siege, Mark only borrows the trial of YHWH (with Assyria as prosecutor), but not the eventual end of the siege brought by God's intervention. God is not there to intervene for Jesus, or Israel, as he did for Hezekiah, the divine son. As we will see in the next chapter, the accusations of absent gods are common in Lucan.

15.16–32 I would not be the first to identify a type of a Roman Triumph in this section of Mark. T.E. Schmidt's article has set the bar for such viewpoints.[68] The basic premise is that the *Via Dolorosa* replaces the Roman *Sacra Via*, the route of the Triumph. One proclaimed the glory of Christ, while the other proclaimed the conquests of the Emperor. The best we can do presently is to summarize Schmidt's article. The scene begins with the gathering of the parade marchers (15.16).[69] This is important because for Mark, the entire cohort of Romans gather in the Praetorium to mock Jesus. In the reverse, the legions would have gathered in the Praetorium to celebrate the returning conqueror. Mocking the glory of Rome, Jesus is ritually clothed in a purple robe (perhaps another allusion to Simon's appearance) and a crown. At the beginning of the triumph the soldiers would hail the conquering emperor. We

---

67. See Psalm 37.14–15 LXX.

68. Schmidt, *The Roman Triumphal Procession*, 1–18.

69. Schmidt argues for the beginning of the Triumph in 15.16, but in 15.5, Jesus presents Pilate with more silence. A moment of silence begins the Triumph. Vespasian and Titus began the Triumph at the dawn of the day. The Emperor accepted the shouts of the solders but gave them the command to quiet. At this point, he offered prayers. After the prayer, a speech followed, and a dismissal for the soldiers to eat and to ready themselves for the Triumph (*B.J.* 7.124-9).

find the same thing, albeit with a satirical tone in 15.18–9. Like the returning hero, Jesus cried out in the streets (15.20). Simon the Cyrenian (15.21) serves as the sacrificial bull, one dressed with purple and the crown of the king. The refusal of the wine is also another connection, in that the returning hero would be offered the wine but instead would pour it out as a libation upon the altar (15.23). The sign above the cross could carry two meanings.[70] The first is the usual one for the Romans, where the criminal carried the sign of his crime. The second, like unto the first, was a sign carried in the triumph indicating the people whom the hero had conquered. The three who were crucified together (Jesus surrounded by two brigands) could symbolize the Emperor and the two consuls who helped to administer the Empire. If the crucifixion scene is pointing to Rome and the Jewish War, it is more profitable to suggest, as I have above, that the positioning of Jesus between the two could be a symbolic tie to the arrival of Vespasian surrounded by his two sons, Titus and Domitian. The figure of two sons following the Emperor in the triumphal procession is not uncommon as Claudius was equally surrounded by his two sons-in-law. Vitellius was surrounded by his two generals, Valens and Caecina. Simon was killed during the Triumph, but alone as he was thrown from the Tarpeian Rock.

The schema of the Roman Triumph fits well into the proposed reading of Mark, as it establishes the memetext as a nonliterary reality an author consumes to issue his reversal. Indeed, the recent scenes in Rome of Vespasian returning, not yet written in minute detail but very present upon the mind of an author enjoying a Roman provenance, serves to provide an actual literary invention, that of recasting the non-ritualistic formality of a crucifixion of a Jewish criminal into that of a sacrifice, or as Mark's Jesus says, the giving of his life as a ransom for many. The basis of the story is that Jesus was crucified, but Mark has taken it and used it to reverse the Roman Triumph as well as to position Jesus against Simon. Simon died alone, vilified. Jesus, while apparently vilified was finally glorified when the Roman Centurion named him the Son of God. One must understand Mark's intended reversal of Rome and Simon before one can fully appreciate Mark's sources.[71]

---

70. It was not uncommon for a brigand to claim the title of King or to have others assume he claimed the title of king. For Pilate and others to charge Jesus with the crime of claiming the throne is historically plausible and verifiable.

71. We should not overlook the theological aspect of the scapegoat either, nor the

Reading Mark Mimetically

15.34-36 Much like we find in Mark 1, where Mark is letting his audience know his intended goals and sources, here he is beginning to draw to a close his story by enumerating his sources. In this section, Mark returns to the familiar territory to recycle his sources (chiasm), using Elijah's battle with the prophets of Baal (1 Kings 18.19-40). The goal of the battle was to test the validity of the deity by acceptance of a sacrifice of the bull, an acceptance signified by fire. Baal was unable to answer his prophets, leading Elijah to ridicule them. This particular scene in Mark is rather oddly placed if it is a reversal of the passage from 1 Kings. Nowhere else in Mark do we find a reversal of the Elijah-Elisha narratives, only their use as intertextual structures and allusions. Here, however, Jesus on the cross is painted in a such a way as to provoke the God of Israel into action. Yet, God forsakes Jesus—and through Jesus, Israel—no doubt clearly representing the desolation felt in Judaea at the time. The Roman soldiers now mock Jesus—and through Jesus, God—in much the same way Elijah mocked Baal and his prophets. No doubt, Mark placed this text here to heighten the dismal state of Jesus and the disciples in preparation for the question of the Resurrection. But the larger question, for the moment, is whether or not God will accept Jesus as a sacrifice. There is no fire or other response from Heaven, at least in Mark's Gospel.[72]

15.38 This is a repeat of the scene in Mark 1.10 (σχιζομένους), or rather, a fitting bookend to Mark's Gospel. Elijah is present in both (John during Jesus's baptism, and now, Elijah as the confusion of Aramaic is seen). However, there is something more. The ripping of the curtain is the tearing of heaven itself. Beyond the mystical symbolism of the cult, we find that the curtain is described by Josephus as containing many symbols. Josephus writes, "πρὸ δὲ τούτων ἰσόμηκες καταπέτασμα

"theatrical mimes" portraying mocked kings who suffered defeat. (See Collins, *Mark*, 723). While I discuss Matthew's mimesis of Mark below, I wish to point out his mimetic expansion of Mark's passion tale. In Matthew 27.26 contains the image of Jesus's beard plucked out by the Roman soldiers. This event is found in the ridiculing Vitellius suffered at the hands of Vespasian's troops. See Dio, *History*, 64.20.

72. A dangerous proposition for reversal is viewing this passage as a way of apology to the Gentiles. I am not sure yet that this is Mark's intent at this juncture, but it does fit well with Mark's insistence on the Gentile mission. One is more dangerous is the acceptance of the abandonment of Jesus by God. When God does appear in the Gospel, it is only to abandon the disciples to hearing only Jesus. The ignoble death on the cross incriminates God more than many would like to accept. See Brown, *Death*, 2:1047-51.

πέπλος ἦν Βαβυλώνιος ποικιλτὸς ἐξ ὑακίνθου καὶ βύσσου κόκκου τε καὶ πορφύρας θαυμαστῶς μὲν εἰργασμένος οὐκ ἀθεώρητον δὲ τῆς ὕλης τὴν κρᾶσιν ἔχων ἀλλ' ὥσπερ εἰκόνα τῶν ὅλων ἐδόκει γὰρ αἰνίττεσθαι τῇ κόκκῳ μὲν τὸ πῦρ τῇ βύσσῳ δὲ τὴν γῆν τῇ δ' ὑακίνθῳ τὸν ἀέρα καὶ τῇ πορφύρᾳ τὴν θάλασσαν τῶν μὲν ἐκ τῆς χροίας ὁμοιουμένων τῆς δὲ βύσσου καὶ τῆς πορφύρας διὰ τὴν γένεσιν ἐπειδὴ τὴν μὲν ἀναδίδωσιν ἡ γῆ τὴν δ' ἡ θάλασσα κατεγέγραπτο δ' ὁ πέπλος ἅπασαν τὴν οὐράνιον θεωρίαν πλὴν ζῳδίων (B.J. 5.212-214)."[73]

15.39 I want to take a moment now to return to the purposely neglected issue of Christology, especially in relation to the titles Son of Man and Son of God found in Mark. The following section is not meant to suggest that Matthew, Luke, or John followed Mark in using the titles the same way. Neither do I suggest Mark corrected the Pauline usage of Son of God (Paul never used the phrase Son of Man), only that he is countering the Roman motif of the Son of God. The Gospel of Mark begins with the key phrase, "This is the beginning of the Gospel of Jesus Christ." The manuscript evidence for adding "the Son of God" is in debate. For Mark to have called Jesus the Son of God is counter to his claim that Jesus was not the Son of God, but instead, the Son of Man. To this end, we will examine the historical use of the "Son of Man," both from canonical and non-canonical sources. The same will be explored in connection with the use of "Son of God." The role demons play and the fact that only the enemies of Jesus use Son of God in Mark's Gospel highlights the mimetic use of the titular phrase. These findings will act then as a gloss as we examine relevant passages in Mark. Finally, we will examine the role of the Centurion and his use of "Son of God" and what it means to Mark's overall purpose.

Sources for the Son of Man

Maurice Casey suggests that the phrase in question comes from the quite stable *lingua franca* of the Assyrian Empire and continued into the Persian Empire of the Jewish Exile.[74] Of course, he suggests that for many passages of Mark, there is an Aramaic original. Tessa Rajak has pointed out that the Septuagint translators, spread out over the course

---

73. For a fuller discussion of this connection, see Ulansey, "The Heavenly Veil Torn: Mark's Cosmic 'Inclusio,'" 123–25.

74. Casey, *Aramaic Sources*, 53.

of several centuries maintained a unique translation language which served to promote a "quiet cultural resistance."[75] Casey further suggests that the titular phrase is rather common in Aramaic (and Hebrew) and used to emphasize the humanity of the person. It was the Gospels, and Mark in particular, who made the phrase a "major Christological title."[76] We must examine the use of this title in the Jewish Scriptures; especially consider the proclivity of Mark's use of the Septuagint in his own Gospel.

We first meet the phrase in Balaam's voice (Numbers 23.19) when the Gentile prophet suggests God is not like us that he should repent or somehow fail on his promises. Following the canonical order, the first use of the title possibly implying something more than the focus on the weakness of humanity is found in Ezekiel. In this book, God refers to Ezekiel as "son of man" an overwhelming number of times. The focus is understood to emphasize not only Ezekiel's humanity, but also his status as prophet. This use of the phrase is picked up in Daniel 8.17 when Daniel quotes the voice of the one calling him the "son of man." However, in the previous chapter, Daniel's infamous vision entertains the scope of heaven where an eschatological figure is seen standing before the "Ancient of Days" (Daniel 7.13). This is arguable considering that, as mentioned, Daniel in just a short space afterwards is being called son of man by the angel Gabriel as the angel, according to God's instructions, relates to Daniel the meaning of several visions.

Fourth Esdras (4.8) picks up the image that Son of Man represents the weakness of the person, the humanity, but that book has little resemblance to one of the more infamous pseudepigraphical books, *Enoch*. In *Enoch*, the Son of Man is positioned as an eschatological figure. In 1 Enoch 46.2, we find a continuation of the scene in Daniel 7 as Enoch is shown the hidden location of the Son of Man and the "Head of Days." The Son of Man is preparing for the final victory of God's army. In chapters 46–48, this image of the Son of Man prevails; however in 60.10, the phrase had returned to the normal usage of emphasizing humanity as now Enoch is called the "son of man." This is the rarer meaning in Enoch, as for the most part, the being who is the "Son of Man" is a figure in God's royal army who will rule the world carrying

---

75. Rajak, *Translation and Survival*, 132.
76. Casey, *Solution to the Son of Man Problem*, 318.

out God's judgment. This image of a very human agent of God is found as well in the *Psalms of Solomon* (17–18).

Mark's use of the title is always applied *to* Jesus, but only *by* Jesus. In 2.10, the Son of Man is now able to forgive sins on earth as well as heal. This is similar to the view in Enoch (62.9) where the Son of Man is worshiped by those who seek his mercy through petitions and supplications. The Son of Man is also the Lord of the Sabbath (Mark 2.28), but is rejected by the rulers of the Temple, suffering many things, even death (8.31; 9.12, 31; 10.33, 45; 14.41). Another connection between the Son of Man in Enoch and Mark is found in Mark 8.38. This connection speaks about the Son of Man sitting in the Glory of the Father causing his persecutors shame (cf. Enoch 62.5–14; 63.11; 69.26; cf. Acts 7). In Mark 9.9, Jesus promises that the Son of Man will rise from the dead (Enoch 62.14). In Mark 14.21 and 14.62, Mark quotes Daniel's vision.

Mark generally follows the Son of Man motif found in Enoch except where it concerns the suffering, betrayal and intended death of Jesus. Mark's Christology always includes the role of suffering divine agent to whom God speaks to and through. It is pulled from Daniel with a strong connection to Enoch but Mark adds to this the role of the suffering servant (perhaps a subtle allusion to Isaiah 53). The use of the Son of Man is consistent, however, in that it is only Jesus who refers to himself as the Son of Man. Angels and divine intermediaries are not present in Mark's Gospel, neither is the Ancient of Days. It is Jesus and Jesus only who uses this title—and only about himself. This is important in our conclusion, but for now, we must examine the sources of the Son of God in Mark's Gospel.

Sources for the Son of God

Mark's prologue begins with John the Baptizer announcing Jesus and then baptizing him. This scene follows *Psalm 2* in declaring the King as God's Son.[77] Yet, this is not the development of the divine Son of God of later Christian dogma, but a ritualistic exercise common in the ancient world. Martin Noth argues that unlike others in the ancient world the enthronement of the Hebrew king was seen as a rejection of the deity of the King in favor of an adoptionistic view. Noth writes, "The use of the

---

77. For an in depth review of the use of Psalm 2 in the early church, see Janse, *You Are My Son*.

formula of adoption shows that the Davidic king in Jerusalem was not god incarnate, was not of divine origin or nature, but is designated 'son' by gracious assent of his God. In this modification, therefore, we have less a proof of Davidic divine kingship in Jerusalem than indeed an indication of a rejection of real divine king ideology."[78] This is echoed by Sigmund Mowinckel.[79] This was not the usual image, however, of the divine kingship. Egypt had their Pharaohs as gods as did the Greeks with their kings, and it was not long that Rome began to develop its own imperial cult, naming Caesar the "son of God."

In 40 BCE, Octavian was identified as "divi filius"—equal to that of the Olympian gods and born of mysterious surroundings.[80] Between the time of the Hasmoneans and the destruction of the Temple, there is a constant clash between imperial cults and Jewish cult. From Antiochus to Caligula, Greek and Roman rulers attempted to force the Jews to accept the Roman imperial cult and declare the foreign king a divine ruler. While there is some controversy of interpretation regarding the *Aramaic Apocalypse*, if one sides with Vermes, then the Qumran community is seen as rejecting the title as one identified in the *topos* of a last world ruler. The divine king, perhaps a Syrian who claimed the throne, plagued the Jewish separatists with pretenses of being a god, but this was met harshly by the one true God.[81] Given the countercultural B.J. and agitprop used by the Jews to deflect the acculturation of Hellenism, as well as the Roman imperial ideology, to allow that the Son of God in Mark is a positive appellation is to essentially deny the rather Jewish character of the Gospel. It is doubtful that the baptismal scene in a Jewish Gospel is anything but the rejection of such concepts as found in the Greco-Roman world. Mark 1.1 presents a rather unique obstacle in exploring the title "Son of God" in Mark's Gospel. It is a textual variant added by certain manuscripts, but absent in the most trusted textual source, א. The choice for modern textual critics seems more dependent upon theological concerns rather than a consistent application of methodology. We must also consider the use of the phrase throughout the rest of the Gospel as well, a usage strikingly different from the other

---

78. Noth, *God, King and Nation*, 172–3.
79. Mowinckel, *He that Cometh*, 78.
80. Collins and Collins, *King and Messiah*, 53.
81. For a complete discussion of the *Aramaic Apocalypse*, see Collins and Collins, *King and Messiah*, 5–73.

Synoptics. Before we return to Mark 1.1, let us examine the other uses of the phrase, or some variation of it throughout the Gospel. In Mark 3.11, the author points out the fact that whenever the demons meet Jesus, they announce that he is the Son of God, only to face a rebuke. In 5.7, the demoniac identifies Jesus as the Son of the Most High God. Even the Jewish accusers at the trial of Jesus are said to call him the Son of the Blessed (God, Mark 14.61). Finally, the Roman Centurion, after Jesus has suffered and died upon the cross, acknowledges Jesus to the true Son of God (Mark 15.39). All of this is preceded by the first exorcism in Mark 1.24 where the demon calls Jesus the Holy One of God, signifying a priest or prophet, rather than a divine son. In each of these instances, unlike the use of the phrase "Son of Man," only the enemies of Jesus identify him as the Son of God. Even Peter, in the great revelation of Mark 8.29, could only allow that Jesus was the Anointed—a reference to a prophet or priest.

Mark 14.62 bears more examination, however. Jesus is standing before the Sanhedrin and was asked if he was indeed the Son of the Blessed. He replied, "ἐγώ εἰμι, καὶ ὄψεσθε τὸν υἱὸν τοῦ ἀνθρώπου ἐκ δεξιῶν καθήμενον τῆς δυνάμεως καὶ ἐρχόμενον μετὰ τῶν νεφελῶν τοῦ οὐρανοῦ." We may take the question as asking if Jesus was the Son of God. The usual stern rebuke of the enemies becomes a sullen answer. He answers affirmatively, but supplies a different interpretation. Jesus's rebuke is best seen as a correction, in that Jesus is saying that he is the Son of Man whom they will see coming in the clouds.[82] It is rather more believable to suggest that the phrase in question contrasted the Jewish version of kingship with the Romans. In Mark 15.1–2, Pilate readily supplies us with this understanding as he asks Jesus if he was indeed the King of the Jews. The reply is yes. Even on the Cross the sign reads "King of the Jews," giving no allowance that Pilate or the Jews understood Jesus to have claimed for himself the mantle of the Son of God. There is no official charge of atheism (i.e., not believing in a pantheon of gods) or other signs Rome saw Jesus as usurping the Emperor's Role. Given that both *Enoch* and the *Psalms of Solomon* saw the future king as still a human agent, there would be no need for the once and future King to be the divine Son of God. Through the horrible details of Jesus

---

82. We must forgo the voice of John in examining Jesus's answer and instead focus on Mark's Gospel.

on the cross, at no time does the author allow for an understanding of Jesus as the Son of God.

Mark 1.1 Reexamined

Ἀρχὴ τοῦ εὐαγγελίου Ἰησοῦ χριστοῦ is the preferred reading of Mark 1.1, or at least according to the SBL's version of the *Greek New Testament*.[83] This, of course, is a major textual accession as many Greek New Testaments, even the most critical ones, still include, if even in brackets, the phrase υἱοῦ θεοῦ. Throughout the Gospel the attribution of divinity rather than humanity is consistently made by the enemies of Jesus. Given that demons and unclean spirits were used by Jewish polemical authors, including the author of the Revelation, to represent Rome, then we may unite the demons with the centurion to allow that they are the same. Considering that all references but one are negative, it is not likely that Mark who emphasized Jesus's humanity and Jewishness, would have pronounced that Jesus is the Son of God at the start of his Gospel. Further weight is added if we consider that Mark's Gospel is written to allow the audience to answer the question of who is Jesus.[84] If Mark reveals to his audience the answer at the beginning, then there is little need to prod his audience into answering the question correctly, except for entertainment value, as it breaks several rules of proper rhetoric to supply the audience with the answer. Following this argument, that the references to the Son of God are always rebuked and made by the enemies of Jesus, save one, we must allow that Mark's incipit is shorter and less divine than we would like.

Mark's use of the Son of Man as anti-Roman Ideology

Jesus refutes the demons forcefully with strong commands of silence. Several passages in Mark mirror Enoch's vision of the Son of Man. The only titles Jesus claims are those of a human agent of God, although a unique one. Yet, his baptism anoints him as the adopted son of God, or the Israelite Prophet and King. Mark is using the contrast between

---

83. Michael W. Holmes, editor, *SBL Greek New Testament*, 2010, Society of Biblical Literature and Logos Bible Software.

84. See Antoinette Clark Wire, *The Case for Mark Composed in Performance*.

the Son of Man and the Son of God as a contrast between Jesus and the Roman Emperor. Whereas the Roman Emperor built a cult around himself, Jesus did not. Indeed, whereas the Roman Emperor thrived on adoration and promotion, Jesus denied it and claimed only humanity. The Emperor became god; Jesus became man.

This leaves us with one final examination purposely ignored until now. In 15.39, the Roman centurion in a judicial proclamation declares "ἀληθῶς οὗτος ὁ ἄνθρωπος υἱὸς θεοῦ ἦν." How are we to understand this? Throughout Mark, the enemies of Jesus declare him the Son of God. Indeed, who is more of an enemy than the one who sees you murdered? If we follow other Jewish polemics of the time, then one may see these demons as Romans themselves. Yet, in this scene is a very human centurion, representing the might of the Roman Empire, and likely the one who had participated in the hammering of the nails. He is, except for Pilate, the only identified Roman in Mark's Gospel. Pilate declares Jesus innocent and intends to free him, choosing instead to let the rabble have the brigand Barabbas. The centurion, following orders, stands before Jesus as he gives up his last breath and declares him not just innocent, but the true Son of God. This is a rather odd judicial pronouncement, although welcomed I am sure. Jesus was not on trial for proclaiming himself the Son of God but was found guilty and crucified under the banner of the King of the Jews.[85]

The Five Books of Mark

Scholars and theological commentators alike see in Matthew five distinct discourses, each representing in some way the Five Books of Moses. Austin Farrer sees much of the same concept in Luke; but as of yet, Mark's brevity allows us to leave this aspect of his work unexamined. This is roundly unfair to the first Gospel writer, but let me correct that

---

85. As Schmidt reminds us, the triumph was a ritualistic exercise that evolved from Dionysus (See Versnel, *Triumphus*) a god what died and rose. It is doubtful that Jesus was meant to cast Jesus as a god, something that Jesus explicitly denied through the Gospel, and it is suggested that Paul did not see Jesus as a god (See McGrath, *The Only True God*). With this said, however, it could be that Mark was in part casting Jesus in the role of this to highlight the resurrection and suggest the eventual outcome to the Gospel. It may also be the reverse that the tradition of the resurrection suggested to Mark a connection to the story of Dionysus which was enforced by the Roman Triumph celebrating Vespasian and his sons.

Reading Mark Mimetically

tragic error now. Mark does contain five distinct sections. His prologue contains the baptism of Jesus, awash with images of Genesis hovering just below the surface. The second section of Mark picks up where the prologue leaves off, continuing to 4.34 with themes of travel, establishing a new covenant, and ironically enough, calling (a) Levi(te). Leviticus, concerned with purity, is Mark's third section, occurring between 4.35 and 9.1. In this section, Mark concerns his readers with the purity of the land by removing demons, diseases, and death while attacking the impure teachings of the Jewish leaders. The fourth component of Mark begins in the second verse of the ninth chapter with a number of teachings related to personal relationships as well as the entry into Jerusalem. The ending of this division, along with the beginning of the final bookend, is difficult to determine.

A natural break takes place in 13.1 when Jesus and the disciples leave Jerusalem. However, the better starting point for the fifth, or the Deuteronomistic, discourse is 12.28, beginning with a quote from Deuteronomy 6.4. In this section, Mark sets right the view of the Messiah, corrects the view of the experts of the law, enacts social justice, and builds a community on the ruins of the Temple. Not only are these themes present in Mark, but so too the Deuteronomistic view of history as well as the decreasing of God's involvement in nature, building a relationship instead between anthropomorphic creatures. The new community, in a land not quite their own, is built through Christ, without a trustworthy priestly class and a Temple. Matthew is not the progenitor of a Torah-based pattern; Mark is; Matthew (and Luke) just announces it better.

Ethnosymbolic Synchronism

As we have seen, Mark is concerned about the Roman and Jewish world around him, although he does not exhibit the literary markers that other authors do, most notably Luke. Synchronism allows for the author, any author, to bring together various historical events to produce an epic moment in history solved by the hero of the story (cf. Acts 3.18–21). For Luke-Acts, the entire world rotated on the axis until the time of Jesus and the church. Now was the time the world stopped and started again, but this time, the axis was Jesus. Mark is not so clear in his obtuseness as Luke in his cultivated literary techniques. Unlike Matthew,

Mark places the Temple's destruction front and center, marking the end of the old world and the beginning of the new. Witherington suggests that the lack of synchronistic markers indicates the Evangelists has no "real interest. . .with the events of the larger Roman world."[86] This is simply not the case, as demonstrated in this volume. Instead, I propose Mark employees synchronism through ethnosymbolism.

Ethnosymbolism brings to this discussion the use of symbols and the adoption of these symbols by mocking or consumption.[87] Symbols mean something, after all, and the national symbols of a ritualistic Rome built on images of authority for the divine Emperor would play a heavy role in how the Empire sustained itself for so long, even with the countless regicides. Ethno-symbolists are modern in the sense they understand the role of a purposed community. National identity is tangible, and made so by the symbols employed and accepted. We see this in origin myths as well as political cults, notably for our discussion in both Rome and the Jewish people. Whereas the Jewish people during the fabled Exile borrowed Babylonian and Persian myths to supplant their own, Rome would equally abuse both Egypt and Greece to build the cult of the Emperor. When Judea met Rome, and Rome met Judea, a certain amount of syncretic sharing occurred, as evidenced by Vespasian. In the Gospels, we see the same thing. Mark borrowed the ethnosymbolism of Rome to counteract their myth of dominance, destroying Rome's symbols through colonial mimicry.[88] This act of defiance is not limited to Mark, however, but is used by Mark's literary predecessor, Lucan, to whom we shall now turn to examine the success of Mark's rhetoric.

---

86. Witherington, *Socio-Rhetorical Commentary*, 3. A.Y. Collins says much the same thing, "There is, however, no theme of opposition to Rome in Mark." (Collins, *Mark*, 269.)

87. See Smith, *Ethno-symbolism and Nationalism: A Cultural Approach* and *Myths and Memories of the Nation*.

88. Michael Peppard labels the ethnosybolism in Mark "colonial mimicry," a process allowing for a disavowal of the represented object by the difference highlighted. He cites birds (the dove at the baptism), among other natural objects. Peppard also sees a divine adoption throughout Mark, something mimicking the Emperor's path to divinity. These things mimic Rome's usual portents for war (birds) and the military power of the emperor (adoption) but rebukes the Roman symbols though the process of imitation. (Peppard, *Son of God*, 123–31.)

7

Reading Mark Mimetically

A Lucan Reading

It is impossible to overcome the great chasm that separates Mark and Lucan, most notably the death of the latter and the faith of the former, but if we were to try we might enjoy hearing the great Roman poet read Mark's Gospel in his own unique way. As we have completed two chapters in reading Mark mimetically, I will take a personal liberty to put forth a Lucan reading of the Gospel of Mark—to tackle several outstanding issues not easily expressed in an analytical fashion. Lucan provides for us a test of Mark's mettle, even preventing our own subjectivity. If the Evangelist used Lucan as a stylistic mentor, it is possible the poet transferred to Mark something else, perhaps something Orphic. After all, by now we can admit Mark existed in Lucan's literary and socio-philosophical environment. This does not mean that since Lucan was at least partially a Stoic that Mark was as well, but as we will discover Stoicism does fit into Mark's Gospel easily, but better, it is easily extracted. How would Lucan have read Mark's characters; how would Lucan have judged his student? Let us see.

The use of language as an element of resistance is Mark's magnet seducing Lucan to the Gospel. Lucan was no dilettante, but he recreated Latin as a barbarous language masterfully. Mark follows perhaps both Lucan and the Septuagintal tradition of mutilating a language so as to preserve a spirit of résistance to counter the *zeitgeist*. Lucan's voice in his epic is one of rage and confusion, as if a civil war is erupting inside of him. It is not a stretch to read Mark with the same psychological confrontation warring in his noumenon. Both Mark and Lucan make use of parataxis, catachresis, puns, and maxims. To some extent, so does the Septuagint. It is not difficult, then, to allow that the choice we must make between the Septuagint and Lucan is one of distraction, with no deciding factor. Given both share a certain style it is plausible Mark would have understood Lucan's method better than most and because of this could have easily found the style a ready-made structure. A Markan reading of Lucan would have found Lucan's style Septuagintal, perhaps something that first attracted Mark to Lucan. Lucan, upon reading Mark, would not need to surmise an Aramaic original or any other hypothesis of historical critics to explain Mark's poor communication, but would have accepted Mark's resistance of Rome even to the smallest detail of our shared existence—language.

Mark's beginning and ending have given pause to commentators. Mark makes use of the Elijah-Elisha narratives, a structure with a recognizable abrupt start and stop; however, this is a feature of Lucan's poem as well. As noted above,, Lucan follows Caesar's historical account by starting on the eve of war and ending before the conflict in Egypt had reached its zenith. Mark begins with Jesus on the eve of his ministry and ends before the audience can see the resurrected Christ, a point of confusion to later scribes. We need only to examine Lucan's full range of sources to understand how the poet would have understood Mark's ending. Augustus was heralded as the bringer of peace—the *Pax Augusta*. Horace and Virgil created myth not from something new, but from existing legends, to herald Augustus as the end of Fate. Augustus, with his new peace, became the end of all history with the new creation to take place upon his ascension as a demigod, leaving his heirs to become the rulers of a new age.[1] Jesus is thus cast to counter this and more, to usurp the role of Caesar as the bringer of the good news (see Mark 1.1 above). Jesus's resurrection was not the end of history, but the beginning of a new age for Israel. Lucan would recognize this ending as one more than dramatic, but deeply theological. And while he would have rejected the underlying ideology, he would not waste as much time as textual critics have in wondering if Mark forgot the rest of the story. The ending is but the true beginning.

As an imitator of Virgil, Lucan awakens us to sleep in Mark's Gospel. In the epics, sleep is as death is, at least in a literary quality; in the

---

1. Fox, *Lucan*, xxii.

Aeneid it is taken as a stand in for the "forgetfulness of death."[2] Indeed, Palinurus dies/sleeps so Aeneas does not have too. In three places in Mark's Gospel key figures are pictured asleep. The first is Jesus, asleep when the storms threaten to destroy the ship killing those on board (Mark 4.38). Jarius's daughter is said to sleep rather than have died (5.39). Finally, as Jesus is preparing for this sacrifice in the Garden, the disciples are unable to resist falling asleep. Each time, those who are asleep are connected in some way to death, either in a possible death, as with Jarius's daughter and the ship in transit, or in preceding a death, as in the Garden. Each time, it is Jesus who awakens the sleeper at the last moments (this is no more boldly expressed than in Mark 14.40 where the author records the disciples could not resist sleep any longer) and it is finally Jesus who dies.

Here we find a comparison between Jesus and Pompey. Lucan would have read the death of Jesus similar to that of the Roman dictator. Pompey is killed by Caesar only indirectly, leaving the actual murder to the Egyptians. Pompey even denies to Caesar any anxiety or guilt for his death. While it is not Caesar's hand that physically strikes the death blow, Lucan intends to nevertheless incriminate Caesar. In death, Pompey remained very much himself, denying to Caesar any hope he would somehow suffer degradation and decay of his image. Lucan writes, "Those who gazed on his mutilated head are witness that death's final stroke did not change the hero's composure and look (8.665–7)." Jesus in Mark 15 is scourged and crucified, yet, on the way to the cross, Jesus gains a crown and a robe along with a placard proclaiming him the King of the Jews. Further, at the moment of his death, a Roman Centurion proclaims him the Son of God. His quick death, perhaps a signal he had allowed himself to die, resembles Pompey's refusal to allow the gods to control his fate. At his burial, he was adorned as a king and treated with spices.

A useful method of imitation is the idea of possession. In Greco-Roman myth, the gods would disguise themselves as mortals to carry out some plan of their own (as in Homer), but in the Latin epics, this is possession (as in Virgil). Lucan borrows this concept moving it into a national embodiment employing the wrathful Furies for his work. In Book 1, the Fury invests Rome with chaotic madness, driving it into a frenzied state of rage. In Book 3, Pompey dreams of Julia's ghost as Fury

---

2. Hardie, *Epic Successors*, 32.

who embodies civil war, destruction, and expulsion from paradise (Elysian Fields). Indeed, Lucan goes so far as to suggest the shades of the underworld have possessed the soldiers (7.772–6). But, what is more profitable in understanding a Lucan reading of Mark is the possession of Pythia by Paean (5.170–90). Mark uses language similar to Lucan's to describe the demonic in 5.1–20. No doubt, Lucan would understand Mark's superstitious refrain of δαιμόνια acting as an inverse to Josephus's use of the word, arguing God was with the Romans, in light of the possession of both gods and men (characters) superimposed upon the author's present situation. Compare Mark 5.1–20 with 9.18. The demonic possessions as noted above are different. One mirrors medical evidence of epileptic seizures while the other clearly rests in mythology.[3] Lucan would have identified the author's poetic license as it were to create *literary* possessions as vehicles while building upon *real* possessions from tradition allowing the former to become reality by the latter. After all, Caesar surely thought himself possessed in a positive sense by the divine.

There is something else to this embodiment. Lucan would discover the idea of transference in Mark's Gospel as well. Lucan was writing about historical events and historical characters, but often times, they are no more fiction than flesh and blood, appropriating various rhetorical tools to create his epic. Historical truthfulness exists only as a second thought. Lucan, unlike modern critics who have not come to a synthesis on the Iscariot and Simon the Zealot, if he had known his history of the Jewish Wars would accept Mark's use of two of the disciples to experience a transference to aid the story. Unlike today's readers who need to see history in the Gospels as an unbiased presentation, a Lucan reading yields a more forgiving one, if not an even more believable one. Lucan willingly rewrote history to slight some and uplift others. We find this too in Mark's use of religious sects that have no historical basis. For example, Lucan transformed history and thus realigned the present. In this instance, the poet has Nero's ancestor Domitius Ahenobarbus die a death intended for another. Caesar's centurion Crastinus is replaced with Pompey's Domitus instead. The overtones of this were not missed. The charge of Nero as an unfit ruler reaches back to his ancestors. Judas

---

3. It bears repeating that 9.18 is most probably a historical scene given its identifiable realistic traits and is archeological of the historical Jesus. Nothing in this volume, however, is meant to recommend avoiding medical doctors and seeking the help of shamans for health issues.

Reading Mark Mimetically

and Simon are read much the same way as Domitus Ahenobarbus, as that of characters imbued with traits to serve a literary purpose. Simon (the Zealot) and Judas (Iscariot) would allow Mark to follow the same historical requirements Lucan did, that of a character invented, or a character suffering transference, to tell a particular story. If only Lucan had taught us historical criticism.

Cosmic dissolution is a Stoic event, with the universe exploding in a fiery conflagration but being reborn in a continuous cycle. We find this in Greco-Roman myths as well as in biblical themes but without the somatic flesh associated with it by today's theologians and interpreters. The authors of the canonical Isaiah speak of the end of the world (exile) and the new creation (return from exile). The magnificent scene in Exodus is a theomachia event in which a new world is created, or perhaps, better, the world is recreated. It is no different, really, than what Lucan was speaking to in his work on the fall of the Roman Republic.[4] Both Wright and Stark have put forth valid explanations as they see it of Mark 13. Their theological agendas mean they are still reading Mark through a Christian lens rather than through the lens of the historical context. Lucan, again, provides us with a sounding board that higher critics and theologians often miss. He too saw the end of the world, or perhaps prophesies the end of the world, and it happened, just as he said it did. How would Lucan have read Mark 13? More than likely, along with Cato's wish in 2.302–30. He would have understood that the world did end when the Temple was destroyed, but would laugh, I think, at our notions of the end of the world that are understood too woodenly.

While the reader of Lucan must be able to read Lucan with Stoicism, it is not necessary to see Lucan as a Stoic. Reading Lucan with a tingle of Stoicism will allow the Lucan reader to gain something lost if the error is made that Lucan is a Stoic fundamentalist, rather than a poet trained by Stoics, using Stoic imagery to tell a story.[5] It is this

---

4. Ovid has provided a model for Lucan here. Ovid writes of the chaos, symbolized by a flood, of the beginning of the world (*Met.* 1.291–2). Lucan uses the imagery to warn of the end of the world caused by the civil war (*BC*, 4.99, 104–5). After flood, once the chaos as subsided, the rivers regain their composure. As described with the desecration of boundaries, the flood symbolizes the transgressions of the war. This cycle of chaos and stability is a Stoic hallmark.

5. Cornutus, the compiler of Chrysippus's writings who is the father of Stoic cosmology, was the teacher of Lucan when he was younger. Seneca was a well-known

Lucan who relates the end of the world in Stoic terms and it is this Lucan who would read Mark's proclamation regarding the end of the world set in a civil war spread across the entire Roman world (including Judea). Without going into a great bit of detail about Stoic cosmology, we will briefly sum it up as a cyclical event beginning and ending with the destruction of the world, trials by fire, and an idea the universe is held together by an invisible bond albeit one stretched at times. This bond is a consensus between the cosmos and humanity, binding and loosening based on human actions. These beliefs are best understood by reading Manilius's work, *Astronomica*. Lapidge insists Lucan was familiar with Manilius (and as such allows for examination as a source of Lucan) but equally insists the rather esoteric metaphors of Stoicism were brought low enough and used by Lucan to describe more human events.[6] Lucan saw the reciprocal bond between the universe and humanity in the surreal world as realistic in examining social structures. In his proem, Lucan speaks of the loosening of those bonds turning the world upside down. Indeed, crimes are now good, a mighty people are brought low, and boundaries are erased. This is not just about Rome, but the world. Of course, Rome *is* the world for Lucan, if not for all Romans. As the State begins to crumble, the world begins to crumble. Lucan is poetic, but he is serious in casting the conflagration upon the back of Caesar as he recreates the Republic into the Empire. One world has passed and "behold," Lucan says, "all things are made new." New, of course, is not always better.

Lucan the Stoic would appreciate Jesus's call to duty. I do not mean to suggest Jesus was indeed a Stoic, but I will go so far as to say Mark was influenced by Stoicism, as were other New Testament writers. I believe if Lucan was found reading the scene taking place in the Garden of Gethsemane, he would note Jesus faces the Cross in a way honoring his father, secures the welfare of his children (or his followers in this case), and does so in the face of achieving nothing good for himself. This is the role of duty and honor in Stoicism. We might compare this to Cato who knowing the war was evil chose to engage Caesar in a desperate attempt to defend the dying Republic. Mark's Jesus, and more importantly the community of Mark, could have very well chosen to side with Rome and to crown Vespasian as emperor, but instead Jesus

---

Stoic as well.

6. Lapidge, *Lucan*, 206.

chose the Cross and Mark's community chose to stand against the false messiahs that litter history, clinging to the crucified criminal instead. Jesus, as the Stoic demands, is not passionate even when faced with the brutality of the cross. He even welcomes his betrayer as a long lost friend. The mind of Jesus is not portrayed as one which is wavering or questioning, but using reason to dictate the future courses of action. His opponents, on the other hand, are irrational creatures that oppose the will of God, slander, react violently with untrained emotions, and thus are the epitome of the anti-Sage. If they are the anti-Sage, Jesus is thus the Stoic Sage.

Foreknowledge of these events was given to humans through portents connecting all things together. For Lucan, the creator of things cordoned off the ages of the world and gave a line of fate for each one.[7] The signs of war served as a means to understand the approach of the end of the age. Granted, other wars preceded Caesar's, but none so far reaching as to destroy the Republic. Returning to the idea of the social bond, Lucan does not afford the gods the blame, but the people who "struck peace from the globe."[8] It is power, greed, and lust pushing Rome to fall into Strabo's mountainous forests—the end of the world. But, while the people are to blame, this is Fate's natural course. Each link in the chain is connected to the previous and to the following so that causality is easily understood. Lucan was a master of synchronicity, or at least the hind sight gave him vision to see the often unseen hand of Fate made clear only after the crisis has passed. Each chain is also met with the heavenly signs so that the people are warned, although it seems to us today rather needless if all was preordained. Perhaps Lucan is merely playing the part of the mad poet railing against the people, only attempting to show the futility of worrying about the crimes of the past, or he could suggest instead a rather non-Stoic theomachy that allows the people to take control of their own fate and remove the Empire forced upon them. For Lucan, though, the moments of the civil war were indeed the final hours of the world. One wonders if he was not also feeling the *zeitgeist*'s final hours before the fall of Nero.

Lucan would not read Mark 13 so causally as Stark or as bombastic as Wright. Indeed, I doubt that he believed so strongly in the portents that he put into verse, as poets often do not take their own words so

---

7. Lucan, *BC*, 2.1–15.
8. Lucan, *BC*, 1.60–2.

strictly as those who attempt to read the work after them. Some of his portents sound rather familiar. He writes of Rome's eventual falling under her own weight, but before this, primal chaos will reign, the signs shall emerge, stars will fall into the sea, lands will dry up, the sun and the moon will turn against one another with the moon claiming the day and then, when all of this is complete, the world will end in riots and discord.[9] This is not all, as comets appear, unique visitors in the sky, and raging storms sweep the earth.[10] There is no peace when the world ends, only horrors until the people cry out in vain to make it stop. Lucan is masterfully depicting the social crisis he believes existed in the civil war and by happenstance is foretelling the great social crisis yet to exist during the civil war taking place shortly after his death. He is not merely a poet and a philosopher but a psychologist, a genographic historian, and a prophet. Lucan concluded his poem with a simple view towards the future, "What Discord ordered came to pass on earth. When Eumolpus had gushed all this out in a monstrous torrent of words, at long last we entered Croton. . ." Lucan no doubt knew the world had indeed gone on after the destruction of the Republic, but only after the fires had rid the cosmos of the remains of the old, beginning a new cycle. After all, he was living in the new world.

When Lucan reads Mark, he would see the cosmic portents and hear the sounds of the promises of the return of Jesus. Mark, I believe, is relating something original to the words of Jesus, whether or not we relate it to the idea of a resurrection as suggested in the Maccabean books or something else, but the (re)author of Jesus's words is now positing them as a sign of the end. Jesus returns at the beginning of a new age brought on by the destruction of the Temple. While this is somewhat of a Stoic notion, it is not foreign to the Hebrew Scripture given that this idea of Temple and (re)Creation is found in Isaiah and Second Temple Jewish literature. Mark is positioning the trial by fire to produce a new world eradicating the boundary of Israel so that the Gentile mission could now occur. The end of the world is not a physical destruction but the eradication of the important social construct. Mark was well aware of what the destruction of the Temple meant, and for him, it was the beginning of the new age. No doubt, Lucan would have understood this and chided us for not understanding simplistic poetry.

9. Lucan, *BC*, 1.60–80.
10. Lucan, *BC*, 1.561–70.

There is another well-rehearsed dilemma Lucan and Mark share. Geography, from our stand point, exists as a major problem for our two authors. Mark is known to have misplaced entire geographical areas or simply renamed them.[11] Jesus is said to have traversed the Sea of Galilee going east several times without ever returning.[12] Geography in Mark leaves the reader with the impression that Mark is either a poor student or an out of touch writer. We could suggest Mark was far removed from the subject area, but given his close proximity with other rather Palestinian features, this is but a flimsy excuse. Lucan, sitting in Rome, with Caesar's journals, Virgil's poem, and Homer's works before him still was able to destroy the geography of the world.[13] He misaligned Pelion and Ossa while providing the wrong travel account between Brundisium and Dyrrachium.[14] Added to this is the use of water from the Alps to fill the Rubicon rather than the water from the Apennines while the Alps also suffer an avalanche flooding the Pillars of Hercules.[15] Lucan calls the Rubicon *puniceus*, positioning Caesar as Hannibal during the

11. Mark 5.1 creates a rather humorous geographical error, where the author misses the mark by nearly 30 miles providing for a rather embarrassing leap for Jesus to from the beach to a town of a great distance to the southeast. Further, there are the rather quick trips taken by Jesus such as the events between 4.35 and 6.45. In 7.31, Jesus heals a deaf man in the Decapolis after meeting the Syro-Phoenician woman in Tyre, but is said to travel north.

12. Jesus would have crisscrossed the Sea of Galilee (an Aramaic construction) several times, heading always east. The phrase εἰς τὸ πέραν is found four times in this pericope (4.35; 5.1, 21; 6.45). It is an idiom which means "from west to east." It is difficult enough to believe that Jesus completed that many journeys across the Sea in such a short time without having to believe that he crossed the breadth of the world to do it.

13. Another example of Lucan's misuse of geography occurs when the author writes about Dorion, a city in Thessaly. The city does not exist, at least not in the place Lucan as written it. Lucan pulls Dorion from Homer who places the city in the western Peloponnese. Masters proposes that Lucan is using an "anti-allusion" to force the towns in Lucan's geography together with those in Homer's world. This would have called attention to Lucan's point in a clear manner for the audience. (Masters, *Poetry and Civil War*, 159–60.)

14. 6.333–6. Bexley suggests, rightly, that the confusion of the two so that both cities appear almost transposed upon on other is meant to symbolize the primal violence of chaos overtaking the Empire (Bexley, *Replacing Rome*, 468). The fissure between the Alps and Apennines act as the same role. Let me also suggest that such confusion aligns well with the flow of the poem pushing the audience into an emotional frenzy.

15. Lucan's rivers flow to us by way of Ovid, a geography model for our poet, although Lucan usually gets them "wrong." The river Inachis may server as an allusion to Ovid, who along with our poet, has written a work that contains the only catalogue of rivers in Latin poetry.

Second Punic War.[16] This creative use of geography as an allusion to a past conflict is carried on throughout the text.[17] Rome trembles before Caesar the way it did before Hannibal.[18] Africa is used throughout the poem to affect the characters. Pharsalus is an African. Pompey meets his doom there. It was Africa that once plagued Rome. But he consistently carved out a specific boundary for his story and violated it, something emblematical of the larger disillusionment of the poem itself. "The contradictory geography Lucan creates symbolizes contested power: Caesar's desperate grab for command literally carves up the world and undermines Rome's assumed role as the political pivot of the globe."[19] As much as Lucan's work is the anti-*Aeneid*, he is still a hopeful Roman. He still believes Rome is the center of the cosmos. But, with the destruction of the cosmos, other centers begin to appear. Along with Rome, Delphi and Ammon arise.[20] Caesar has Rome, Pompey has Delphi, and Cato has Ammon. Lucan is a master of *geopoetic* politics.

We should remember the role cities play, even today. The United States and most countries are identified by their capitol city. Rome was no different; neither was Palestine. In Mark's Gospel, Jesus vacillates between Galilee (more specifically, the home of Peter in Capernaum) and Jerusalem. There is a tension shared between the two areas. The further into perceived Gentile territory Jesus goes, the more friendly his acceptance. When he begins to go to Jerusalem, the heart of the Israelite people, the more hostile his enemies become. Even the disciples seem to lose faith and Jesus loses power the closer the distance to Jerusalem. Rome is split in two. The Senate sits in the city and Caesar outside. The closer Caesar comes to Rome, the place of peace and rest, the more the world trembles. While Rome remains virtually unscathed, the rest of the world is laid waste; except Lucan wants his audience to realize that it is the city of Rome itself laid waste. Further, the control of Rome is

16. Lucan, *BC*, 1.214.

17. Geography is closely associated with language. For example, see Chapman, "Locating the Gospel of Mark: A Model of Agrarian Biography;" Stewart, *Gathered Around Jesus*; Willis, *Now and Rome*; Smith, *Map is not territory*.

18. 1.303–5

19. Bexley, *Replacing Rome*, 459.

20. The reader cannot help to notice that the three centers of power in Lucan's poem mimic the First Triumvirate. Lucan was against the Empire, and in some ways, this was translated into removing the space of that one ruler and divesting it. No doubt, this was a sign of the end as the cosmos needed a central anchor point.

Reading Mark Mimetically

not settled in Rome, but in a distant city, Pharsalus; the final action of Caesar's dominance is not made in Rome, but in Pharsalus. Jesus makes it to Jerusalem, but it is outside the city he offers his sacrifice and it is outside the city he must escape to become a captive. Boundaries, space, and time all play a part in the way both authors toy with geography and the movements of their characters. The clearest example of this in Mark is, again, the thirteenth chapter where the Temple of God in Jerusalem serves as both the end and the beginning of the world, as if Judaism flows into it and out into the Gentile world. It is from there geography is redefined.

If the three pivotal cities each represent three pivotal characters in Lucan's poem, can we expect such a scene in Mark's Gospel? Jesus is centered in Galilee while the Pharisees and the Romans are centered in Jerusalem. Lines are drawn by Mark, however, preventing Jesus from going to the city for some time. The same lines continue to draw Jesus back to Galilee, or at the very least, away from Jerusalem.[21] How do the cities represent those who are attached to them? Galilee is still a Jewish country, but Gentiles are making inroads. It is the barrier that holds back the Parthians. It is also the place where the Jewish Revolt first started. This fits Jesus and Mark's community well. As discussed in the previous chapter, Mark sees the beginning of the Gentile mission with the destruction of the Temple. The community is still Jewish, but they are Jews learning to live with Gentiles. Jesus as head of the community serves to protect the community from invasion (or at least, Mark does through the Gospel of/about Jesus). The Romans, in Jerusalem, are the center of power, albeit a corrupt power. They are claiming the role of God's appointed nation (Vespasian). The Pharisees who brought in Simon as messiah are the holders of a corrupt religion. The two pivotal cities are well attached to their respective captains and as such are not discarded as extras in the scene. Lucan would have most certainly recognized the role of Markan geography, more so, than we do.

Might Lucan have applauded the lack of a divine force in Mark? God appears two times in Mark, once at the baptism of Jesus and the other at the transfiguration. Each time the audience only hears God as a voice in the clouds. Worse, God remains remarkably absent when Jesus was in the direst of circumstances. No doubt, this is what many

---

21. These lines are utilized in Luke's Gospel in a concentric fashion to slowly move Jesus deliberately to Jerusalem.

Jews felt during the Jewish Revolt when it seemed God had abandoned them. Lucan excludes the usual role of the gods from his epics. Gone are the positive views of the gods who guide humanity on their way. Theodicy still plays a part, but it is not a positive one. When there is no other thing to do but to bow to the will of the gods, Cato does so. While Lucan's characters and the poet himself resist the gods, the control of the gods is still something that factors into the poem. In Mark, Jesus is suddenly confronted with helplessness in front of the will of God—a God who would not answer him in the moment of distress—but he still proceeds forward. A short perfunctory note here cannot explain the role of the divine in either Lucan or Mark but we must realize the unusual absence of the gods in Lucan and Mark are telling of a theological principle larger than the words themselves. After all, it would appear the gods had abandoned Rome during the civil war. Lucan would see in Mark the creation of a new theology, one where Jesus is the proxy for YHWH, but in a condemning sort of fashion. It was Jesus who had not forsaken Israel contra God. Just as the gods had forsaken Rome, leaving only Pompey and Cato to give their lives in a desperate attempt to save it, God is read by Lucan as forsaking Israel (something even Josephus would allow) and the divine messenger when both—Israel through Jesus—are crucified. Further, Mark's use of prophecy, unlike the other Evangelists, is seen as more like the oracles of Delphi than long cast visions of divine promises. The gods are absent, leaving Lucan to find no answers and Mark to posit only questions.

Lucan would have relished this act of one man serving as a sacrifice for the people, I believe, since the idea of a sacrifice was prevalent in the Latin epics of the time. The scene of Jesus between the brigands were enough, but the conversation in Mark 10, where James and John surrounded Jesus as sacrifices fit well with the role of sacrifice in preserving order. As Rome fell during the first Civil War, chaos reigned even in religious rituals. A sacrifice was needed, as demonstrated in *Aeneid 12*. Indeed, such violence is often beneficial because the social disorder is characterized by the life and death of one man. When Jesus said he would give himself as a ransom (to Rome), Lucan would understand that the social order disrupted by both the Roman Civil War and the Jewish Revolt as restored only through Jesus, but more, it was through the duality of Jesus juxtaposed with both Vespasian and Simon that this could only happen. Bandera notes "Virgil is making Aeneas fight his own double, his enemy twin."[22] This duality is not limited to Virgil but found in other poets as well, such as Statius.[23]

Sacrificial duality is not the only theme Lucan would identify in Jesus, so too the idea of the ransom of one for the many. As Hardie notes, the sacrificial *human* victim is found at the start of the *Aeneid* with the sacrifice of Iphigeneia (*Aen.* 2.116–9). Lucretius has an inaugural sacrifice as well when he tells his story of Epicurus. Hardie proposes that Sinon serves as the evolution of this concept further when Virgil brings into focus *unus/omnes*. Indeed, Sinon is chosen. Virgil writes, "all consented, and the fate that each man had feared for himself, they did not oppose when turned to the death of one poor retch."[24] Hardie notes the atoning sacrifice of one is replete in Virgil, involving generals and even a woman—Dido. Dido is seen in Lucan's poem as well as is the idea of a blood sacrifice. Lucan, above all, is the one with the most intensive view of atoning sacrifices.[25] Ahl sees in Lucan an atoning sacrifice as well, even going so far as to suggest the Roman Civil War served as a blood offering to the ghosts of Africa for the gladiatorial games.[26] The importance of the sacrifice is made clear in the violent suicide of Cato. This devotion is *the* example of Stoic virtue. His death was seen as one of duty, a Stoic trait. Cato's acceptance of his duty to Rome, either through warfare or personal sacrifice, gave rise to his legend and his legend gave rise to the Cato that we read in Lucan's poem.[27]

How might Lucan have read Jesus? He would have found a suitable reminiscence in Cato. The third character in Lucan's story wages war against Caesar and in some way, at least by his character, Pompey. Jesus is fighting against Vespasian and Simon bar Giora.[28] While

---

22. Bandera, "Sacrificial levels in Virgil's Aeneid" 217–39.
23. Hardie, *The Epic Successors of Virgil.*
24. Virgil, *Aen.,* 2.130–1.
25. Hardie, *Epic Successors,* 26–8.
26. Ahl, *Lucan: An Introduction.*
27. Lucan's grandfather was among the first to welcome Cato into the pantheon of exemplar heroes. His suicidal death was no longer seen as that of a loser, but as that of what the individual must be willing to do to in his line of duty. Cato's death gave rise to the political martyr. (See Griffin, "Philosophy, Cato, and Roman Suicide II," 192–202.) The political martyr's death had to meet several qualifications for it to be considered worthy. These were theatricality, eliciting a public reaction, calmness of the victim, and for a valid philosophy. (Geiger, *Political Biography,* 63.)
28. The Roman civil war was set between Pompey and Caesar, but Cato became a

Mimetic Criticism and the Gospel of Mark

Mark's contestants are more subtle, they are present as we have seen. Had Lucan picked up on this, there is little reason to think otherwise, the poet would have read Jesus as the one who did his duty even in chaotic times. There is more to this, however. The Roman General, as Lucan writes him, begged the gods that he alone provide full atonement for the crimes of the civil war and thus save Rome.[29] Cato wished to provide his body as the space of the cosmic struggle instead of watching stars fall, the earth shaking apart, and nations feasting on the remains of Rome.[30] The suicide of Cato is something Lucan's audience was expecting because Cato kept promising it.[31] Cato judges as the gods do and by his actions attempts to fill in for the absent gods. He even speaks with the voice of the gods.[32] Might we say the same for Jesus who acts as God on earth by both healing and raising the dead while giving new commands? Lucan would view Jesus as the idyllic Cato because it was within his body that the ransom was provided for the sins of the people. Jesus is also the one who saves his people, taking upon himself many of the theophonic qualities given to YHWH in the Hebrew Scriptures. Cato is the divine superman in Book 2, presented in such a way to become more god than human.[33] In fact, Plutarch in his biography of Cato

---

major player, allying with Pompey. Once Pompey was dead, the civil war ceased in a way, because it was no longer between two men who sought to control Rome, but between a general who defended Roman *libertes* and the Roman General who sought to conquer Rome. The same can be seen in the response to the Jewish Revolt. For at least a little while, two men claimed to be the Jewish messiah. This civil war was ideological, but no less violent than the physical war. But, when Simon died, it was left to Mark's Jesus to finally be proclaimed the true Jewish messiah.

29. Mark Allen Thorne completed his dissertation on Cato's memory in Lucan (*Lucan's Cato: The Defeat of Victory, the Triumph of Victory*) arguing that Cato's memory in the poem enacts the epic as a funeral *monumentum* that retold the death of Rome in the civil war. Cato embodies Rome and as such, future generations are meant to look to Cato as the glory of Rome. We might go so far as to say that Jesus is meant to embody Israel in much the same way Cato is meant to embody Rome.

30. Lucan, *BC*, 2.302–30. As far as sources and underlying structures go, this scene in Lucan is expanded by them. The Stoic Lucan would have had a difficult time writing his Stoic character who challenges orthodoxy. Lucan uses Stoic concepts as a structure but turns to Virgil for the intertext (compare *Aeneid* 7.461). One should not miss the comparison with Seneca's *Controversiae*.

31. Lucan, *BC*, 6.311; 9.208–14; 9.582–3. The comparison is rather simple to see between the three prophecies of Cato's death and the same number given for Jesus's death. However, Cato's suicide is never seen in the poem.

32. Lucan, *BC*, 9.564.

33. The divinization of Cato is a rather important one in the scope of the poem,

attempted to correct this view by writing of Cato's more human qualities rather than his exploits.[34] If we compare Cato's words in this passage to the words of Jesus in Mark 10 and Mark 13, we come to a certain semblance. Add to these passages the entirety of the passion (defined by Mark 10 and 13) and we find a savior figure taking within his body the chaos of the ages to banish it. Lucan recognized what modern Girardian theorists have seen, that Jesus is meant to act as the sacrifice undoing not only the destruction caused by Rome, but also the lingering evil presence caused by the Jewish Revolt. This is much more than Jesus merely acting as a good faith pledge in Simon's stead; this is a messiah who defeats the spirit of the age and quite reasonably is seen as a figure that defies and decimates the gods.

I mean, *if* we were reading this with Lucan.[35]

Conclusion

In chapters 5 and 6 we demonstrated the possibility of reading Mark's Gospel through the use of mimetic criticism. Our theory is made better by a Lucan reading of Mark. While Mark was a Jewish writer, he was living in a violence besotted Rome enlivened with poetry, rhetoric, and the skills to shape a civilization. He knew his Isaiah but so too his Lucan. He, like all of us, contextualized his tradition with his recent experiences. A Lucan reading of Mark, then, will give birth to answers

---

especially in contrast with the apparent absence of the gods. For more on Cato's quasi-god like status in Lucan's poem, see Tipping, *Terrible Manliness*, 224–7, 236.

34. According to Plutarch, Cato the Elder, in his raging thirst was known to drink sour wine (*posca*) and maybe a little wine (*Vit. Cato Major* 1.7). In Lucan's account of Cato the Younger in Libya, the virtue of the Roman is seen when he refuses water so that others may drink first. The scene in the desert contains many allusions to thirsty men willing to drink anything (9.760–1175).

35. Lucan did not create a theological crisis with Cato, at least not one that would have pressed the Markan community. But, unlike Odysseus, Cato provides the model for understanding the death of Jesus; or rather, Lucan using the legends surrounding Cato developed the model understood next to the atonement model of Jesus in the Gospel. The most symbolic use of this model is the open ended question found in both works. Cato, after the defeat of Pompey, becomes the opponent of Caesar. The war has been won and settled but Cato begins to defend Rome's liberty, not so that he could become emperor, but that Rome would be free. This open ended question by Lucan allows the audience to consider whether or not they will follow Cato to victory for Roman freedom.

raised and doubts cast on the text. It is to some of these questions we now turn. For now, however, let us conclude these three chapters of mimetic commentary in suggesting that unlike other sources, such as Homer, we can show that Mark's audience would have readily picked up on his agenda. The purpose of Mark's Gospel was to dispel the remnants of the Jewish War, namely the false messiahs populating the landscape and healing the wounds. By using current sources, Mark is able to make use of several decades of theological reflection upon Jesus and then to use this to suggest that Jesus's gospel not only has the power to reverse Rome's triumph, but is the one true gospel of the Jewish messiah who brings life—unlike the desolation caused by Simon.

8

Reading Mark's Scholia

Introduction

As with any work, some subjects are not worth the length of a chapter.[1] There are two subjects fitting this quandary, at least for what I hope is an introduction to mimetic criticism. First, we shall endeavor to establish mimetic criticism not just as a method of reading Mark, but as one giving us ground to reexamine theories long thought settled. I will examine the weaknesses in the heavily fortified Synoptic problem and then turn to the more stable Farrer Theory.[2] Mimetic criticism allows the Farrer Theory to do away with the Two-Source Theory and the Q Hypothesis altogether. In the second part of this chapter we will examine the light mimetic criticism sheds on the Historical Jesus. We will then end with, what is my opinion, the identification of Mark's genre. It is my hope not to end—or even pretend to end—the conversation, but to suggest a stage of evolution in the discussion of the Gospels. At the end of this present volume, we find only the beginning of the story.[3]

---

1. The title for this chapter comes from the scholia compiled on ancient works that included glosses and other data later authors used to interpret the work at hand. This chapter contains subjects not large enough for individual chapters, so I have decided to put them all here.

2. Crossley, *Reading the New Testament: Contemporary Approaches*, 19. For the most of the scholastic record, the theory which will be explained later is either called Farrer or Farrer-Goulder, but it would be somewhat disingenuous to exclude Mark Goodacre as he is, as far as I know, the larger promoter the theory in the United States and has contributed many facets in his own right. However, he has insisted in at least one work that it simply be called the Farrer Theory. We will honor his request.

3. It is difficult to see any work on the *Gospel of Mark* complete without the examinations of other themes in Mark's Gospel such as discipleship, Christology, the family

Mimetic Criticism and the Gospel of Mark

Answering the Synoptic Problem

The Synoptic Problem has caused scholars to lay waste to countless trees as book after book has been printed in favor of one theory or another.[4] I suspect some of issues revolve around a motivated desire to defend the criterion of multiple attestations. Until recently, New Testament scholarship resided in the hands of those with a sympathetic ear to the texts, assuming the texts existed outside of their social situation. Only recently has this begun to change so while sympathetic scholars still remain, more are willing to explore the New Testament texts alongside texts from the temporal location. Before we get to how we may finally hope to solve a solution, let us briefly examine the supposed problem.

There are several issues surrounding proposed solutions to the Synoptic Problem and there are as many solutions as there are views of the problem. The Patristic authors argued Matthew wrote first.[5] Nearly every modern scholar holds Mark as the first Gospel fully composed. While Thomas Brodie, as discussed above, holds to a proto-Luke, his theory still allows for a Markan priority. Some modern scholars, however, follow the Griesbach Theory in some form, suggesting Mark is not the first Gospel, but the last of the Synoptics.[6] This is the minority view. Returning to the idea of Markan Priority, the inclusion of added material in Matthew not found in Luke and material not in either Mark or Matthew, as well as various rearrangements of the Matthean material by Luke, has led to the creation of the Two-Source Theory—a theory best articulated in 1924 by B.H. Streeter. His theory positioned Mark as the first Gospel writer, but suggested he used a now lost document, known as "Q," which Matthew and Luke used in conjunction with Mark to write their own Gospels. Q, the biblical scholar's Thalia, gives us many answers to questions, forming an *argumentum ad ignorantiam*.

---

of Jesus, and other Jewish themes (such as Watts' *New Exodus*), but that is not the goal of this volume.

4. I have attempted to source every detail of my thought that may seem to arrive from the tome of Mark Goodacre's contribution to the issues of the Synoptic problem. If I have missed even one, I apologize, but Goodacre's work has become something of a foundation for my own, so much so, that I have adopted phrases and thoughts I know are found in his works. I, of course, claim all responsibility for any misrepresentation.

5. Black, and Beck, *Rethinking the Synoptic Problem*.

6. Johnson, *The Griesbach Hypothesis and Redaction Criticism*; Peabody, Cope, and McNicol, *One Gospel From Two*; Tuckett, *Revival Griesbach Hypothesis*.

Each point has its strengths. The Matthean Priority proponents have the combined weight of history and tradition on their side, leaving all others with a deficit of trust. The Two Source Theory allows for simplistic explanations of literary connections and allows for the theory of multiple attestations. The Q Hypothesis presents a richly heuristic possibility, allowing scholars to mine for possible "original" words, meanings, and so on. However, none of the theories as such are empirically valid as the supporting data for each theory is based upon either circular reasoning or presuppositions ignoring the temporal location of the Evangelists. While these theories have advanced us almost to a point of overexposure to the Synoptic problem, there is one theory, popular in the United Kingdom, which has found a minority voice in the United States. This theory occupies our thought on this matter, but before we discuss it further, we should endeavor to explore not only Q, but a newer theory as well.

Since Q is the prevailing hypothesis, we will examine it more closely with as few criticisms as possible.[7] According to the International Q Project, "(t)he evangelists Matthew and Luke used, and from their point of view improved, a very archaic written Greek Sayings Gospel. Hence it was no longer copied by Christian scribes, who preferred to copy Matthew and Luke, for which reason no manuscripts of this lost Gospel have survived."[8] No doubt the discovery of an actual sayings "Gospel," the Gospel of Thomas, has bolstered Q a great deal. In a recent work, however, Goodacre shows how the author of Thomas derives the sayings found therein from the canonical Gospels.[9] An Aramaic Q is a considerable proposal given Casey's thesis, however, no such document is needed to explain Mark's language. The preeminent Q scholar, John Kloppenborg, would seem to agree, calling the theory of an Aramaic Q "extraordinarily weak" and "legendary."[10]

Writing in 1965, Helmut Koester identified and developed Q as a collection of the sayings of Jesus transmitted through oral tradition.[11]

---

7. The intent of this work is not to debunk Q; that is just the natural side effect.

8. The Q Project maintains an extensive website which can be found here, http://www.cgu.edu/pages/8074.asp.

9. Goodacre, *Thomas and the Gospels*.

10. Kloppenborg, *Excavating Q*, 66–73, 80.

11. In the hands of form critics, Q became a tool for the *kerygma* of the early Christian community. Bultmann held to the idea of an Aramaic Q but allowed that

In of itself, this oral tradition is not problematic, but once it becomes theologically orientated, we are forced to consider what caused this. Theological reflection does not occur overnight, not without crisis. If Paul is the example of a proto-Christian in the aftermath of the death of Jesus, such a theological reflection as the Gospels is quite impossible. For Paul, the death of Jesus was not a crisis but the logical end to God's plan. Tradition allowed Koester to separate what Jesus said and did not say, such as the mini-apocalypse. Koester also had the availability of Thomas to build his thesis and thus it ignited the interest of scholars again, such as Kloppenborg who began to work on Q as if it was an independent work written by an actual author, and as such, was submitted to the rigors of redaction criticism. He was able to narrow down what scholars believed Q to represent to six speeches set well within the Jewish Wisdom tradition.[12] His redaction of the sayings into six essential speeches produced imitations in varying numbers and density by other well-known scholars such as Hans Dieter Betz, who dated the Sermon on the Mount to after the Jerusalem Council.[13] While these scholars have contributed much to the discussion, I suspect they have started with the wrong foundation.

There is, however, another theory that has now landed at the doorstep of New Testament scholars.[14] It is promoted almost single handedly by Delbert Burkett.[15] His first work in this series purports to show the Gospel writers would not need Mark as a basis and therefore write *independently* of one another. Citing the history of the discussion and his new data, or the data presently newly by him, he advocates doing away with the simpler theories. He holds to a proto-Mark differing from

the original document existed as the original presentation of the Gospel from Jesus. Not taking into consideration the later debates at the start of the twenty-first century, Bultmann, Barth, and others insisted that Q was the kerygmatic foundation, or law, for the earliest communities. However, it was simply not important, and one can understand why, considering that for several of the middle twentieth century critics, it was the traditions of the church that had become important. It was not until the time of the form critics had passed to the time of the redaction critics that Q once against became important. The brief interlude allowed Q scholars enough time to formulate a solid justification for the eradication of forests.

12. Kloppenborg, "The Sayings Gospel Q: Literary and Stratigraphic Problems," 1–66:48.

13. Betz, *The Sermon on the Mount*, 1, 3, 5 and 6.

14. This theory is a stand-in for other proto-document theories.

15. Burkett, Delbert. *Rethinking the Gospel Sources* and passim.

Markan priority, positing only there is still an unknown and impossible source Matthew, Luke, and Mark borrowed for their literary creations. Like Q and other variations, it depends on first suggesting such a source exists and then allowing each of the writers to have used it, acting more as compilers than authors. Due to the nature of the hypothesis, we will spend a short time covering the basics of how Burkett has arrived to this conclusion.

Burkett's premise is rather simple when it comes to Mark. "The Gospel of Mark did not serve as a source for either Matthew or Luke."[16] His theory is instead a rather more complicated version of Q. He supposes there was once a Proto-Mark subsequently revised by two editors, producing Proto-Mark A and Proto-Mark B. Matthew, Mark, and Luke made use of these sources to then edit their own work. This is how he accounts for the lack of material in various Gospels and the inclusion of shared material among, for lack of a better term, the copyists. If his theory is carried to the logical conclusions, the Evangelists are not authors or even compilers, but little more than mildly creative copyists who have committed scribal errors. For instance, instead of supposing Matthew, who gave a strong place to Peter in his Gospel, sought to correct Mark's omission of Peter's remorse (Mark 14.72; cf. Matthew 26.75) and it was accepted by Luke (Luke 22.62), he simply told near the same time as the original letter from Clement to Rome, he simply creates a hidden source.[17] His source, then, is free of any of the usual human conventions of memory, interpretation, contextualization and ideological creation but borders on a source recorded as an eyewitness free from theological reflection. If this is the case, then one would have to assume the close parallels between Josephus's socio-political history and the Gospels (as shown in this volume with regards to Mark) are abductions by Josephus.[18]

In the end, Burkett's solution is unscientific and does not deal with the evidence at hand. In regards to comprehensiveness, Burkett simply does not take into account any external data to the Gospels, such as

16. Burkett, *Rethinking*, 42.

17. Burkett, *Rethinking*, 8.

18. In earlier drafts and in conversation with others, I toyed with a section suggesting that Josephus borrowed from Mark, bringing in the criticism of Justus Tiberius. In the end, the only point to make here, upending any suggestion that Josephus borrowed his story of Vespasian from Mark's story of Jesus is that Vespasian would then become second to Jesus, something Josephus did not allow.

time, date, and location of composition as well as authorial intent. He dismisses modern experiments and data revealed by these experiments as based only on the idea Matthew and Luke were not original in their composition, but instead were attempting to somehow correct Mark.[19] It would seem for him the Greco-Roman practices as well as the Jewish practices of *Pesher* and rewritten Scripture are more trivial concerns. I cannot accurately test Burkett's theory because his sources are simply hypothetical. He can derive these sources because he believes they are in the Gospels. His theory is not economical but moves steadily in the opposite direct with not just one pre-existing source, but with several pre-existing sources that predate our canonical Gospels. These esoteric constructs are simply unnecessary. All of this must prohibit such a theory as being scientifically feasible. In his effort to create a more complex solution he has pulled Mark, Matthew, and Luke out of their historical context to place them squarely into ours denying them their own unique purpose, setting, and theology. However, a theory Burkett chides gives us the most reasonable, and I would argue the only reasonable, solution to the problem of the Synoptic Gospels.[20]

The theory I find most reasonable in light of mimetic criticism is the Farrer theory. Initially named after Austin Farrer due to an essay he wrote in 1955, this theory has subsequently expanded under the guidance of Michael Goulder, Austin's student, and Mark Goodacre, Goulder's student.[21] Farrer's premise was simple: dispense with Q and allow Matthew and Luke to stand out as unique literary creators. Allowing Luke to read Matthew as a redactor is not something unfamiliar

---

19. For a thorough going critique of the experiments performed by McIver and Carroll in relation to memory and the Synoptics, see Poirier, "Memory Written Sources, and the Synoptic Problem: A Response to Robert K. McIver and Marie Carroll," 315–22. Poirier, whom I count as a colleague now that we've dealt with the NLT issue well enough (yes, John, you were right), has written an excellent rebuttal on why such experiments, while helping with traditional oral and scribal cultures are too anachronistic to be used in the Synoptic Problem.

20. I owe much on the discussion on the scientific feasibility of analysis to Richard M. Ryckman (*Theories of Personality*). Criticism is analysis and as such should not be separated from scientific theories that tackle such processes. Part of the goal in this chapter is to show how FGG is a scientifically feasible theory.

21. Nineham, *Studies in the Gospels*, 55–88. To be sure, however, while Farrer was the first to properly address the theory, it was Morton S. Enslin, who in 1947, began to ponder if Matthew and Luke weren't reflected solely on Mark. (See Enslin, "The Artistry of Mark," 385–399.)

with those who hold to the Matthean Priority.[22] Farrer places the composition of Mark before 65 with Matthew and Luke coming between 75 and 90. There is not much to disagree with these dates in regards to Matthew and Luke, and for the most part, they should stand. He argues that given that there is no independent evidence of a Q document, but substantial evidence that would allow for Matthew and Luke to have read Mark, and Luke Matthew, then we can more easily base our arguments on proper sources. These sources aid the (re)author(ing) of a Gospel moving from Mark to Matthew to Luke. Using Luke, then, as the end result of this literary trend, Farrer inspects the house Mark built, Matthew added too, leaving Luke to do a complete remodel.

In Luke's proem, he suggests he is writing regarding the things already fulfilled among the Christian community.[23] Farrer notes artifacts found in the text, such as the death and resurrection of Jesus. Given Q does not have such things as a Gospel would entail, Luke could not have then used such an ancient constitution to build his Gospel; a source of sayings does not provide a structure of "good news." If the Jesus community was founded at the very least on the death of Jesus as Paul illuminates, then we could reasonably expect Q to include the passion narrative instead of simply documenting Jesus' teachings. Farrer suggests, "to postulate Q is to postulate the unevidenced and the unique." Why? Farrer is able to appreciate the remarkable development between the Gospels often missed by Q scholars. Indeed, Farrer gives credit where credit is due and suggests Matthew began a "pattern of symbolism" Luke developed. Farrer sees in Luke a more natural and happy method of storytelling destroying thematic barriers for the audience, unlike Matthew. Matthew, as commentators have long recognized, has a set of five sections. Luke does not dismiss this, but adopts Matthew's novel idea. Granted, Luke weights the sections differently, organizing the pieces of the puzzle to better fit his audience and even taking some poetic license.

Farrer ends his 1955 essay with an important statement that bears repeating. He writes, "The literary history of the Gospels will turn out to be a simpler matter than we had supposed. St. Matthew will be seen to be an amplified version of St. Mark, based on a decade of habitual preaching, and incorporating oral material, but presupposing no other

---

22. Dungan, Peabody, McNicol, *Beyond the Q Impasse*.

23. Luke's proem (Luke 1.1–4) is written in higher Greek than the rest of the Gospel, possibly imitating Sirach's prologue.

literary source beside St. Mark himself. St. Luke, in turn, will be found to presuppose St. Matthew and St. Mark, and St. John to presuppose the three others. The whole literary history of the canonical Gospel tradition will be found to be contained in the fourfold canon itself, except in so far as it lies in the Old Testament, the Pseudepigrapha, and the other New Testament writings." And then, "The surrender of the Q hypothesis will not only clarify the exposition of St. Luke, it will free the interpretation of St. Matthew from the contradiction into which it has fallen. For on the one hand the exposition of St. Matthew sees that Gospel as a living growth, and on the other as an artificial mosaic, and the two pictures cannot be reconciled."[24] From here, we'll turn to Mark Goodacre's work and examine the latest developments in the case against Q.

Mark Goodacre's 2002 work, appropriately named *The Case Against Q*, spells out in detail the Farrer Theory supported not only by himself, but E.P. Sanders and others.[25] Calling it a derivative hypothesis based on presuppositions and assumptions, Goodacre goes to work to make quick work of the supposedly ironclad hypothesis, which has somehow of its own accord, become a theory.[26] Goodacre notes Q is no longer seriously questioned, but more easily assumed than even the historical presence of Jesus! As a scholar and a teacher, this gives him pause to consider how this is limiting students of the New Testament who no longer question their forbearers' scholarly assumptions. Calling it a fragile consensus, Goodacre suggests Q is supported by the weakest of links, but supported against even the various disputes between the leading scholars. Citing the various ideas of Goulder (such as a lectionary as the basis of Matthew's work) used by others as reasons why many do not accept the Farrer Theory, Goodacre upbraids those who simply turn a blind eye to the possibility of such a theory as proposed by Farrer. Finding pause in the scholarly community for a new round of questioning of Q, Goodacre moves to assert his position, using the words of E.P. Sanders and Margaret Davies, "We think that Matthew used Mark and undefined other sources, while creating some of the sayings mate-

---

24. Farrer, "On Dispensing with Q," 55–88.

25. Goodacre, *The Case Against Q*. As much as Adam Winn has influenced this author in regards to the purpose of Mark's Gospel as well as the use of sources, Mark Goodacre has secured for me the permanent resistance against Q.

26. Goodacre, *Case*, 3–18, passim.

rial. Luke used Mark and Matthew, as well as other sources, and the author also created sayings material."[27] The reader of this volume will recognize the appeal of using the Farrer Theory along with mimetic criticism because it allows for Matthew and Luke to remain as creative authors in their own right with Mark as such a one as these from the very start. I hope the satisfaction Farrer gives to mimetic criticism is likewise returned.

Much of the rest of the work is dedicated to examining the reasons of Q's rhetoric and showing the errors of these assumptions. This volume has no need to restate fully those arguments, but only to summarize. First, the various minor and major agreements with Matthew and Luke against Mark suggests they were using a similar document Mark either did not have access to or simply decided not to use. The problem with this is the assumption Mark, Matthew, and Luke were not authors, but simply copyists who were reporting history. Mark reported history in a haphazard fashion. Matthew attempted to correct, but failing to do so, was rescued by Luke. This is hardly the only explanation. Instead, Mark wrote first followed by Matthew who used the same Greco-Roman style as Mark to set the story of Jesus to paper for his audience. Luke understood this and did much the same thing. These are not copyists then, but (re)authors who are (re)presenting the previous Gospel to their audience in such a way as to preserve and expand the text. We assume additions, omissions, and corrections were caused by ignorance or knowledge instead of creativity. What Farrer gives us is a group of creative and intelligent authors existing within their own time, writing as they intended, following not the dictates of modern copyright rules and plagiarism but imitation and invention. What Goodacre accomplishes is to cause us to pause and consider that Luke is not destroying Matthew and Matthew is not correcting Mark, but that Matthew is recreating Mark for his community, and Luke is doing the same for his.

Why have Q scholars and those who rely on multiple sources for the Gospels not seen the light so to speak? In my opinion, it is because for the most part they are still working as redaction critics instead of answering the challenge of Goodacre. He writes, "This is a weakness

---

27. Goodacre, *Case*, 13.n53. This undefined sources are hardly a Q document. Below, I will discuss Matthew's identification of Stoicicism in Mark. This, then, becomes an undefined source.

of the current scene, in which scholars have become so besotted with responding to the texts in isolation from one another that they have forgotten that the texts have, and have always been perceived as having, an intimate interrelationship."[28] And further, "While the newer, emerging discipline of narrative criticism pronounces itself firmly uninterested in the matter of sources, focusing purely on the individual text at hand, narrative criticism of Mark nevertheless aligns itself with redaction criticism of Mark in avoiding comparison with the other Synoptics."[29] Through his 2001 work, Goodacre calls for the use of narrative criticism, a call lost in the deafness around Q. Indeed, in several places in *Thought the Maze*, Goodacre points to the idea that narrative criticism refuses to show superiority in Luke's rearrangement, but only attempts to make narrative sense of the supposed problems. In *Case Against Q*, Goodacre devotes an entire chapter to showing how narrative criticism helps the critic to understand various questions in the issues of the Sermon on the Mount. This follows Farrer's suggestion that Luke arranged his teachings in such a way as to combine them. As stated above, mimetic criticism uses narrative criticism and as such, I believe answers Goodacre's challenge.

*Testing Mimetic Criticism and Farrer Theory—
Mark's First Reader, Matthew*

Dennis MacDonald writes, "Unfortunately, these flags seem to have been invisible to actual readers, even to a sophisticated Greek like the author of the Gospel of Luke. Mark was long on concealing, short on revealing."[30] He goes on to suggest that, "readers for two thousand years apparently have been blind to this important aspect of Mark's project." Goodacre disagrees, citing Matthew as Mark's first reader and

28. Goodacre, *Synoptic Problem*, 29.
29. Goodacre, *Maze*, 86.
30. MacDonald, *Homeric*, 6; He does attempt to correct this damning statement with a follow-up book in which he postulates that the author of Luke-Acts has followed Mark's lead (MacDonald, *Four Cases*, 14) but previously, he writes that the author of Luke-Acts is the only New Testament author "capable of imitating Homer." (MacDonald, *Four Cases*, 7.) MacDonald seems to base the change of attitude on a work published shorting after his Homeric Epics in which the author suggests that Luke-Acts is modeled after Virgil's Aeneid. (Bonz, *The Past as Legacy: Luke-Acts and Ancient Epic*.)

suggesting Matthew knew Mark's clues.[31] While not issued as a challenge to MacDonald, Goodacre nevertheless has an argument against him.[32] If Mark's mimesis is as vague as MacDonald suggests, then we should not expect to find a replication of it in Matthew. The idea of a plausible first reader is not one well received by some literary theorists. For instance, MacDonald roughly cites Stephen Hinds who suggests the reception of the clues left in the text and what they build for the audience "will always in the final analysis be unattainable."[33] Perhaps this is true for the great majority of allusion-filled texts, but in the case of Mark's volume, it is not. Indeed, we have the first and second generations of readers (Matthew and Luke respectively) who not only show us they knew what Mark was doing, but doing it themselves.

Anne M. O'Leary has bestowed upon our argument a better way to validate the Farrer Theory.[34] After building up a sizeable argument in favor of Greco-Roman writings styles, O'Leary easily shows Matthew adding his own *inventio* to and *imitatio* of Mark.[35] Her thesis is rather simple: Matthew took Mark as his source to imitate, (re)presenting the Gospel to his audience. Placing Matthew near 80 in a Jewish context, her census reveals Matthew as neighbors with Plutarch and other Greco-Roman writers, a community affording Matthew flexibility in constructing a biography more virtuous than factual.[36] This *bios* genre is applied to the Gospels and in succinct fashion O'Leary is able to demonstrate more clearly than her predecessors Matthew is employing both *imitatio* and *bios* to (re)build Mark's Gospel. O'Leary cites the use of parallelism, conflation, omission, addition, and positivization as literary tools Matthew used to to bring Mark into a more traditional Jewish context. The allowance here, she notes, is because Mark is writing with a

---

31. Goodacre, *Maze*, 89.

32. Goodacre has taken to task those who do not allow for Matthew to serve as a guide in interpreting Mark. See Goodacre, "Mark, Elijah, the Baptist and Matthew: The Success of the First Intertextual Reading of Mark," 73–84.

33. Hinds, *Allusion and Intertext: Dynamics of Appropriation in Roman Poetry*, 46; MacDonald cites this in his allowance that we do not have a recorded reception from Mark's first readers. MacDonald, *Homeric*, 7.

34. It is no small hobby of mine to trace the students and their teachers, so I would be remiss to note that O'Leary was a student of Thomas L. Brodie.

35. O'Leary, *Matthew's Judaization of Mark*.

36. O'Leary, *Judaization*, 92–3.

Roman provenance while Matthew is writing to a more Jewish audience situated near Palestine.[37]

O'Leary sees several Matthean Judaizations of Mark. First, as is often noted, Matthew has taken the structure of Mark and made it into a rather unique construction based on the key numerals of the Torah, with this latter part recognized easily enough. She also sees Matthew has "Deuteronomized" Mark with the Temple tax issue and the "brotherly correction." Other areas include the parables and the move to a more appreciation of classes in the social situation. She ends her work by suggesting Matthew's social situation involved an impetus to write regarding the continuity between the followers of Jesus and the more mainline religion of the Jews.[38] Jesus is the new Moses.[39] We can also note Mark contains a close theme to Isaiah's new exodus, something better detailed by Rikki E. Watts.[40] Matthew, then, even in the barest of examinations, has moved (Mark's) Jesus' assumption of the role of Elijah/Elisha to allowing a more prevalent assumption of Moses' role by Jesus. All of this is well within Jewish religious structure with no need to feel a theological crisis from a dying influence of Hellenistic poetry. Now, let us add our own contribution to Matthew's mimetic (re)presentation of Mark in order to show Matthew, Mark's first reader, knew and appreciated Mark's literary genius and attempted to rival it in his own way.

Before we stray too far from O'Leary, let us return for a moment to her suggestion of a more positive presentation of Jesus by Matthew than what we find in Mark. Specifically, Mark's Jesus experiences the range of human emotions while Matthew's Jesus has become rather stoic.[41] The Jesus of Matthew is logical and does not suffer from the frailty of human emotions. As noted above, both Mark and Lucan have recognizable Stoic elements, given Stoicism was part of the cognitive environment. Matthew seizes upon the Stoicism in Mark to develop Jesus in a more divinely Christological fashion. Not only does a more Stoic view of Jesus give us

---

37. O'Leary, *Judaization*, 104–5. See also Stark, *Social History of the Matthean Community*.

38. O'Leary, *Judaization*, 169–70.

39. O'Leary, *Judaization*, 171.

40. Watts,.*Isaiah's New Exodus in Mark*.

41. O'Leary, *Judaization*, 114–5. Matthew as removed Jesus' emotional responses and ignorance (Mark 1.17, 45; 3.21; 5.9; 6.5, 38, 48; 7.24; 8.12, 23; 9.16, 21, 33; 11.13; 14.14; cf. Matthew 1.4; 3.5; 6.6; 8.12; 10.14, 21; 14.33).

license to suggest Matthew found cause to omit some of Mark's accounts of the emotional Jesus, but it should also give us cause to suggest Jesus is portrayed as teacher in Matthew's Gospel is due in part to the level of Stoic influence by the author.[42] Paul's Jesus was one of a single purpose, namely, to die. Paul does not teach the ethics Jesus taught but relies heavily on Deuteronomy to provide a moral law for the foundation of the new sect of Judaism. It is not difficult to observe the influence of Deuteronomy and Stoicism in several of Jesus' teachings in Matthew, especially the Sermon on the Mount, something Stanley Stowers has pointed out.[43] The positivism O'Leary suggests is answered easily by a more focused Stoicism giving rise to the distinctive Matthean teachings of Jesus.[44]

Matthew has decided, for his Jewish audience, to reinforce the fact of Jesus' insistence on the continuity with the Torah. Mark 7 details several conservations between Jesus and others essentially saying the same thing, while Matthew overhears this conversation, he has decided to put the abolishment of the Law into the eschatological realm. In Matthew 5.17–18, Matthew's Jesus says the Law will only be fulfilled when heaven and earth pass away. Mark does not record any scene like this except where he describes the end of the age brought about by the destruction of the Temple (13.31). Matthew has the same line in nearly the same place in his discourse, but I would contend Matthew 5.17–18 not only evolves from Mark 13.31, but the latter is rewritten to present Jesus as the new Moses. Contrary to the words of Moses, Jesus' words will not pass away. This allows for the extension of Mark's eschatological concept to include the new authority given to Jesus as found in Matthew 28.19–20. Further, it requires Matthew to take the onus off the destruction of the Temple (something Luke did as well by moving this scene further away from the Passion than Matthew's placement) and place it upon the cross, utilizing Mark's ripping of the veil (see above) as a key factor in this. As we have previously proposed, a

---

42. A letter dated to near the time of Mark's composition suggests that Jesus was known as a Stoic in Syria. (See Theissen and Merz, *Historical Jesus*, 76–9.)

43. Rasimus, Engberg-Pedersen, and Dunderberg, *Stoicism in Early Christianity*.

44. Farrer, in his essay noted above, has already presented us with the validation of Matthew's use of Deuteronomy to add to Mark, so much so that we do not intend to address it further in this volume. Stoicism, something Matthew extends from Mark, also accounts (in part) the genealogy of Jesus. See Van Kooten, "Philosophical Criticism of Genealogical Claims and Stoic Depoliticization of Politics: Greco-Roman Strategies in Paul's Allegorical Interpretation of Hagar and Sarah."

part of Mark's theological goal is the need for the Gentile mission, yet Matthew is writing for the need of the continuity with Judaism. This is why he pushes the passing away of the heavens and the earth back from the destruction of the Temple to the crucifixion of Jesus.[45] This need for the authority of Jesus and the continuity with Israel gives us the theological sources for Matthew's expansion of the hour of Jesus' death to include dead-raising earthquakes and why writing the Resurrection's aftermath is so important to Matthew.

A few more observations are important. One such is Matthew's rehabilitation of Peter and immediate punishment of Judas. Unlike in Mark where Judas simply fades from history, Matthew suggests Judas, feeling remorse, goes and hangs himself. Mark suggests Peter merely weeps while Matthew (and Luke) shows Peter weeping bitterly. As discussed above, Simon b. Giora had his own Judas who was hanged, as was Matthew's Judas. In regards to Peter, Matthew is rehabilitating Peter to fulfill a special role—something detected in Jesus' anointing of Peter as Prime Minister in Matthew 16, a scene not present in Mark but extracted from Isaiah 22.15–20.[46] Peter becomes the spokesperson for the group as well as an imitator of Jesus when he attempts to walk on water. Indeed, it seems the curia around Jesus makes as dramatic a character realignment as Jesus himself. Another Matthean mimetic use of Mark is the creation of the Lord's Prayer, explained simply with *inventio* and the reading of Mark's Gospel. Matthew takes the scene in the Garden of Gethsemane (Mark 14.35–41) as his influence and from out of the address to God, prayer against testing, the allowance for God's will instead of our own, the delivering to/from evil, and the use of sinners he shapes the prayer. Luke easily takes Matthew 6.15 for his 11.4.

For Matthew, the impetus of crisis had passed, or rather, the Markan imperial crisis. Matthew, on the other hand, felt a different crisis—one of community. He is seeking continuity with the religion of the Jews and goes to great lengths to suggest Jesus is the new Moses and a true son of David, a concept experiencing quick evolution in the time between Mark and Matthew. This continuity becomes important in a

---

45 For more on the passion interpreted as the end of the age, see Allison. *End of the Ages Has Come.*

46 See Goodacre, "The Rock on Rocky Ground: Matthew, Mark and Peter as 'Skandalon,'" 61–73. Michael P. Barber will argue in an upcoming essay ("Jesus as the Davidic Temple-Builder and Peter's Priestly Role in Matthew 16:16–19,") Peter's role is also understood as a priest. A special thanks to Dr. Barber for an advanced read of the article.

post-70 world with the rise of two Judaisms. This is where the inclusion of the ἐκκλησίαν in Matthew is generated. The new Christian community is well within the old Jewish community and is given legitimacy because it is following in a line reaching back to David, to Moses, and even hollowed Abraham. Further, Peter is said to have explicit charge over the Jesus community, however one may need to interpret that. Whereas Mark uses the title "son of David" in a negative sense, Matthew uses it in the positive sense. The crisis for Matthew is not the rise of dual messiahs and the destruction of the Temple and the intervening social upheaval. That has already passed. Instead, the crisis is the peace after the closing days of the Revolt as well as the institution of the Flavian dynasty, spurred in part by Mark's Gospel, which pushed the Christian community to begin severing ties with Judaism, not out of aggressive attitudes, but because of the exposed differences in theology. Matthew aims to strengthen the continuity between Christianity and the Judaism of Abraham, Moses, and David. As such, Matthew is not only imitating Mark, but also adding *inventio* to solve his own theological crisis.

This lack of imperial crisis is not to say Matthew was friendly with Rome.[47] Indeed, as Warren Carter has shown, Matthew's Gospel still contains an anti-imperialistic edge to it. He regards Matthew as writing to sustain "an alternative community of disciples of Jesus in anticipation of the coming triumph of God's Empire over all things, including the destruction of Rome's empire."[48] This imperial challenge still presents us Vespasian as pretender, as Mark does, but is focused on the community rather than securing Jesus as the Messiah. This power

---

47. The purpose of this section in this volume is not the argument of Matthew, but serves only to show that Matthew recognized Mark's ideology and used it in somewhat the same manner. As I stated above, the impetus was not so much the messianic claims, as it was Rome's new community. Mark secured Jesus as the messiah against Vespasian and Simon b. Giora, leaving Matthew the assurance of the community. Carter draws this point out in his work in multiple places, showing that the community in Matthew is one which is not just waiting for the end of the world, but one which is founded on a constitution with certain duties (4.17, 18–22; 10.7–8). This community has Jesus at the center and is a direct confrontation to Roman communal ideology as well as to the slight against them that they were not in continuity with Judaism. In a future volume, it may be necessary to explore further a mimetic synopsis of the Gospels, as it moved from Mark to Matthew to Luke, but for now, we must understand that the crisis was different for Matthew than it was for Mark; however, this did not preclude Matthew from using Mark in the same way. Indeed, there are the words of Jesus in Matthew 23.35 bearing a striking resemblance to *B.J.* 4.335–45.

48. Carter, *Matthew*, 1.

dynamic of the community is felt in such places as Matthew 20.25–27, a place where Jesus challenges the power structure of Rome. Just as Mark has placed himself in Rome, Matthew has placed himself in the vicinity of Syria. Antioch, according to Josephus, ranked as the third wealthiest city in the Empire (*B.J.* 3.29). This city on a hill protected the Roman citizens often times at the expense of the Jewish inhabitants. Carter details the history of the establishment of temples, one containing a statue of Vespasian with the honor given to the destruction of Judaea.[49] Against Parthia, the city served as a frontline and became the administrative capitol of the area. No doubt, the community of those seeking Roman favor challenged the community that did it. With the destruction of Judaea and the reconstruction of Rome at the expense of the defeated people, Matthew found a palatable version of theological events in Mark's Gospel and used it as a foundation.

Vespasian, who had by the time of Matthew's writing had expired, nevertheless haunts the Gospel. The thunderous legacy of his sons still flourished and tormented the Christian community, as evidenced by the persecution enacted by Domitian.[50] Vespasian and the notion of *Pax Romana* are decried by Jesus in 10.12–34. Here, Jesus is sending out his twelve disciples to wage war and to conquer Judaea. It is no usual war, however, as it is accompanied by a mimetic reversal. The sick are cured, the dead are raised, and the demons are driven out. Jesus only asks the populace to welcome his twelve disciples. If Judaea refused them, they are to turn and leave the place without bestowing their peace upon it.[51] Here is another mimetic expansion as Jesus gives warning about standing before kings (Matt 10.17–20) something Matthews recreates from Mark 13.[52] At the end of the instructions, he speaks about his un-peaceful mission, the exact opposite of the proceeding

---

49. Carter, Matthew, 39–40.

50. Or, at least according to the fourth century Christian historian Eusebius. although no real record of the persecutions has been found, it is enough that we have the Gospel of Matthew and the Book of Revelation to suggest that the Jewish-Christian community felt persecuted without making judgments either on the historicity or the psychological aspects of their claims.

51. Matthew is asking his audience to contemplate the story of Elijah and Elisha who were rejected by various kings and others as prophets. Luke picks up this theme in 4.24–7 (cf. 1 Kings 17.9 and 2 Kings 5.1).

52. I would contend that Matthew 10 can easily be traced as a whole to various parts of Mark.

instructions about giving peace. This is a challenge to *Pax Romana*, a false notion. Peace is not the opposite of war; Roman peace does not startle the cliché. Further, Vespasian would go on to build the Temple of Peace in Rome—a temple housing the loot taken from the Jerusalem Temple. This section of chapter ten surrounded by instructions for giving and restoring peace, is set against the proclaimed *Pax Romana*, peace Vespasian and his progeny supposedly brought.

Carter suggests a second Vespasian intrusion as well, this one involving a tax. It comes from Matthew 17.24–27. His thesis is paying the tax, one leveled by Vespasian against the defeated Jews to rebuild pagan buildings in Rome, is a subversive argument by Matthew to challenge the usual dichotomy between God and Caesar; there is no dichotomy for Matthew; God is ultimately sovereign. We find a similar scene in Mark 12.14–17, albeit with a different interpretation and ultimate outcome. For Mark, there is a dichotomy, but for Matthew, the separation between the kingdom of Caesar and the kingdom of God is overcome. Indeed, we might call attention that here Simon is named simply Simon, not Simon Peter or some variation as is common (although Matthew's narrator makes sure to inform his reader this is indeed Simon Peter), perhaps a throwback to Mark's Simon b. Giora as after all, Jesus had just renamed Simon Peter. Carter argues the fish is the key to understanding the rebellious nature of the story. For him, he sees connections with Martial and Juvenal wherein fish are used in parodies against Domitian.[53]

To sum, Matthew may use undefined sources to add additional material to Mark. As O'Leary showed, Mark is the subject of a more traditional approach to imitation, wherein the basic story is kept but the new author adds some of his own unique invention. This Judaization, as she calls it, is met by other efforts to place more sectarianism into Mark's Gospel. While Mark retains Jewish elements but generally in the form of subtle cultic cues and a reluctant nationalism, Matthew breathes a distinctively seminal rabbinical air not in Mark's atmosphere. In regards to the teachings of Jesus, Matthew provides ethical teachings via the Stoicism latent in Mark's Gospel without diverging too far from Judaism by use of Deuteronomy. Further, his crisis is shown as Jesus builds a community. Mark's loose ends (Judas and the Temple of Peace) are tied up neatly in Matthew. Matthew was Mark's first reader

---

53. For the discussion in this paragraph, see Carter, *Matthew*, chapter 8.

and knew full well the goal of Mark. Without doubt, we can dispense with both Q and Homer.

Before we move on to the final part of this chapter, I want to examine the Farrer Theory as a scientific model. The reason I am somewhat insistent upon using a scientific evaluation is we are not simply studying ancient texts when we are studying the Synoptic Gospels. Nor are we simply studying theology. We are indeed deciphering idiographic personal experiences, both internal (as in the case of the Historical Jesus) and external (as in the case of the author *and* the community). The perception, reception, and transmission of memory, tradition, and texts in cultures are scientifically measurable. We are also not free to simply suggest a hypothesis, a scientific term, and suppose it will become, on its own fruition and without any substantial testing whatsoever, a theory. We must establish some sort of criteria for suggesting new theories when we are engaging texts we posit as having ideological intents and making use of techniques many deem merely the license of the poet. These techniques, such as intertextuality and mimesis, are more than literary tools to tell a good story, but are deeply concerned with psychological aspects. It is not merely the psychology of the reader, but of the author as well, especially in the case of those writing in crisis. Thus, a scientific method of disposing theories safely grounds us but also allows us to fashion appropriate hypotheses. Once tested these hypotheses become theories if not laws.

Farrer's Theory is a rather sound one, and much more sound than any one currently present. First, Farrer's Theory is comprehensive. As it is based on narrative criticism, he can explain the development of both Matthew and Luke (and in my opinion, John as well). While Goulder's use of the lectionary hypothesis is testable only in part, he insists there is no great need for undefined sources (per E.P. Sanders) to have developed the remaining Gospels. Farrer requires us to accumulate more data, instead of, as with Q, requiring firm facts otherwise unprovable.[54] I would argue Farrer's Theory takes into account the personality of Matthew and Luke, a personality developed by their experiences and social situation, as much as Mark is. Further, it requires us to take into account the most trivial changes exhibited by Matthew and Luke upon Mark's work asking for an interpretation, not as the clue to some hidden document but as a clue to the authors themselves.

54. For such testing, see: Goodacre, *Goulder and the Gospels*.

We can test Farrer's Theory. As we have demonstrated against Hinds and MacDonald, Matthew is Mark's first reader, an item giving us a sound starting point to experiment. Farrer discussed at great length Luke's expansion of Matthew. O'Leary has discussed Matthew's process of making Mark more Jewish. Every road leads to Mark and no one needs to ask Q for directions. Not only this, but as demonstrated above, it is now possible through understanding the role of *imitatio* and *inventio* that we can test Farrer's Theory with precision. While doubters of such a process remain, we can show, for example as with the Lord's Prayer, Matthew pulled from Mark much the same way Mark pulled from the Septuagint, with bits and pieces. Luke in turn organized his stories to fit a better pattern for his goal. This testing is only possible because we have the data to support it. If we examine Matthew and Luke apart from Mark and as individuals, they become authors.

The Farrer Theory is parsimonious because it allows for undefined sources, but not does require historical documents.[55] It is economical because all we need to give allowance for Matthew and Luke is an understanding of Greco-Roman literary rhetoric. To understand Mark, we need a little more data and better methods. The same methods we use to understand Mark (looking for social situation, etc. . .) can then find use when we examine Matthew and Luke as expansions of Mark's work. This leads us to the heuristic value of Farrer's Theory. Once we understand Matthew and Luke are authors in their own right, instead of simply digging through their work looking for clues to a nonexistent document, we can relaunch the last century of Synoptic Gospel studies not as attempting to identify Q, but in attempting to identify the psychology of the expansions. These are new concepts, and if applied appropriately, will help us understand and better appreciate the Synoptic Gospels, not merely as religious literature, but as literary masterpieces in their own rights standing in close connection to the epics of Rome. Farrer's Theory, as modified by Goulder, by Sanders, and now by Goodacre is the perfect scientific answer to the Synoptic Problem. Now, let us turn to Part II of this chapter, in an attempt to argue in favor of allowing for the historical figure of Jesus, even in light of mimetic criticisms.

---

55. For serious study of these undefined sources, the critic should turn to the Jewish-Christian Gospels, of which we only have fragments. (See Theissen and Merz, *Historical Jesus*, 51–4.)

Mimetic Criticism and the Gospel of Mark

Catching the Historical Jesus

I do not intend to argue for Jesus as the Son of the Only True God, the second person of the Trinity, or any such other thing developed after serious theological reflection over the last two thousand years.[56] However, given many will view this work as license to doubt the historical presence of Jesus, and some have even gone so far as to use mathematical formulas based on subjective data to deny the historical person of Jesus, I feel it is necessary to spend a small amount of time identifying how mimetic criticism may lead us to a better Historical Jesus.[57] To do this, we will examine several criteria and propose a new one. Then we will examine whether Jesus is a literary vehicle or historical figure. Finally, we will examine Mark 1.1 as either subjective or objective—and why this impacts understanding the *reliability* of Mark's work.

Historically, scholars and theologians who examine the Historical Jesus through the historical critical method have established a set of criteria meant to allow for the plausibility of historical events of the Gospels.[58] The primary set includes the criteria of coherence, discontinuity, embarrassment, dissimilarity, and multiple attestations. A new work has leveled some serious charges at these criteria, moving the discussion to a better place.[59] Gerd Theissen and Dagmar Winter have proposed the criterion of plausibility as a replacement for the criterion of dissimilarity, so that events in the Gospel(s) are examined for their historical situation in light of their plausibility regarding the time and location they claim.[60] There is another criteria I would like to introduce: the criterion of apologia. It is well within line with our previous focus

---

56. Although, I am not opposed to that in that Christian theology is sometimes different from historical events.

57. I fear drawing a connection to closely to Bruno Bauer who, in his 1841–2 work, declared that history was produced in the Gospels. My divergence produces a wide gulf. History is not produced, but the future *affected* by, following Williams, changing the present's perception of the past, something not uncommon in Mark's social situation.

58. Theissen and Merz (*Historical Jesus*, 91) present the battle between the Historical Jesus and the Mythological Jesus in Hegelian terms. The authors note that mythicists ("outside theological skepticism") seek to rob Christianity of its legitimacy while theologians seek to make it legitimate.

59. Keith and Le Donne, *Jesus, Criteria, and the Demise of Authenticity*.

60. Theissen and Winter, *The Quest for the Plausible Jesus*.

on thesis, antithesis, and synthesis and is based on the psychological crisis that caused the impetus of writing.

As given above, the crisis for Mark is one where the messiahship of Jesus, a relational term still yet undefined, was challenged. It is only through the challenge to a conquering messiah who brought world peace (Vespasian) and a messiah who promised a free Judaea in the mold of King David (Simon) that the early community of Jesus followers found their theology coalescing around what messiah meant. This is not uncommon and occurs not just in the Christian Tradition but in other religious and political climates as well. To reinvent a person to fit the present needs of a community is not uncommon today when such a reinvention is logically impossible given the vast resources of recording actual history. For example, David Barton has written a book showing Thomas Jefferson as a deeply pious Christian something nearly every critical historian and most school children know is a complete falsehood.[61] Another recent example is the considerable makeover given to Ronald Reagan, the fortieth president of the United States. Modern Republican Party proponents have created a Ronald Reagan who was anti-tax, anti-budget deficit, pro-millionaire, anti-gay rights and abortion rights, among other newly minted Republican Party talking points, all the while ignoring the facts as preserved not just in the historical record of Congress and the White House, but so too in popular media where we have the actual words of Reagan recorded showing him less the miracle worker many claim him as. The crisis precipitating the rise of the Christian Thomas Jefferson and the Conservative Ronald Reagan is one much less of political expedience than it is of the disease of nostalgia and the need to justify the actions of a few by a perceived image of the past. Myth-making is more than a hobby; it is as sustaining for the community as air is for the human body.

The criterion of apologia, then, acknowledges the critical impetus as one causing the Jesus of Paul who did nothing more than die on the cross and experience some form of resurrection to become in Mark's Gospel the essential Messiah of Israel.[62] Paul mentions nothing personal about

61. Barton, *The Jefferson Lies*.

62. Examining Paul's Jesus by the Gospel's Jesus produces the crisis. Paul's Jesus is the pre-existent Son of God who will return. This could give Paul the impetus not to record his teachings or miracles, only to focus on the victory achieved by his death. The Synoptics, then, become the new Torah. They, sensing that Paul was wrong about the return of Jesus in physical form to establish a new kingdom, begin to feel the impact of

Jesus except he was a Jew, he died by the hands of the Romans, was resurrected, and he had a final meal with his closest followers along with the fact Jesus had a brother. How then could a theological reflecting community of Jesus followers have created such a figure as Jesus the Christ? Through the push to define who Jesus was against whom Vespasian and Simon claimed to be, the Christology of Jesus began to include a finalized belief of the messiah. The crisis, then, forced them to mythologize Jesus, but not completely. One cannot have a crisis if one does not have an impetus. The Jesus community was existent before the Jewish Revolt, as we know from Paul's letters, but as we also know, longed for the return of Jesus, something that did not happen. The question of who Jesus was and what messiah meant was not truly asked until the crises developed by the Jewish Revolt and its aftermath. We, in any case, can detect Paul's inconsistent theological constructs of Jesus, moving from human to divine, from equal to subordinate. His only crisis was suggesting Jesus was the one who died in the Jewish tradition of prophets. Mark's community faced the question of the identity of the Jewish messiah. The peace some of them promised found fulfillment only in Vespasian, who had brought peace (a peace Matthew sees as transparent) and, unlike the dead Jesus, built a new visible community under heaven.

The Jesus Mark started with was a Jesus who had already suffered through theological reflection. As demonstrated above, we must avoid the temptation to match every line or episode in Mark's Gospel to either the Jewish Scriptures or the Jewish Revolt. Parallelomania is as debilitating as nostalgia. Mimetic criticism cannot even account for all miracles as demonstrated with the exorcism in Mark 9.17–27, an exorcism too real for both Matthew and Luke who turned it into a more divine event. Does this mean we are to believe Jesus was a miracle worker able to cast out demons, or rather, to heal those with seizures? Hardly, but we do not yet fully understand how these healing rituals were employed and accepted by the audiences as accomplishing something tangible. This cognitive science of religion is still new, and is too broad to discuss in so short a space, but it is important to understand how rituals were used

---

the crisis. They respond, as we have seen, by drafting the story of Jesus against Rome, setting his death in a different light, and proclaiming the new kingdom, something Paul looked forward too, as already in existence. This new kingdom, then, needed the teachings of Jesus and a new law, something Paul did not need because Jesus would return with the kingdom.

and accepted as effective in ancient cultures.[63] If such a tradition existed about Jesus, or came to exist about Jewish before Mark wrote, it would have easily served as the foundation for the audience to believe in other exorcism accounts. However, even then, we need not worry if they did or not, as in all except one case, exorcisms can be best understood in a political light. The only acceptable conclusion is to consider that a tradition of Jesus as exorcist existed before Mark's writing that allowed the author to use it and cast the story around the tradition. If Mark had invented a Jesus *ex nihilo*, his community—nor Matthew, Luke, and John—would not have accepted the work.

Apologia also allows us to understand the why of Mark's story. His community was in danger due to the ideological currents battering their coracle. His Jesus was disappearing into history with no hope of return. We must understand Mark's purpose is defense, then, and to defend something, you must have some realistic notion about what you are defending. As demonstrated above, Mark could very well have made himself known in his work beyond that of narrator and lived as a young man around Jesus and an older man during the Jewish Revolt. However, even if we deny what the author says about himself and his place in the story of Jesus, we cannot deny Mark was in a community that believed in a historical Jesus. We know this by simple deduction, not counting the work of this volume. A spiritual Jesus would not have faced such a severe crisis as presented by Rome. Mark's Jesus, attested to by biographical footnotes, is one who operated in the early first century. Indeed, a spiritual Jesus as messiah requires not only a well-defined persona of Jesus, but also a well-defined concept of the messiah including the atoning work and other theological facets, something we do not receive from Paul. It has a genesis in Mark and continues in Matthew, Luke, and finally, John. What we find is this:

---

63. Sax, Quack, and Weinhold, *The Problem of Ritual Efficacy*. The question of ritual efficacy is one not easily answered. I do not suggest that Jesus had extranatural powers, but if he was a Rabbi or even a mystic, he would know certain rituals meant to suggest healing. After all, the institution of a common meal lasting until the return of Jesus is a ritual, as is baptism. Given the supposed healing effects of baptism, both inwardly and outwardly, a healing ritual is not completely unbelievable. Whether it worked in any real sense is another matter, only what the cognitive provocation such rituals issues. In *Ritual Efficacy*, Theissen tackles the issue of symbolic healing in early Christianity by examining how pre-modern cultures today act as anthropological museums to allow investigations into such concerns. Hardly considered charlatans, these ritualistic physicians offer something difficult to inject with modern science, faith.

Mimetic Criticism and the Gospel of Mark

Q is more plausible than the mythicist Jesus.[64] To defend something that needs no defending, such as a spiritual Jesus, makes the Gospels an exercise in futility, something a mimetic reading easily refutes. Plausibility helps us to examine the historical possibility of events in the Gospel(s) happening within their own purported time frame; apologia allows us to examine the critical impetus of the Gospels and even why some events simply do not align with the historical records.

So, was Jesus a mere literary vehicle to challenge Rome, as part of Jewish agitprop?[65] Where a challenge does not exist, one should not so easily supposed to challenge Rome. To create a literary response to a nonexistent challenge would be pure madness. Lucan had a challenge presented to him, that of the failure of the line of Caesar and the Empire to make a better world. He gave a response. Mark had a challenge as well, that of Jesus as merely another dead messiah. He gave a response as well. The Gospel, then, is the literary vehicle to challenge Rome, not Jesus. Jesus becomes transformed in Mark's Gospel through redefinition and is thus presented as the one who challenges Rome. To view Jesus as a mere literary vehicle, or otherwise a myth, is not to have a good grasp of either facts or methods; however, to question the historicity of the actions of the Jesus of the Gospels is to rest well within reality of literary and historical criticism.

If we ask ourselves what is real about the *Gospel of Mark*, we are missing the nonsensical nature of the question and our own arrogance.

---

64. Chapter four in Theissen and Merz's book on the Historical Jesus puts to rest the arguments of mythicists.

65. It is possible, rather probable, that Jesus viewed himself in some light as a prophet. This self-contextualization is not uncommon as we have seen with the brigands. To suggest Jesus exists only in the literary imagination is to not understand either literary or imagination. My hypothesis is along the lines of Sanders (*Historical Figure*, 85–90). Jesus, believing himself a prophet, preached a Deuteronomistic message. If he considered himself a prophet, he knew that his ultimate validation was martyrdom. Also, as a prophet, Jesus was expected to act a certain way. Perhaps he did act the part of Moses or Elijah/Elisha. As with others of the time, he was a leveler and foresaw the destruction of the Temple. Of course, this foreknowledge is nothing more than a calculation or a proclamation calling for the destruction of the Temple. He practiced rituals and most likely could perform healing ceremonies. Jesus was surrounded by a group of followers that listened to his message and followed him around Judaea. A new wave of violence began in 26 CE. Jesus, preaching during this time, was mistaken as a brigand. His death was taken as a sign to his followers that he was a prophet. (I refrain from discussing the Resurrection until Sunday.) We cannot expect the Jesus who exists as part of history to act contrary to observable facts and evidences.

There are no real/unreal aspects to Mark's story, but a new reality formed by experience, both external in the lives of Mark's audience and internally with the interaction between the audience and the author. My overarching thesis in this volume is Mark's transformation of reality by effecting the present. This is clearly possible, as we have seen in Lucan and his history. There are no coincidences, only connections, so to have a suicidal poet die just literary minutes away from a civil war, the topic of his anti-temporal work, testifies to the profound impact of his work. Mark is able to accomplish the same miracle. With rampant apostasy, a war-torn Judea, and a deep depression caused by the destruction of the Temple, absolute Roman victory, and no sign of the return of Jesus, challenging the community, Mark begins to craft a document that will change the face of Christianity, and with it, the world. This is not impossible, as esoteric as it sounds. R. Bartsch suggests the concepts of events and individuals are used to understand specific situations, after those ideas are formed. At this junction, our ontology comes into play, something changed through Mark's language; the contexualization and conceptualization of history is always formed in the present. Mark embeds his history into the minds of his audience in such a way as to create new concepts of reality.[66] While aspects of historical fact are interpreted through theological reflection and human memory, there is a simulation taking place.[67] This simulation is an act with some basis in reality, but it is the reality of the dynamic social situation of the author and audience. It is a semiotic praxis cultural critics understand and recognize.[68]

---

66. See Bartsch, *Generating Polysemy*, 54–6.

67. There is no doubt that the Jesus of early Christian memory and tradition existed, contrary to those who wish to express doubt as a matter of stubborn pride. However, if doubt does remain, especially with those who cannot grasp that all language is figurative, that memory adds to history, and that all history is narrative interpreted through the lens of the both the narrator and the audience, then we should note that if Mark was indeed an embarrassment to the early Church, as indicated by our discussion regarding Papias above, then we understand why Matthew and Luke developed their Gospels according to more of a tangible tradition. Indeed, many of the parables as well as other embedded archeological evidence point to a Jesus and a community found in the first half of first century Palestine. We also can look at such embedded literary archeology as found in Luke 19.12–26, a passage that without a doubt refers to Herod Archelaus. What is Mark doing? Mark is simply doing what other first century writers, and indeed, what we all do, is to contextualize the present day via our own experiences.

68. Baudrillard, *Simulacra and Simulation*.

Mimetic Criticism and the Gospel of Mark

The entirety of Mark's story is not mimetic and while we should not develop a Jesus-of-the-gaps view, we can seek better to understand Mark's overarching premise as one allowing for use of previous traditions, even if we are cautious in seeking their identification. The translation of Mark 1.1 is often disputed. It is either objective or subjective; either it is the good news about Jesus or it is Jesus as the good news. It is, in my estimation, it is best to understand that 1.1 contains both ideas. For Mark, the victory of God is Jesus, and as such, news about Jesus will bring victory. When Mark speaks about Gadara/Gerasa, Mark is challenging Roman destruction by suggesting Jesus can reverse the curse through the acceptance of the Gospel. The gospel is Jesus and is about Jesus and it is the response to Rome. We need not question the living dynamic Mark is attempting to present throughout his historical-present tinged work, or the way he rather abruptly concludes. Finding in Lucan a suitable method of conclusion, Mark also finds a suitable method of pushing the audience to engage Jesus, to discover if he really is in Galilee—to continue in the faith.

What of genre? I am nearly averse to placing Mark's Gospel into an ancient genre. Once we do, we limit the creativity of Mark as an author and suggest he follow the rules others have, especially if we follow Hermann Gunkel over our friend Bakhtin. Perhaps Mark was a rather unique writer who employed various literary rules with a certain fluidity. Why then should we suppose he had a set genre? He clearly followed the rules of Lucan for the Roman Epic, but to suggest he was writing an Epic is just a bit of a stretch, although I have to admit I toyed with this idea for a long time. Perhaps O'Leary is correct when she reads the Gospels next to Plutarch's *bios*. It is neither history, nor poetry, but involves many of the elements of each. It is not myth, unless we compare it to Virgil's myth-making about the beginning of Rome. Instead, before we waste any more ink on suggesting a novelistic genre for Mark in the manner of *Tobit*, let us become a little more green and instead acknowledge that placing Mark in a genre will limit our ability to read him according to the rules he used, instead of the rules we *think* he used. Removing the quest for genre allows us to consider the more heuristic value allowing for different rules of various genres when reading Mark.

Mimetic Criticism is a testing ground for both the Farrer Theory as well as the Historical Jesus.[69] It is foremost, however, a method at discovering the sources of composition. We now turn to our conclusion.

---

69. For further discussion on memory and the evidence of a Jewish Jesus as a historical figure in first century Palestine, see recent works by Bailey, *Jesus Through Middle Eastern Eyes*; Le Donne, *Historical Jesus* and *The Historiographical Jesus*; and Stern, *A Rabbi Looks at Jesus' Parables*

9

Conclusion

A CRITICAL THEORY SHOULD be judged by its methodology, not by its conclusions that may go against the grain. It has been the intent of this volume to present mimetic criticism as fitting well within historical criticism while not denying the historical place the Gospel of Mark occupies, namely, that of a literary work composed in a first century Roman provenance. This social and rhetorical situation must then inform us how to read the Gospel, what rules and tools to apply, and whether or not to judge it for historical accuracy or for ideological purpose (although I would argue that there is no line between history and ideology, between event and interpretation of the event). If there is anything of a valuable contribution here, it is only because I stand upon the shoulders of great scholarly minds who in turn stand upon more great scholarly minds. My goal is not to slight in anyway those who have gone before, and if I have, then it is my egregious error that I can only hope to correct with the rest of my work, if there be any such work to come. If there is nothing here, then I claim all fault as my own. I must make a confession, then, as throughout this work, I have attempted to litter it with clichés, pop culture references, and even references to parts of a symphony as well as other arts along with references buried for friends to find; if you have picked up on this, and found your mind wondering as why I have done so blatantly, even to the point of beginning this work in mid-sentence—even to the point of making the conclusion no more than eight sentences—it is because I am attempting to prove my point of allusion, intertextuality, mnemonic clues, and mimetic sources.

From here, we should endeavor to translate our *jouissance* into

Bibliography

Works Cited and Consulted

Abrams, M. H., and Geoffrey Harpham. *A Glossary of Literary Terms*. 10th ed. Wadsworth Publishing, 2011.
Achtemeier, Paul J. "Person and Deed Jesus and the Storm-Tossed Sea." *Interpretation* 16, no. 2 (April 1, 1962): 169–176.
———. "Toward the Isolation of the Pre-Markan Miracle Catenae." *Journal of Biblical Literature* 89, no. 3 (September 1970): 265–291.
Ahl, Frederick. *Lucan: An Introduction*. First ed. Cornell Univ Pr, 1976.
Allen, Graham. *Intertextuality*. 2nd ed. Routledge, 2011.
Allen, James, Eyjolfur Kjalar Emilsson, Benjamin Morison, and Wolfgang-Rainer Mann, eds. *Oxford Studies in Ancient Philosophy: Essays in Memory of Michael Frede Volume 40*. Oxford University Press, USA, 2011.
Anderson, William S. *The Art of the Aeneid*. 2nd ed. Bolchazy-Carducci Publishers, 2005.
Asso, Paolo, ed. *Brill's Companion to Lucan*. Leiden: Brill, 2011.
Auerbach, Erich. *Mimesis: The Representation of Reality in Western Literature*. Translated by Willard R. Trask. 50 anniversary. Princeton University Press, 2003.
Aus, Roger David. *My Name Is Legion: Palestinian Judaic Traditions in Mark 5:1–20 and Other Gospel Texts*. University Press Of America, 2003.
Bagnall, Roger S., and Bruce W. Frier. *The Demography of Roman Egypt*. Cambridge University Press, 2006.
Bailey, Kenneth E. *Jesus Through Middle Eastern Eyes: Cultural Studies in the Gospels*. IVP Academic, 2008.
Bakhtin, M. M. *The Dialogic Imagination: Four Essays*. Edited by Michael Holquist and Vadim Liapunov. Translated by Vadim Liapunov and Kenneth Brostrom. University of Texas Press, 1982.
Bakker, Egbert J. *Poetry in Speech: Orality and Homeric Discourse*. Cornell University Press, 1997.
Balch, David L., ed. *Social History of the Matthean Community: Cross-Disciplinary Approaches*. Fortress Pr, 1991.
Baldick, Chris. *The Oxford Dictionary of Literary Terms*. 3rd ed. Oxford University Press, USA, 2009.

Bibliography

Bandera, Cesário. "Sacrifical Levels in Virgil's Aeneid." *Arthusa*, no. 14 (1981): 217–39.
Barthes, Roland. *Image-Music-Text*. Translated by Stephen Heath. Hill and Wang, 1978.
Barton, David. *The Jefferson Lies: Exposing the Myths You've Always Believed About Thomas Jefferson*. Thomas Nelson, 2012.
Bartsch, Shadi. *Ideology in Cold Blood: A Reading of Lucan's* Civil War. Harvard University Press, 2001.
Baudrillard, Jean. *Simulacra and Simulation*. Translated by Sheila Faria Glaser. University of Michigan Press, 1995.
Beard, Mary. *The Roman Triumph*. Belknap Press of Harvard University Press, 2009.
Beardslee, William. *Literary Criticism of the New Testament*. Philadelphia: Fortress Press, 1977., 1977.
Behr, Francesca D'Alessandro. *Feeling History: Lucan, Stoicism, and The Poetics of Passion*. 1st ed. Ohio State University Press, 2007.
Beilby, James K., and Paul R. Eddy, eds. *The Historical Jesus: Five Views*. IVP Academic, 2009.
Berger, Klaus. *Formgeschichte Des Neuen Testaments*. Quelle & Meyer, 1984.
Betz, Hans Dieter. *Galatians Hermeneia*. Augsburg Fortress Publishing, 1989.
———. *Sermon on the Mount Hermeneia*. Edited by Adela Yarbro Collins. Augsburg Fortress Publishing, 1995.
———. *The Greek Magical Papyri in Translation: Including the Demotic Spells: Texts*. 1st ed. University Of Chicago Press, 1997.
Black, David Alan, and David R. Beck, eds. *Rethinking the Synoptic Problem*. First ed. Baker Academic, 2001.
Black, Matthew. "The Use of Rhetorical Terminology in Papias On Mark and Matthew." *Journal for the Study of the New Testament* 12, no. 37 (September 1, 1989): 31–41.
Bock, Darrell L. *Studying the Historical Jesus: A Guide to Sources and Methods*. Baker Academic, 2002.
Bockmuehl, Markus, and Donald A. Hagner, eds. *The Written Gospel*. Cambridge University Press, 2005.
Bonner, Stanley. *Routledge Library Editions: Education Mini-Set H History of Education 24 Vol Set: Education in Ancient Rome: From the Elder Cato to the Younger Pliny*. Routledge, 2011.
Brodie, Thomas L. *The Birthing of the New Testament: The Intertextual Development of the New Testament Writings*. Sheffield Phoenix Press Ltd, 2006.
———. *The Crucial Bridge*. The Liturgical Press, 2000.
Bryant, Donald C. "Aspects of the Rhetorical tradition-II: Emotion, Style, and Literary Association." *Quarterly Journal of Speech* 36, no. 3 (1950): 326–332.
Buchanan, George Wesley. *An Additional Note to "Mark 11.15–19: Brigands in the Temple."* Hebrew Union College, 1960.
———. "Symbolic Money-changers in the Temple?" *New Testament Studies* 37, no. 02 (1991): 280–290.
Bultmann, Rudolf. *New Testament & Mythology*. Fortress Press, 1984.
———. *The History of the Synoptic Tradition*. Translated by John Marsh. Revised. Hendrickson Pub, 1994.
———. *Theology of the New Testament*. Translated by Kendrick Grobel. 2nd ed. Baylor University Press, 2007.
Burkett, Delbert. *Rethinking the Gospel Sources: From Proto-Mark to Mark*. T&T Clark Int'l, 2004.

Bibliography

Buss, Martin J. *Biblical Form Criticism in Its Context*. 1st ed. T&T Clark, 1999.

———. *The Changing Shape of Form Criticism: A Relational Approach*. Sheffield Phoenix Press Ltd, 2010.

———. *The Concept of Form in the Twentieth Century*. Sheffield Phoenix Press Ltd, 2008.

Cameron, Alan. *Greek Mythography in the Roman World*. First Edition, First Printing. Oxford University Press, USA, 2004.

Campbell, Charles L., and Johan H. Cilliers. *Preaching Fools: The Gospel as a Rhetoric of Folly*. Baylor University Press, 2012.

Carrier, Richard. *Proving History: Bayes's Theorem and the Quest for the Historical Jesus*. Prometheus Books, 2012.

Carter, Warren. *Matthew and Empire: Initial Explorations*. Trinity Press Int'l, 2001.

Case, Shirley Jackson. *Jesus: A New Biography*. Gorgias Press LLC, 2006.

Casey, Maurice. *An Aramaic Approach to Q: Sources for the Gospels of Matthew and Luke*. Cambridge University Press, 2005.

———. *Jesus of Nazareth: An Independent Historian's Account of His Life and Teaching*. 1st ed. T&T Clark, 2010.

———. *The Solution to the "Son of Man" Problem*. 1st ed. T&T Clark, 2009.

Chancey, Mark A. *Greco-Roman Culture and the Galilee of Jesus*. 1st ed. Cambridge University Press, 2008.

———. *The Myth of a Gentile Galilee*. Cambridge University Press, 2004.

Chapman, Dean W. "Locating the Gospel of Mark A Model of Agrarian Biography." *Biblical Theology Bulletin: A Journal of Bible and Theology* 25, no. 1 (February 1, 1995): 24–36.

Collins, Adela Yarbro, and John J. Collins. *King and Messiah as Son of God: Divine, Human, and Angelic Messianic Figures in Biblical and Related Literature*. William B. Eerdmans Publishing Company, 2008.

Collins, Adela Yarbro. *Mark: A Commentary*. Edited by Harold W. Attridge. Fortress Press, 2007.

Collins, John J. *Between Athens and Jerusalem: Jewish Identity in the Hellenistic Diaspora*. 2nd ed. Wm. B. Eerdmans Publishing Co., 1999.

Combs, Jason. "A Ghost on the Water? Understanding an Absurdity in Mark 6:49–50." *Journal of Biblical Literature* 127, no. 2 (June 15, 2008): 345–358.

Conte, Gian Biagio. *Saggio Di Commento a Lucano, Pharsalia VI, 118–260, lAristia Di Sceva*. Goliardica, 1974.

———. *The Rhetoric of Imitation: Genre and Poetic Memory in Virgil and Other Latin Poets*. Translated by Charles Segal. Cornell University Press, 1996.

Corbeill, Anthony. (2001). Education in the Roman Republic: Creating traditions. In Too, Y.L. (Ed.) Education in Greek and Roman antiquity. New York: Brill. 261–288.

Corley, Jeremy. *New Perspectives on the Nativity*. T&T Clark Int'l, 2009.

Crawford, Sidnie White. *Rewriting Scripture in Second Temple Times*. Wm. B. Eerdmans Publishing Co., 2008.

Crossan, John Dominic. *The Historical Jesus: The Life of a Mediterranean Jewish Peasant*. HarperOne, 1993.

Crossley, James G. *Reading the New Testament: Contemporary Approaches*. Routledge, 2010.

———. *The Date of Mark's Gospel: Insight from the Law in Earliest Christianity*. T&T Clark, 2004.

Bibliography

Danove, Paul. *The Rhetoric of Characterization of God, Jesus and Jesus' Disciples in the Gospel of Mark*. 1st ed. T&T Clark, 2005.

Dawkins, Richard. *The Selfish Gene: 30th Anniversary Edition--with a New Introduction by the Author*. 30th Anniversary. Oxford University Press, USA, 2006.

Dewey, Joanna. *Disciples of the Way*. Women's Division Board of Global Ministries, 1976.

———. *Markan Public Debate: Literary Technique, Concentric Structure, and Theology in Mark 2:1–3:6*. Society of Biblical Literature, 1980.

Dickey, Eleanor. *Ancient Greek Scholarship: A Guide to Finding, Reading, and Understanding Scholia, Commentaries, Lexica, and Grammatiacl Treatises, from Their . . . Association Classical Resources Series)*. Oxford University Press, USA, 2007.

Dirven, René, and Ralf Pörings, eds. *Metaphor and Metonymy in Comparison and Contrast*. Mouton de Gruyter, 2003.

Doble, Peter. *The Paradox of Salvation: Luke's Theology of the Cross*. Cambridge University Press, 2005.

Dominik, William, and Jon Hall, eds. *A Companion to Roman Rhetoric*. 1st ed. Wiley-Blackwell, 2010.

———. *The Historiographical Jesus: Memory, Typology, and the Son of David*. Baylor University Press, 2009.

Doty, William G. *Contemporary New Testament Interpretation*. Prentice Hall, 1972.

Downing, Crystal L. *Changing Signs of Truth: A Christian Introduction to the Semiotics of Communication*. IVP Academic, 2012.

Duncan, Anne. *Performance and Identity in the Classical World*. Cambridge University Press, 2006.

Dungan, David, David B. Peabody, and Allan J. McNicol, eds. *Beyond the Q Impasse. Book and Access*. Trinity Press International, 1996.

Eco, Umberto. *A Theory of Semiotics*. First Paperback ed. Indiana University Press, 1978.

———. *Semiotics and the Philosophy of Language*. Indiana University Press, 1986.

———. *The Name of the Rose: Including the Author's Postscript*. Translated by William Weaver. 1 Harvest Ed. Harvest Books, 1994.

Edmunds, Lowell. *Intertextuality and the Reading of Roman Poetry*. The Johns Hopkins University Press, 2003.

Elsner, Jas, ed. *Art and Text in Roman Culture*. Cambridge University Press, 1996.

Enos, Richard Leo. *Roman Rhetoric: Revolution and the Greek Influence*. Rev Exp. Parlor Press, 2008.

Enslin, Morton S. "The Artistry of Mark." *Journal of Biblical Literature* 66, no. 4 (December 1947): 385.

Evans, Craig A. *Jesus and His Contemporaries: Comparative Studies*. Humanities Pr, 2001.

———. *Journal of Greco-Roman Christianity and Judaism*. Sheffield Phoenix Press, 2004.

Fairweather, Janet. *Seneca the Elder*. 1st ed. Cambridge University Press, 2007.

Feeney, D. C. *The Gods in Epic: Poets and Critics of the Classical Tradition*. Oxford University Press, USA, 1993.

Finkelberg, Margalit, ed. *The Homer Encyclopedia, Three Volume Set*. 1st ed. Wiley-Blackwell, 2011.

Fisher, Kathleen M., and Urban C. von Wahlde. "The Miracles of Mark 4:35–5:43 Their Meaning and Function in the Gospel Framework." *Biblical Theology Bulletin: A Journal of Bible and Theology* 11, no. 1 (February 1, 1981): 13–16.

Fishwick, Duncan. *The Imperial Cult in the Latin West: Studies in the Ruler Cult of the Western Provinces of the Roman Empire : Provincial Cult : Institution and Evolution*. Brill Academic Pub, 2002.

Fowler, Robert M. *Let the Reader Understand: Reader-Response Criticism and the Gospel of Mark*. Trinity Press International, 2001.

Freedman, David Noel. *The Anchor Bible Dictionary*. Bantam Doubleday Dell Publishing Group, Inc., 1992.

Garrels, Scott R., ed. *Mimesis and Science: Empirical Research on Imitation and the Mimetic Theory of Culture and Religion*. Michigan State University Press, 2011.

Giora, Simon Bar, and Otto Michel. "Studien Zu Josephus." *New Testament Studies* 14, no. 03 (1968): 402–408.

Girard, René. *Deceit, Desire, and the Novel: Self and Other in Literary Structure*. The Johns Hopkins University Press, 1976.

———. *The Scapegoat*. Translated by Yvonne Freccero. The Johns Hopkins University Press, 1989.

———. *Violence and the Sacred*. Translated by Patrick Gregory. The Johns Hopkins University Press, 1979.

Goodacre, Mark. *Goulder and the Gospels: An Examination of a New Paradigm*. Sheffield Academic Press, 1996.

———. *Synoptic Problem: A Way Through the Maze*. T&T Clark Int'l, 2004.

———. *The Case Against Q: Studies in Markan Priority and Synoptic Problem*. 1st ed. Trinity Press Int'l, 2001.

———. *Thomas and the Gospels: The Case for Thomas's Familiarity with the Synoptics*. Wm. B. Eerdmans Publishing Company, 2012.

Goodman, Martin, George H. Van Kooten, and Jacques T. A. G. M. Van Ruiten, eds. *Abraham, the Nations, and the Hagarites: Jewish, Christian, and Islamic Perspectives on Kinship With Abraham*. Brill Academic Pub, 2010.

Goodman, Martin. *The Ruling Class of Judaea: The Origins of the Jewish Revolt Against Rome, A.D. 66–70*. Cambridge University Press, 1993.

Goodyear, F. R. D. "Gian Biagio Conte: Saggio Di Commento a Lucano Pharsalia VI 118-260; l'Aristia Di Sceva. (Biblioteca Degli Studi Classici e Orientali, 2.) Pp. 86. Pisa: Editrice Libreria Goliardica, 1974. Paper." *The Classical Review (New Series)* 27, no. 01 (1977): 113–114.

Green, Joel B., Scot McKnight, and I. Howard Marshall, eds. *Dictionary of Jesus and the Gospels*. IVP Academic, 1992.

Griffin, Miriam. "Philosophy, Cato, and Roman Suicide: II." *Greece & Rome (Second Series)* 33, no. 02 (1986): 192–202.

Grunewald, Thomas. *Bandits in the Roman Empire: Myth and Reality*. 1st ed. Routledge, 2008.

Gundry, Robert H. "The Language Milieu of First-Century Palestine: Its Bearing on the Authenticity of the Gospel Tradition." *Journal of Biblical Literature* 83, no. 4 (December 1964): 404.

Habib, M. A. R. *Literary Criticism from Plato to the Present: An Introduction*. 1st ed. Wiley-Blackwell, 2011.

———. *Modern Literary Criticism and Theory: A History*. 1st ed. Wiley-Blackwell, 2008.

Bibliography

Hadas-Lebel, J. *Jerusalem Against Rome (Interdisciplinary Studies in Ancient Culture & Religion)*. Peeters Publishers, 2006.

Halliwell, Stephen. *The Aesthetics of Mimesis: Ancient Texts and Modern Problems*. Princeton University Press, 2002.

Hardie, Philip. *The Epic Successors of Virgil: A Study in the Dynamics of a Tradition*. Cambridge University Press, 1993.

Hatina, Thomas. *Biblical Interpretation in Early Christian Gospels: Volume 2: The Gospel of Matthew*. 1st ed. T&T Clark, 2008.

Hays, Richard B. *Echoes of Scripture in the Letters of Paul*. Yale University Press, 1993.

Henderson, John. *Fighting for Rome: Poets and Caesars, History and Civil War*. 1st ed. Cambridge University Press, 2006.

Hinds, Stephen. *Allusion and Intertext: Dynamics of Appropriation in Roman Poetry*. Cambridge University Press, 1998.

———. *The Metamorphosis of Persephone: Ovid and the Self-conscious Muse*. Reissue. Cambridge University Press, 2007.

Holmes, Michael W. *The Greek New Testament: SBL Edition*. Society of Biblical Literature, 2010.

Hooker, Morna D. *Gospel According to Saint Mark, The*. Reprint. Baker Academic, 2009.

Horsley, Richard A. *Bandits, Prophets, and Messiahs: Popular Movements at the Time of Jesus*. 1st ed. T&T Clark, 1999.

———. *Jesus and Empire: The Kingdom of God and the New World Disorder*. First ed. FORTRESS PRESS, 2002.

———. "Menahem in Jerusalem a Brief Messianic Episode Among the Sicarii: Not 'Zealot Messianism.'" *Novum Testamentum* 27, no. 4 (October 1985): 334.

———. *Revolt of the Scribes: Resistance and Apocalyptic Origins*. Fortress Press, 2009.

———. "The Zealots. Their Origin, Relationships and Importance in the Jewish Revolt." *Novum Testamentum* 28, no. 2 (April 1986): 159.

Horsley, Richard A., ed. *In the Shadow of Empire: Reclaiming the Bible as a History of Faithful Resistance*. Westminster John Knox Press, 2008.

Horsley, Richard. *Jesus and the Powers: Conflict, Covenant, and the Hope of the Poor*. Fortress Press, 2010.

Humphrey, Hugh. *He Is Risen!: A New Reading of Mark's Gospel*. Paulist Press, 1992.

Humphrey, Hugh M. *From Q to Secret Mark: A Composition History of the Earliest Narrative Theology*. T&T Clark Int'l, 2006.

Hyde, Michael J., and Craig Smith. "Hermeneutics and Rhetoric: A Seen by Unobserved Relationship." *Quarterly Journal of Speech* 65 (1979): 347–63.

III, Ben Witherington. *The Gospel of Mark: A Socio-Rhetorical Commentary*. Wm. B. Eerdmans Publishing Company, 2001.

Incigneri, Brian J. *The Gospel to the Romans: The Setting and Rhetoric of Mark's Gospel*. Brill Academic Pub, 2003.

Iverson, Kelly. *Gentiles in the Gospel of Mark: "Even the Dogs Under the Table Eat the Children's Crumbs'*. 1st ed. T&T Clark, 2007.

Iverson, Kelly R, and Skinner Christopher W. *Mark as Story: Retrospect and Prospect*. Edited by Kelly R. Iverson and Christopher W. Skinner. Society of Biblical Literature, 2011.

Jackson, T. Ryan. *New Creation in Paul's Letters: A Study of the Historical & Social Setting of a Pauline Concept*, 2010.

Bibliography

Janse, S. *You Are My Son: The Reception History of Psalm 2 in Early Judaism and the Early Church*. Peeters Publishers, 2009.
Johnson, Sherman E. *The Griesbach Hypothesis and Redaction Criticism*. Society of Biblical Literature, 2003.
Johnson, Walter Ralph. *Momentary Monsters: Lucan and His Heroes*. Cornell Univ Pr, 1987.
Jr, Arthur J. Bellinzoni, Joseph B. Tyson, and William O. Walker Jr, eds. *The Two-Source Hypothesis: A Critical Appraisal*. First ed. Mercer Univ Pr, 1985.
Jr, Dale C. Allison. *End of the Ages Has Come: Early Interpretation of the Passion and Resurrection of Jesus*. Augsburg Fortress Publishing, 1985.
Keane, Catherine. *Figuring Genre in Roman Satire (American Classical Studies*. Oxford University Press, USA, 2006.
Keith, Chris, and Anthony Le Donne, eds. *Jesus, Criteria, and the Demise of Authenticity*. T&T Clark Int'l, 2012.
Kelber, Werner H. *Mark's Story of Jesus*. Fortress Press, 1979.
———. *The Oral and the Written Gospel: The Hermeneutics of Speaking and Writing in the Synoptic Tradition, Mark, Paul, and Q*. Indiana University Press, 1997.
Kennedy, George A. *A New History of Classical Rhetoric*. Princeton University Press, 1994.
———. *Classical Rhetoric and Its Christian and Secular Tradition from Ancient to Modern Times*. 2 Rev Upd. The University of North Carolina Press, 1999.
———. *New Testament Interpretation Through Rhetorical Criticism*. The University of North Carolina Press, 1984.
Klawans, Jonathan. *Josephus and the Theologies of Ancient Judaism*. Oxford University Press, USA, 2012.
Kloppenborg, John S. *Excavating Q: The History and Setting of the Sayings Gospel*. Fortress Press, 2000.
Koskenniemi, Erkki. *Rewritten Biblical Figures*. Edited by Erkki Koskenniemi and Pekka Lindqvist. Eisenbrauns, 2010.
Kraus, Christina S., and Jane D. Chaplin. *Livy*. Edited by Christina S. Kraus and Jane D. Chaplin. OUP Oxford, 2009.
Kristeva, Julia. *Desire in Language: A Semiotic Approach to Literature and Art*. Edited by Leon S. Roudiez and Alice Jardine. Translated by Thomas Gora. 1st Edition in English, 4th printing. Columbia University Press, 1980.
Kurzinger, Josef. *Papias Von Hierapolis Und Die Evangelien Des Neuen Testaments: Gesammelte Aufsatze, Neuausgabe, Und Ubersetzung Der Fragmente, Kommentierte ... Philosophie Und Theologie)*. F. Pustet, 1983.
Lacoue-Labarthe, Philippe, ed. *Typography: Mimesis, Philosophy, Politics*. 1st ed. Stanford University Press, 1998.
Laird, Andrew, ed. *Ancient Literary Criticism*. Oxford University Press, USA, 2006.
Lange, Armin, Matthias Weigold, and Jozsef Zsengeller, eds. *From Qumran to Aleppo: A Discussion with Emanuel Tov About the Textual History of Jewish Scriptures in Honor of His 65th Birthday*. Vandenhoeck & Ruprecht, 2009.
Larsen, Kevin W. "The Structure of Mark's Gospel: Current Proposals." *Currents in Biblical Research* 3, no. 1 (October 1, 2004): 140-160.
Lebel, Hadas. *Flavius Josephus*. Simon & Schuster, 2001.
Le Donne, Anthony Le. *Historical Jesus: What Can We Know and How Can We Know It?* Wm. B. Eerdmans Publishing Company, 2011.

Bibliography

Leoussi, Athena S., and Steven Grosby, eds. *Nationalism and Ethnosymbolism: History, Culture and Ethnicity in the Formation of Nations*. Edinburgh University Press, 2007.

Levick, Barbara. *Vespasian*. New. Routledge, 2005.

Levine, Amy-Jill, Dale C. Allison, and John Dominic Crossan, eds. *The Historical Jesus in Context*. Princeton University Press, 2006.

Lincicum, David. *Paul & the Early Jewish Encounter With Deuteronomy*, 2010.

Lucan. *Civil War*. Translated by Matthew Fox. Penguin Classics, 2012.

Luke, Trevor S. "A Healing Touch for Empire: Vespasian's Wonders in Domitianic Rome." *Greece & Rome (Second Series)* 57, no. 01 (2010): 77–106.

MacDonald, Dennis R. *The Homeric Epics and the Gospel of Mark*. First ed. Yale University Press, 2000.

MacDonald, Professor Dennis R. *Does the New Testament Imitate Homer?: Four Cases from the Acts of the Apostles*. Yale University Press, 2003.

Mali, Joseph. *Mythistory: The Making of a Modern Historiography*. 1st ed. University Of Chicago Press, 2003.

Marcus, Joel. "The Jewish War and the Sitz Im Leben of Mark." *Journal of Biblical Literature* 111, no. 3 (1992): 441.

Martindale, Charles, ed. *The Cambridge Companion to Virgil*. Cambridge University Press, 1997.

Marxsen, Willi. *Mark the Evangelist: Studies on the Redaction History of the Gospel*. Abingdon Press, 1979.

Mason, Steve. *Josephus and the New Testament*. 2nd ed. Baker Academic, 2002.

———. *Josephus, Judea, and Christian Origins: Methods and Categories*. Baker Academic, 2008.

Masters, Jamie. *Poetry and Civil War in Lucan's Bellum Civile*. 1st ed. Cambridge University Press, 2007.

McCasland, S. V. "Portents in Josephus and in the Gospels." *Journal of Biblical Literature* 51, no. 4 (December 1932): 323.

McKnight, Edgar V. *What Is Form Criticism?* 0 ed. Wipf & Stock Publishers, 1997.

Meier, John P. *A Marginal Jew: Rethinking the Historical Jesus: The Roots of the Problem and the Person, Vol. 1*. Anchor Bible, 1991.

Mitchell, Margaret M. *Paul and the Rhetoric of Reconciliation: An Exegetical Investigation*. Westminster John Knox Press, 1993.

Mowinckel, Sigmund. *He That Cometh: The Messiah Concept in the Old Testament and Later Judaism*. First ed. Wm. B. Eerdmans Publishing Co., 2005.

Myers, Alicia D. *Characterizing Jesus: A Rhetorical Analysis on the Fourth Gospel's Use of Scripture in Its Presentation of Jesus*. 1st ed. T&T Clark, 2012.

Nagy, Gregory. *Pindar's Homer: The Lyric Possession of An Epic Past*. The Johns Hopkins University Press, 1994.

Nagy, Professor Gregory, and Lynn Sawlivich, eds. *The Concept of the Hero in Hellenic Civilization: A Sourcebook*. Gregory Nagy, 1992.

Neusner, Jacob, William Scott Green, and Ernest S. Frerichs, eds. *Judaisms and Their Messiahs at the Turn of the Christian Era*. Cambridge University Press, 1988.

Neusner, Jacob. *Messiah in Context: Israel's History and Destiny in Formative Judaism: The Foundations of Judaism: Method, Teleology, Doctrine*. Augsburg Fortress Publishing, 1984.

Bibliography

Niehoff, Maren R. *Jewish Exegesis and Homeric Scholarship in Alexandria*. 1st ed. Cambridge University Press, 2011.

Nineham, Dennis Eric (1921-) Ed. *Studies in the Gospels : Essays in Memory of R. H. Lightfoot*. 1St ed. Oxford : Basil Blackwell, 1957.

Noth, Martin. *The Laws in the Pentateuch and Other Essays*. Reprint ed. Oliver & Boyd, 1967.

O'Leary, Anne M. *Matthew's Judaization of Mark: Examined in the Context of the Use of Sources in Graeco-Roman Antiquity*. T&T Clark Int'l, 2006.

Oden, Thomas C. *The African Memory of Mark: Reassessing Early Church Tradition*. IVP Academic, 2011.

Ong, Walter J. *Orality and Literacy*. 2nd ed. Routledge, 2002.

Pasquali, Giorgio. *Conversazioni Sulla Nostra Lingua*. Edizioni Radio Italiana, 1953.

———. *Storia Della Tradizione e Critica Del Testo*. Felice Le Monnier - Firenze, 1971.

Peabody, David B., Lamar Cope, and Allan J. McNicol. *One Gospel From Two: Mark's Use of Matthew and Luke*. Trinity Press International, 2002.

Peabody, David Barrett. *Mark as Composer*. Mercer University Press, 1987.

Peppard, Michael. *The Son of God in the Roman World: Divine Sonship in Its Social and Political Context*. Reprint. Oxford University Press, USA, 2012.

Perri, Carmela. "On Alluding." *Poetics* 7, no. 3 (September 1978): 289–307.

Perrin, Norman. *What Is Redaction Criticism?* Wipf & Stock Publishers, 2002.

Pietersma, Albert, and Benjamin G. Wright, eds. *A New English Translation of the Septuagint*. Oxford University Press, USA, 2007.

Poirier, John, and Jr. Walker. "Memory, Written Sources, and the Synoptic Problem: A Responce to Robert K. McIver and Marie Carroll." *Journal of Biblical Literature* 123, no. 2 (June 15, 2004): 315–322.

Potolsky, Matthew. *Mimesis*. New Ed. Routledge, 2006.

Powell, Mark Allan. *What Is Narrative Criticism?* Fortress Press, 1991.

Pucci, Joseph. *The Full-Knowing Reader: Allusion and the Power of the Reader in the Western Literary Tradition*. Yale University Press, 1998.

Rajak, Tessa. *Josephus*. 2nd ed. Bristol Classical Press, 2002.

———. *The Jewish Dialogue With Greece and Rome: Studies in Cultural and Social Interaction*. Brill Academic Pub, 1999.

———. *Translation and Survival: The Greek Bible of the Ancient Jewish Diaspora*. Oxford University Press, USA, 2011.

Rasimus, Tuomas, Troels Engberg-Pedersen, and Ismo Dunderberg, eds. *Stoicism in Early Christianity*. Baker Academic, 2010.

Reed, J. D. *Virgil's Gaze: Nation and Poetry in the Aeneid*. Princeton University Press, 2007.

Reese, Gustave. *Music in the Renaissance*. Revised. W. W. Norton & Company, 1959.

Rhoads, David, Joanna Dewey, and Donald Michie. *Mark As Story: An Introduction to the Narrative of a Gospel*. 3rd ed. Fortress Press, 2012.

Rhoads, David M. *Israel in Revolution, 6–74 C.E: A Political History Based on The Writings of Josephus*. Fortress Press, 1976.

Ricks, Christopher. *Allusion to the Poets*. Oxford University Press, USA, 2004.

Riggs, Christina, ed. *The Oxford Handbook of Roman Egypt*. Oxford University Press, USA, 2012.

Rives, James B. *Religion in the Roman Empire*. Wiley-Blackwell, 2006.

Bibliography

Robbins, Vernon K. *Jesus the Teacher: A Socio-Rhetorical Interpretation of Mark*. New ed. Augsburg Fortress Publishers, 2009.

Robinson, James McConkey, Paul Hoffmann, and John S. Kloppenborg. *The Critical Edition of Q: Synopsis Including the Gospels of Matthew and Luke, Mark and Thomas with English, German, and French Translations of Q ... & Historical Commentary on the Bible)*. Augsburg Fortress Publishers, 2000.

Robinson, John A. T. *Redating the New Testament*. Wipf & Stock Publishers, 2001.

Romm, James S. *The Edges of the Earth in Ancient Thought*. Princeton University Press, 1994.

Rothschild, Clare K. *Luke-Acts and the Rhetoric of History: An Investigation of Early Christian Historiography*. Mohr Siebeck, 2004.

Ryckman, Richard M. *Theories of Personality*. 9th ed. Wadsworth Publishing, 2007.

Sadie, Stanley, and John Tyrrell, eds. *The New Grove Dictionary of Music and Musicians: 29 Volumes with Index*. 2nd ed. Oxford University Press, USA, 2004.

Ryou, Philip Ho-Young. *Apocalyptic Opening, Eschatological 'inclusio': a Study of the Rending of the Heaven and the Temple Curtain in the Gospel of Mark With Special References to the Motif of 'seeing'*. University of Glasgow, 2004.

Sanders, E. P. *The Historical Figure of Jesus*. Reprint. Penguin Books, 1996.

Sandmel, Samuel. "Parallelomania." *Journal of Biblical Literature* 81, no. 1 (March 1962): 1–13.

Santayana, Santayana. *Interpretations of Poetry and Religion*. Forgotten Books, 2012.

Sax, William, Johannes Quack, and Jan Weinhold, eds. *The Problem of Ritual Efficacy*. Oxford University Press, USA, 2010.

Schmidt, T. E. "Mark 15.16–32: The Crucifixion Narrative and the Roman Triumphal Procession." *New Testament Studies* 41, no. 01 (1995): 1–18.

Schneidau, Herbert N. *Sacred Discontent: The Bible and Western Tradition*. Univ of California Pr, 1977.

Sellew, Philip. "Composition of Didactic Scenes in Mark's Gospel." *Journal of Biblical Literature* 108, no. 4 (1989): 613.

Seward, Desmond. *Jerusalem's Traitor: Josephus, Masada, and the Fall of Judea*. First ed. Da Capo Press, 2009.

Smith, Anthony D. *Ethno-symbolism and Nationalism: A Cultural Approach*. 1st ed. Routledge, 2009.

———. *Myths and Memories of the Nation*. Oxford University Press, USA, 2000.

Smith, Jonathan Z. *Map Is Not Territory: Studies in the History of Religions*. University Of Chicago Press, 1993.

Smith, Rebekah M. "Deception and Sacrifice in Aeneid 2.1–249." *American Journal of Philology* 120, no. 4 (1999): 503–523.

Soulen, Richard N., and R. Kendall Soulen. *Handbook of Biblical Criticism, Fourth Edition*. 4th ed. Westminster John Knox Press, 2011.

Stanley, Christopher D. *Arguing With Scripture: The Rhetoric of Quotations in the Letters of Paul*. 1st ed. T&T Clark, 2004.

Stark, Thom. *The Human Faces of God: What Scripture Reveals When It Gets God Wrong*. 1st ed. Wipf & Stock Publishers, 2010.

Statius. *Silvae IV*. Edited by K. M. Coleman. Oxford University Press, USA, 1988.

Stern, Frank. *A Rabbi Looks at Jesus' Parables*. Rowman & Littlefield Publishers, 2005.

Stewart, Eric C. *Gathered Around Jesus: An Alternative Spatial Practice in the Gospel of Mark*. James Clarke & Co, 2010.

Stowers, Professor Stanley K. *A Rereading of Romans: Justice, Jews, and Gentiles*. Reprint. Yale University Press, 1997.

Stowers, Stanley K. *Letter Writing in Greco-Roman Antiquity*. Westminster John Knox Press, 1986.

Stroup, Sarah Culpepper. *Catullus, Cicero, and a Society of Patrons: The Generation of the Text*. 1st ed. Cambridge University Press, 2010.

Such, W. A. *The Abomination of Desolation in the Gospel of Mark*. University Press Of America, 1999.

Tannehill, Robert C. "Tension in Synoptic Sayings and Stories." *Interpretation* 34, no. 2 (April 1, 1980): 138–150.

Telford, W. R. *The Theology of the Gospel of Mark*. Cambridge University Press, 1999.

Telford, William R. *Writing on the Gospel of Mark*. Deo Pub, 2009.

Tesoriero, Charles, Frances Muecke, and Tamara Neal, eds. *Lucan*. Oxford University Press, USA, 2010.

Theissen, Gerd, and Annette Merz. *Historical Jesus: A Comprehensive Guide*. Fortress Press, 1998.

Theissen, Gerd. *The Gospels in Context: Social and Political History in the Synoptic Tradition*. Translated by Linda M. Maloney. 1st English-language ed. Fortress Pr, 1992.

Theissen, Gerd, and Dagmar Winter. *The Quest for the Plausible Jesus: The Question of Criteria*. Westminster John Knox Press, 2002.

Thiselton, Anthony C. *The First Epistle to the Corinthians*. Wm. B. Eerdmans Publishing Co., 2000.

Thomas, Richard F. *Virgil and the Augustan Reception*. 1st ed. Cambridge University Press, 2006.

———. "Virgil's Georgics and the Art of Reference." *Harvard Studies in Classical Philology* 90 (1986): 171.

Thomas, Richard Felstead. *Reading Virgil and His Texts: Studies in Intertextuality*. University of Michigan Press, 2000.

Thompson, Thomas L. *The Messiah Myth: The Near Eastern Roots of Jesus and David*. Export Ed. Basic Books, 2005.

Thompson, Thomas, and Thomas Verenna, eds. *Is This Not the Carpenter?* Equinox Publishing Limited, 2012.

Thorne, Mark Allen. *Lucan's Cato, the Defeat of Victory, the Triumph of Memory*. ProQuest, UMI Dissertation Publishing, 2011.

Tobin, Thomas H. *Paul's Rhetoric in Its Contexts: The Argument of Romans*. Baker Academic, 2005.

Tolbert, Mary Ann. *Sowing the Gospel: Mark's Work in Literary-Historical Perspective*. Augsburg Fortress Publishers, 1996.

Tuckett, C. M., and F. Van Segbroeck. *The Four Gospels 1992. Festschrift Frans Neirynck*. Peeters Publishers, 1992.

Tuckett, Christopher M. *Q and the History of Early Christianity: Studies on Q*. T. & T. Clark Publishers, 1997.

Tuckett, Christopher. *Revival Griesbach Hypothes*. Cambridge University Press, 2005.

Ulansey, David. "The Heavenly Veil Torn: Mark's Cosmic Inclusio." *Journal of Biblical Literature* 110, no. 1 (1991): 123.

Vermes, Geza. *Jesus the Jew*. 1st Fortress Press ed. Fortress Press, 1981.

Bibliography

Viladesau, Richard. *The Beauty of the Cross: The Passion of Christ in Theology and the Arts from the Catacombs to the Eve of the Renaissance.* Oxford University Press, USA, 2008.

Vines, Michael E. *The Problem of Markan Genre: The Gospel of Mark and the Jewish Novel.* Brill Academic Pub, 2002.

Volosinov, V. N. *Marxism and the Philosophy of Language.* Translated by Ladislav Matejka and I. R. Titunik. Harvard University Press, 1986.

Walsh, P. G. "Livy and Stoicism." *The American Journal of Philology* 79, no. 4 (1958): 355.

———. *Livy; His Historical Aims and Methods.* Cambridge, at the University Press, 1967.

———. "Livy: His Historical Aims and Methods." *Rheinisches Museum Für Philologie* 97, no. 2 (1954): 97–114.

Wasserman, Tommy. "The 'Son of God' Was in the Beginning (Mark 1:1)." *The Journal of Theological Studies* 62, no. 1 (April 1, 2011): 20–50.

Watts, Rikki E. *Isaiah's New Exodus in Mark.* Rev Upd Su. Baker Academic, 2001.

Wilder, Amos N. "Scholars, Theologians, and Ancient Rhetoric." *Journal of Biblical Literature* 75, no. 1 (March 1956): 1.

Wilder, Amos Niven. *Early Christian Rhetoric: The Language of the Gospel.* Hendrickson Pub, 1999.

———. *Theopoetic.* Academic Renewal Press, 2001.

Williams, James G. *Gospel Against Parable: Mark's Language of Mystery.* Sheffield Academic Pr, 1985.

Willis, Ika. *Now and Rome: Lucan and Vergil as Theorists of Politics and Space.* Continuum, 2012.

Winn, Adam. *Mark and the Elijah-Elisha Narrative: Considering the Practice of Greco-Roman Imitation in the Search for Markan Source Material.* Pickwick Publications, 2010.

———. *The Purpose of Mark's Gospel: An Ealry Christian Response to Roman Imperial Propaganda*, 2008.

Wire, Antoinette Clark. *The Case for Mark Composed in Performance.* Cascade Books, 2011.

Wiseman, T.P. *Clio's Cosmetics: Three Studies in Greco-Roman Literature.* Bristol Phoenix Press, Univ of Exeter, 2004.

Witherington, Ben, III. *New Testament Rhetoric: An Introduction Guide to the Art of Persuasion in and of the New Testament.* Wipf & Stock Publishers, 2008.

Witmer, Amanda. *Jesus, the Galilean Exorcist: His Exorcisms in Social and Political Context.* 1st ed. T&T Clark, 2012.

Wright, N. T. *Jesus and the Victory of God.* Fortress Press, 1997.

Young, George W. *Subversive Symmetry: Exploring the Fantastic in Mark 6:45–56.* Brill Academic Pub, 1999.

Zahn, Molly M. *Rethinking Rewritten Scripture.* BRILL, 2011.

Zahn, Theodor. *Introduction to the New Testament, Vol. 2 of 3.* Forgotten Books, 2010.

Zeitlin, S. "Zealots and Sicarii." *Journal of Biblical Literature* 81, no. 4 (December 1962): 395.

Author and Subject Index

Aristotle, 5, 24–28
Aeneid, 87–88, 90–97, 116, 197, 204, 206–208, 220
Ahl, Frederick, 90, 94, 107, 110, 207
Allusion, 40–43
Analogy, 14, 17, 160
Antetext, 7
Antimimesis, 31–34
Antithesis, 4, 7, 31–32, 102, 231
Apologia, Criterion of, 230–234
Apostrophe, 88–91, 108–109
Aristophanes, 32
Bakhtin, Mikhail, 38–40, 49, 236
Bar Giora, Simon, 59, 63, 107, 126–127, 133, 150–155, 163, 167, 176, 179, 207, 224–225, 227
Bartsch, Shadi, 88–89, 91, 94, 98–99, 131, 235
Belfoire, Elizabeth, 24
Brody, Thomas L., 18–23, 34, 86 113, 212, 221
Burkett, Delbert, 214–216
Carter, Warren, 225–227
Casey, Maurice, 52–53, 75–78, 158–159, 177, 186–187, 213
Cato, 91, 94–95, 102, 199, 200, 201, 206–209
Corbeill, Anthony, 16–17
Crossley, James, 52–53, 76, 177–178, 211
Damon, Cynthia, 21
Doubling, 111, 137, 146–147
Eco, Umberto, 33–34
Education in Antiquity, 15–17, 61, 72, 79, 112
Emotions, Use of, 15, 26, 28–29, 37, 41, 72, 90–92, 108, 120–121, 137, 201, 203, 222–223

Enthosymbolism, 193–194
Euripides, 16–17, 93, 99
Farrer, Austin, 192, 211, 216–221, 223, 228–229, 237
Fox, Matthew, 84085, 89, 196
Gischala, John of, 59, 63, 65, 145, 155
Goodacre, Mark, 211–213, 216, 218–221, 224, 228
Graves, Kersey, 2–3
Halliwell, Stephen, 24, 28, 32
Hardie, Philip, 93, 95, 197, 207
Hegelian-Fichte Dialectic, 31–33, 102, 230
Henderson, John, 86, 89, 98–100
Hinds, Stephen, 13–14, 18, 42, 43, 221, 229
Historical Criticism, 8, 9–10
Homer, 6, 8, 10, 18, 20, 22–25, 27–28, 32, 38, 41, 61, 71, 83, 87–90, 93, 95–98, 100–101, 116, 131–132, 141, 143, 160, 197, 20
Hypertext, 7
Hypotext, 7
Iliad, 10, 12, 26, 87
Imperial Ideology, 3, 69, 107, 116, 189, 225
Intercalation, 109–111, 118, 139–140, 182
Intertextuality, 36–40
Inventio, 20–23, 86, 92, 219, 221, 227, 229, 231
Irenaeus, 49–53
Irony, 110–111, 161, 166
Kennedy, Duncan, 36
Kristeva, Julia, 36, 38, 39, 42
Lacoue-LeBarthe, Philippe, 32
Levick, Barbara 59–134
Livy, 20, 36, 86–87, 89, 91–92, 101–102

MacDonald, Dennis, 10–15, 17–18, 20–23, 33–34, 61, 83, 113–114, 116, 131–132, 141, 160–161, 220–221, 229
McNelis, Charles, 15
Melberg, Anre, 23, 27
Memetext, 7
Merism, 8
Metonymy, 8
Mimetic Theatre, 26
Mimicking, 7
Mnemonic, 8
O'Leary, Anne, 221–223, 227, 229, 236
Odyssey, 12, 131–132
Papias, 49–51, 166, 235
Paradox, 32, 88, 99, 100, 102, 110–111, 128, 142, 144
Parallelomania, 2, 6, 12, 154, 232, 248
Parataxis, 77, 80, 98–99, 112, 121, 158, 196
Plato, 5, 10, 15, 17, 24–27, 32, 83, 87, 101, 115
Posidonius, 27
Potolsky, Matthew, 23–26
Pucci, Joseph, 34, 36, 39–44
Q, 1, 6, 19, 141, 211–220, 228–229, 234
Quintilian, 15, 18, 21, 28–29, 42, 84, 91, 103. 108
Rajak, Tessa, 17, 73–74, 78–80, 186–187
Repetition, 23, 93, 111
Resemblance, 122–123, 154, 187, 225
Ritual Efficacy, 232
Roman Triumph, 65, 74–75, 150, 159, 162, 180, 183–184
Sandmel, Samuel, 2
Scott, James, 31
Seutonius, 3, 67–68, 84
Seward, Desmond, 73, 155
Sicarii, 63, 126–127, 155
Statius, 84–85, 87, 93–94, 102, 159, 207
Stoicism, 15, 27–28, 71, 85, 90, 102, 114, 185, 199, 200–202, 207, 208, 219, 222–223, 227
Strabo, 27, 23, 201
Synthesis, 4, 7, 14, 20, 27, 31, 37, 43, 102, 107, 198, 231
Thesis, 4, 31, 102, 136

Thomas, Richard, 13, 40, 42
Transcript, 31, 71, 88, 113
Transfer, 40–41, 95–97, 118, 195, 198–199
Virgil, 5, 6, 8, 10, 12–13, 20, 22, 38, 41, 43, 83–102, 108, 116, 196–197, 203, 206–208, 220, 236, 240–241, 244, 246–249
Walsh, P.G., 86–87
Winn, Adam, 11, 18, 22–23, 34, 41, 52–54, 68–69, 86, 108, 114, 116–117, 121, 132–133, 142, 145, 177–178, 218
Witherington, Ben III, 15, 142, 194
Zealots, 57–58, 62, 65, 108, 125–127, 137, 154–155, 163–164, 171

www.ingramcontent.com/pod-product-compliance
Lightning Source LLC
Chambersburg PA
CBHW051104230426
43667CB00013B/2441